Revised and Enlarged Edition

weekendLearning
Series

Islamic Studies

Level 5

Mansur Ahmad and Husain A. Nuri

weekend
Learning

ISBN: 978-1-936569-61-8

First edition: 2008
Second edition: 2009
Third edition: 2011
Fourth edition: 2012
Reprint: 2014, 2016
Revised and enlarged edition: 2018
Reprint: 2018, 2020

Cover Design and Photography: Mansur Ahmad
Illustrations: Mansur Ahmad, Husain A. Nuri and Abira Das

Weekend Learning Publishers
5584 Boulder Crest St.
Columbus, OH 43235, USA
www.weekendlearning.com

Printed in India

Preface

The concept of a series of Islamic Studies books was conceived in 2002 when both of us were teachers or principals of two weekend schools in two different states. We used several excellent textbooks and reference books in these schools. However, we soon realized there was no single textbook available that could meet our classroom needs. Some of the available books had too many or too few lessons for an academic year. Some lessons were too long for a class hour, and some were too short. Some lessons were too difficult for the ages involved or too basic for higher-level classes. Some books were not written with a 12-year curriculum in mind. The lessons in higher grades, therefore, did not develop from the knowledge base of prior years. Sometimes, extra emphasis was placed on one topic at the expense of other important topics. Thus, we thought a balanced knowledge base was lost.

We always felt there was a better way. We began writing the lessons ourselves to meet the needs of our schools. We involved other teachers in this process. For the next two years, we conducted classes based on the lessons we had prepared. In the meantime, both of us met with other principals and teachers across the country. We wanted to find out how they taught Islamic Studies and what their major concerns were. Most of the principals and teachers we talked to expressed their inability to find or develop a good curriculum. If they had a curriculum, they could not find lessons to complement the curriculum.

This survey prompted us to develop a functional, comprehensive curriculum for weekend schools in the West. We wanted to create a curriculum that would include everything that Muslim students growing up in the West would ideally need to know. We wanted to include topics based on the life experiences of students growing up in the West. Muslim children growing up in the U.S., Europe, and Australia are facing diverse challenges and conflicting pressures at schools and in social circles. They are constantly influenced by the mainstream youth culture. We wanted lessons to address their issues from their perspectives.

The curriculum alone would not be of any use unless there were lessons based on the curriculum. The lessons had to be age-appropriate and suitable for the typical class duration of most schools. As we continued to write and edit lessons over the next two years, we discovered ways to make the curriculum increasingly meaningful.

In 2007, we published coil-bound versions of these books. More than 30 schools in the U.S. and UK used the books. We also received a large number of inquiries from many other schools. Based on the suggestions, comments, and reviews received from many of these schools, we have edited the series of books and made other changes as appropriate.

We are thankful to Allāh for giving us the ability to write these books. We pray to Allāh to accept our labor and make us successful in communicating the message of Islam. We hope Islamic schools and home schools in the U.S. and other countries will find these books useful. Any errors in the books are our responsibility. We appreciate receiving meaningful comments and suggestions to improve the series.

"Our Rabb! Accept from us, you indeed are the all-Hearing, all-Knowing." (2:127)

January 15, 2008

Mansur Ahmad
Husain A. Nuri

Preface to the Revised and Enlarged Edition

All praise is due to Allāh﷾ alone. We are indebted to Him for giving us time, energy, and resources to publish this book and other books in this series. The first edition of the book was published in 2008. Over the next 10 years, we made small editorial changes in some of the lessons. During this time, our books became one of the most-sought-after series all over the world for teaching Islam in weekend schools. Thousands of schools on all the continents adopted our series, and we are indebted to the teachers, students, and above all, to almighty God.

We do not want to remain idle with the success of the series. We have been constantly striving to improve the books to meet the changing and growing needs of the weekend schools. Many schools wrote to us requesting additional materials in some of the lessons. In view of their requests, we have revised and enlarged all the lessons, adding more information and resources. Our utmost focus all along has been to remain extremely loyal and true to the teachings of the Qur'ān and authentic sunnah of the Messengerﷺ. With the enlarged lessons, teachers are now equipped with many more materials, but the teaching time in class remains the same. Therefore, the challenge will be to maximize the time available in a class by getting the most out of the lessons. This will be possible only when teachers review the lessons before coming to class and prepare themselves to do their best.

We are grateful to Brenda Rusch for editing and proofreading the book. She has not only eliminated some grammatical, punctuation, and spelling errors, but has also improved content flow, transitions, and overall organization. May Allāh﷾ accept our small effort.

April 15, 2018

Husain A. Nuri
Mansur Ahmad

Table of Contents

How to use this book effectively
Instructions for teachers and parents

The lessons for fifth-grade Islamic Studies expand upon the key information on Islam learned in the previous years. As with other books in the series, this book also begins with a few topics on Allāh. The lives of Rasūlullāh, Ibrāhīm, and Yūsuf (A) are discussed in greater detail. Messengers Ayyūb (A), Zakariyyāh (A), and Yahyā (A) are introduced this year. Some related **Interesting Facts** and **Points to Remember** are included in certain lessons to impart knowledge about the creations of Allāh, and to make a connection between the *deen* and the *dunya*. Islamic views on dating and opposite-gender socializing will be discussed in higher-level books. However, the foundation of these issues is introduced in lesson for weekend 23, *My Mind, My Body*.

For maximum benefit, each lesson should be completed within one class hour. We recommend that a test be administered after every fifth or sixth lesson. An annotated Teacher's Edition of this book is available. This version provides additional text, explanations, and āyāts from the Qur'ān related to the lesson. The Teacher's Edition also contains a CD-ROM featuring question banks, ready-to-print exam questions, and homework assignments in PDF and Word files.

Homework:

Teachers are requested to assign and grade homework regularly. The time commitment for homework is approximately 10–15 minutes per lesson. Parents are strongly encouraged to supervise the student during the homework assignment. Regular supervision of homework by a parent indicates that education is valued.

Regular Interaction with the Qur'ān:

Every Muslim student should develop the habit of interacting with the Qur'ān. To complete some homework assignments, an acceptable English translation of the Qur'ān is required. The purpose of such homework is to build a strong connection between the student and the Qur'ān. Insha-Allāh, these homework assignments will plant a seed in the minds of children to continue a lifelong interaction with the Qur'ān.

Teaching Respect:

From an early age, students should be taught to show respect for Allāh, His Messengers, and His Angels. Teachers and parents are requested to mention the following:

Whenever the word Allāh appears in the book, please add the glorification, "Subhāna-hu wa-Ta'ālā." We used a symbol that states "Azza wa-zal," and also a symbol that states "Subhāna-hu wa-Ta'ālā."

Whenever the word Muhammad appears, or other words appearing indicating Nabi Muhammad, for example, Rasūlullūh, the Prophet, or Nabi—, please add the prayer, "Salla-llāhu 'alaihi wa Sallam." We have used ﷺ in the book as a reminder of the prayer. Whenever a student reads the name of a messenger or an angel, please add the prayer, "Alai-hi-s Salām." This is noted by (A). Students should be taught to add the prayer, "Radi-allāhu 'an-hu" for a khalifah, or a male companion of Rasūlullāh. For a female companion, the prayer "Radi-allāhu 'an-hā" should be used. These are noted by (R) or (ra) respectively.

Suggestions:

Please provide suggestions, corrections, ideas, and comments to improve the book by sending an email to the publisher at info@weekendLearning.com. It is a combined effort of the publisher, authors, teachers, and parents to prepare our future ummah. May Allāh guide us all. Amin.

A Guide to Features

Interesting Facts

Interesting Facts

Wolves are of two types: gray or timber wolves, and red wolves. Only a small number of wild, red wolves exist now.

Wolves are not fast runners, but they can run for a long time.

Wolves usually hunt small animals, but if their pack is large, they may attack animals as big as a moose. Unless wolves are desperate, they do not usually attack people.

Wolves are social animals—usually live in a group of 5–11. Their groups are called a pack.

Wolves howl to locate their members or to alter others if there is danger.

Wolves are common motif in legends, mythology and folklore. The *Little Red Riding Hood* is one of the most famous fairy tale involving a wolf.

Interesting Facts are provided in most chapters. These notes are intended to provide additional information pertaining to a theme. The idea is to increase awareness of the subject and to enhance the knowledge base. These facts will develop curiosity in the minds of students to explore wider areas of learning that might otherwise remain unnoticed.

Points to Remember

Points to Remember

The word Qur'ān literally means "The Reading."

A total of 86 suwar (plural of surah) were revealed in Makkah, while 28 were revealed in Madinah.

The longest sūrah is Al-Baqarah.

The Qur'ān has total 6,236 verses.

All surah start with Bismillah, except surah Taubah (#9)—it does not have Bismillah in the beginning,

Points to Remember are provided in most chapters. These key points are intimately related to the theme of the chapter and should be remembered to broaden the knowledge base. Students should be quizzed on these points.

Definition

Definition

Blood money: It is the money paid in compensation to the family of someone who has been killed. In return for the receipt of blood money, the family of the deceased would forgive the killer.

Definitions of unfamiliar and novel terms are explained in a small box for quick learning.

From Hadīth

From Hadīth

One or two Hadīth pertaining to the theme of the lesson are quoted in many lessons.

It is narrated by 'Abdullah: When the following Verse was revealed: "It is those who believe and confuse not their belief with wrong" (6:83), the companions of Allāh's Apostle asked, "Who is amongst us who had not done injustice [wrong]?" Allāh revealed: "No doubt, joining others in worship with Allāh is a great injustice [wrong] indeed." (31.13) (Bukhārī)

Time to Review or Points to Ponder

Time to Review

1. Why should everything in the universe follow Allāh's rule?
2. Unlike a human CEO, can Allāh be at multiple places at the same time?
3. What are some of the unique things about Allāh's knowledge?

Points to Ponder

No one else created anything in the universe, therefore no one else can be worthy to be a deity. So why do so many people invent deities and idols and worship these objects?

Throughout the chapters, these features ask students to stop, reflect on, and review the content learned in the chapter. This enables students to raise intelligent questions from their perspective and reinforce learning.

Unit 1: The Creator and His Messengers

Knowing about Allāh 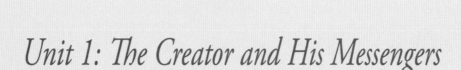 is one of the most important areas of learning for young readers. Since time immemorial, human beings have sought to understand who God is and what He does. In their inability to adequately understand God, human beings often idolized God using images, objects, and their own imaginations. Throughout the Weekend Learning Series, we include a few topics on Allāh so that students can learn about their Creator. The first two lessons in this unit attempt to address specific concepts about Allāh found in the Qur'ān. The third chapter focuses exclusively on the Qur'ān—the last book from Allāh. The final lesson discusses some of the common characteristics of Allāh's nabis and rasuls. Biblical interpretations of many of the Judeo-Christian messengers appear to influence many Muslims. Therefore, a proper understanding of what the messengers did and did not do will help students dispel many of the prevalent misconceptions and myths about the messengers.

The Creator, His Message, and His Messengers

Tawhīd, Kāfir, Kufr, Shirk, Nifāq

In this lesson students will learn a few common Islamic terms and their significance. One of the fundamental teachings of Islam is belief in tawhīd. A person can respond to tawhīd with acceptance, denial, or partial denial. Each of the response gives rise to other problems that are identified by some other Islamic terms. An understanding of these terms will enable students comprehend the principle of believing in One God.

Why Should We Worship Allāh?

Why do people worship objects, and why do they worship idols? These simple questions do not have simple answers. But we can try to understand why we should worship only Allāh. This lesson explains the reasons in simple terms by using a story about a robot.

Revelation of the Qur'ān

The revelation of the Qur'ān was a long process involving several steps and requiring several years. It was revealed under different circumstances, and in different locations, in order to solve different problems. This lesson introduces students to the process of the revelation of the Qur'ān.

Characteristics of the Messengers

The messengers of Islam came during different periods, to different communities, and to solve different problems. Yet all of them showed a similar nature, behavior, and activities. This lesson discusses some of the qualities in common of all messengers and explains why these qualities made them righteous servants of Allāh.

Tawhīd, Kāfir, Kufr, Shirk and Nifāq

Objective of the Lesson:

In this lesson students will learn a few common Islamic terms and their significance. One of the fundamental teachings of Islam is belief in tawhīd. A person can respond to tawhīd with acceptance, denial, or partial denial. Each of the response gives rise to other problems that are identified by some other Islamic terms. An understanding of these terms will enable students comprehend the principle of believing in One God.

In English writing, we normally do not make any distinction between **faith** and **belief**. Both words seem to mean the same thing. These words mean "having complete trust in someone or something." Islamic scholars make a fine distinction between faith and belief. They make this distinction because it is not enough to just believe or have faith. It is not enough to say, "I have faith in God." Faith must contain other elements in it, and unless one has complete faith in all the elements, our faith will not be counted as Islamic faith.

Belief is acceptance that a statement is true or that something exists. For example, Muslims believe Allāhﷻ is One. Someone might say, "I believe in the government," "I believe in education," or "I believe most people are good." These are just statements. There is no action involved in these beliefs.

On the other hand, faith means not only believing in a statement, but also to acting on that belief. Therefore, in Islam, when we say, "We have imān," we actually mean not only do we believe in Allāhﷻ and His teachings, but also we act on His teachings. Our

Nabi Muhammad ﷺ once said, "Faith is a knowledge in the heart, a voicing with the tongue, and an activity with the limbs."

In previous grades, we learned about the **Arkān of Islam** or Pillars of Islam. The first pillar, Shahadah, is about our belief. The rest of the pillars translate this belief into action. Belief and action in the arkān of Islam allows a person to feel the presence of Allāh ﷻ in his or her life and provides meaning to his or her existence.

Definition

Arkān of Islam: It means the pillars of Islam. The five pillars of Islam are: Shahadah, Salāt, Zakāt, Fasting and Hajj.

With this basic understanding of imān, belief, faith, and the arkān of Islam, let us learn some of the common Islamic terms that have a direct connection to imān.

Tawhīd

The concept of **tawhīd** is the central theme in the Qur'ān. It refers to the Oneness of Allāh ﷻ. In the Qur'ānic concept, Allāh ﷻ is the only Creator, the only entity who deserves our sincere worship. To believe in this single entity is tawhīd.

The word tawhīd (توحيد) derives from the root word **wahada** (وحد), which means "to be one," "to be unique," or "unparalleled." Two other words derive from this root word expressing Divine Unity. These two words are "**Ahad**" (احد) and "**Wahid**" (اوحد). The word "ahad" means "one who is, and has ever been one and alone." The word "wahid" means "one" or "alone."

Heaven and earth declare tawhīd

Nabi Muhammad ﷺ taught us the religion of Islam. However, he was not the first nabi to share the concept of tawhīd. In the past, all nabis and rasūls conveyed the message of tawhīd. For example:

Nūh (A) told his people, "O my people! serve Allāh, you have no deity other than Him."[7:59] and "You do not worship anyone except Allāh."[11:25] and "O my people! worship Allāh, there is no deity for you other than Him."[23:23]

Sālih (A) said, "O my people! worship Allāh, you have no deity other than Him."[7:73] Hūd (A) said, "O my people! worship Allāh, you have no deity other than Him."[7:65] The same message of tawhīd can be seen in the teachings of Shu'aib (A).[7:85] These are just a few examples.

In fact, long before human beings were created, heaven and earth declared the glory and unity of Allāh ﷻ. If there were multiple gods in heaven and on earth, they would have destroyed heaven and earth. These points are beautifully explained in the following āyāt:

$$لَوْ كَانَ فِيهِمَا آلِهَةٌ إِلَّا ٱللَّهُ لَفَسَدَتَا ۚ فَسُبْحَانَ ٱللَّهِ رَبِّ ٱلْعَرْشِ عَمَّا يَصِفُونَ ﴿٢٢﴾$$

Had there been in them deities except Allāh, both of these would certainly have been disordered. Therefore glory be to Allāh, the Author of the Throne, above what they attribute! (21:22)

$$وَلَهُ أَسْلَمَ مَن فِي ٱلسَّمَوَاتِ وَٱلْأَرْضِ طَوْعًا وَكَرْهًا وَإِلَيْهِ يُرْجَعُونَ ﴿٨٣﴾$$

...while to Him submits whoever is in the heavens and the earth willingly or unwillingly; and to Him they will be returned. (3:83)

$$سَبَّحَ لِلَّهِ مَا فِي ٱلسَّمَوَاتِ وَٱلْأَرْضِ ۖ وَهُوَ ٱلْعَزِيزُ ٱلْحَكِيمُ ﴿١﴾$$

Whatever is in the heavens and the earth declares the glory of Allāh; and He is Exalted in Might, most Wise. (57:1)

Greatest testimony of tawhīd

The Qur'ān rejects the idea that alleged semi-gods or gods had any influence in the dominion of Allāhﷻ. In the past, many ancient civilizations believed in multiple gods. Ancient Persians believed in the **duality** of god, that is, two gods—one God for good, another for evil. Hindu and Greek civilizations believes in multiple gods. Christians believes in the **Trinity**—a triple manifestation of God.

The Qur'ān rejects the idea of the plurality of god. The most important form of testimony on the oneness of God comes from God Himself. The Qur'ān contains several āyāt that testify to this fact.

$$وَإِلَهُكُمْ إِلَهٌ وَاحِدٌ ۖ لَّا إِلَهَ إِلَّا هُوَ ٱلرَّحْمَنُ ٱلرَّحِيمُ ﴿١٦٣﴾$$

And your God is the One God, there is no god but He, the most Gracious, the most Rewarding. (2:163)

$$۞ وَقَالَ ٱللَّهُ لَا تَتَّخِذُوا إِلَهَيْنِ ٱثْنَيْنِ ۖ إِنَّمَا هُوَ إِلَهٌ وَاحِدٌ ۖ فَإِيَّايَ فَٱرْهَبُونِ ﴿٥١﴾$$

And, Allāh says: "Do not adopt two gods, He is only One God; therefore Me, only Me, should you then fear." (16:51)

هُوَ ٱللَّهُ ٱلَّذِى لَآ إِلَٰهَ إِلَّا هُوَ عَٰلِمُ ٱلْغَيْبِ وَٱلشَّهَٰدَةِ هُوَ ٱلرَّحْمَٰنُ ٱلرَّحِيمُ ﴿٢٢﴾

He is Allāh, the One besides Whom there is no god; Knower of the invisible and the visible; He is the most Gracious, the most Rewarding. (59:22)

وَلَا تُجَٰدِلُوٓا۟ أَهْلَ ٱلْكِتَٰبِ إِلَّا بِٱلَّتِى هِىَ أَحْسَنُ إِلَّا ٱلَّذِينَ ظَلَمُوا۟ مِنْهُمْ وَقُولُوٓا۟ ءَامَنَّا بِٱلَّذِىٓ أُنزِلَ إِلَيْنَا وَأُنزِلَ إِلَيْكُمْ وَإِلَٰهُنَا وَإِلَٰهُكُمْ وَٰحِدٌ وَنَحْنُ لَهُۥ مُسْلِمُونَ ﴿٤٦﴾

And do not dispute with the People of the Book except by that which is the best, barring those who do wrong among them, and you say: "We believe in that which has been revealed to us and what has been revealed to you, and our God and your God is One, and to Him we have surrendered." (29:46)

Kufr

Just as tawhīd is a common word, we also hear another word and its derivatives from time to time. This word is **Kufr** (كفر), which means "to cover," or "to hide." In Islamic terminology, the word "kufr" means the denial of something. The act of denial also has other underlying meanings, for example, non-belief or rejection. Thus, kufr also means hiding or rejecting the truth. For this reason, kufr is considered the opposite of imān or faith. In short, kufr is covering over and concealing the truth that one knows.

Imān begins with the recognition of the truth in one's heart. Once this truth is recognized in the heart, a sense of gratitude results for recognizing the truth. Kufr begins with the denial of truth in one's heart. With this denial, there is a sense of ingratitude toward God who creates, provides, sustains, and nourishes.

Different forms of kufr

After learning the concepts of tawhīd, a person can respond in one of two ways: accept it or deny it. If someone denies it, then this is the act of kufr. Several forms of kufr can be observed among people. For example:

1. **Complete denial:** A person may completely deny the existence of God or reject the idea that God is the Supreme being, the Creator of heaven and earth. If a person holds this view, he or she is an **atheist**.

2. **Partial denial**: A person may partially deny one God, that is, he or she believes God is not the only deity—there are other deities. According to this view, one can worship the Supreme God as well as other gods. This form of kufr makes a person a **polytheist**. Here the word "poly" mean "many," and "theism" means "belief in the existence of one God."

3. **Refusal to act**: One may believe in One God, but he or she refuses to act upon God's teachings or rejects His laws.

4. **Refusal of God's Messengers**: There are people who believe in One God, but they refuse to believe in all of His messengers.

For the sake of simplicity, we mentioned four forms of kufr. Islamic scholars mention many other forms. In short, any form of denial of One God or His messengers is considered kufr.

Kāfir

A **kāfir** (pl. kuffār) is a person who displays the qualities of kufr in faith and activities. The word kāfir is primarily used for the nonbelievers in Arabia at the time of Nabi Muhammad. In ordinary usage, a kāfir is a person who does not accept Islam. Therefore, if Muslims are the believers, the kuffār should be the nonbelievers. However, we previously noted that "belief" is not the best meaning for the word "imān," therefore, "non-belief" is only a partial meaning of kufr.

The Qur'ān uses the term kāfir with three meanings—one meaning is someone holding opposite views of imān, another is someone displaying ingratitude. The Qur'ān also uses the term kāfir in its original sense, which means someone who hides or covers. In sūrah Hadīd, a cultivator is termed as kāfir because he sows the seeds and covers them up with soil.[57:20]

Punishment of kufr

The Qur'ān offers stern words of warning towards anyone who displays kufr in belief and activities. Well over 175 verses in the Qur'ān use the word kāfir. Of these well over 100 verses cautions those who display kufr. For example:

Time to Review

1. What is the basic meaning of the words kufr and kāfir?
2. What are the four forms of kufr discussed in the lesson?
3. Where and from whom will we find the greatest testimony of tawhīd?

"But those who disbelieve and belie Our Messages, these shall be the fellows of the Fire, in that they will abide." (2:39)

As to those who disbelieve, surely neither their wealth nor their children will avail them anything against Allāh. And these are themselves the fuel of the Fire. (3:10)

Surely those who have disbelieved and done wrong, it is never that Allāh should pardon them nor should He guide them to any path. (4:168)

Shirk

Another word we often hear is **shirk**. In Islam, it means "to share," "to be a partner," "to associate someone with someone **else**." Shirk means to associate someone or something with Allāh. The direct outcome of this is to worship the associates along with Allāh or to exclusively worship these associates.

One of the important teachings of the Qur'ān is to avoid associating anyone or anything with Allāh because this violates the concept of tawhīd. Associating does not always mean giving God a partner; it also means giving someone or something God's attributes, power, rights and so forth.

As students of Islam, we should guard ourselves from participating or engaging in any form of shirk. We should remember that others do not share the essential attributes of Allāh. No living or dead saint could solve problems or difficulties. Visiting the shrines of dead saints, offering food at the shrines, showing devotional homage to the saints, or even praying to Allāh while at the shrine—believing such prayer has greater value—are all forms of shirk.

The Qur'ān strongly condemns all forms of shirk. It clearly commands people not to indulge in any form of shirk.

And worship Allāh and do not associate with Him anything ... (4:36)

Come, I shall recite what your Rabb has forbidden to you,—that you do not associate with Him anything ... (6:151)

...Do not associate with Allāh. Surely polytheism is indeed a grievous wrongdoing. (31:13)

Points to Ponder

In many parts of the world, people visit the shrines of saints and offer fruit or other food. People pray at these shrines to invoke the shrine's alleged power to fulfill some wishes. Why do such activities amount to shirk?

Nifāq

The root word "nafaq" means an underground burrow or passageway that opens at both ends. A chipmunk, mouse, or other animal can enter one side of the burrow and escape through the other. From this root word derives the word **nifāq**, which means "hypocrisy." It describes the practice of claiming to have certain standards or beliefs but acting in a manner that is opposite to the standards or beliefs.

A **munāfiq** is a hypocrite who has dual standards about belief. This person symbolically enters Islam from one side and exits from the other. Hypocrites are never fully committed to Islam. If Islam benefits them, they pretend to be Muslim. But when the situation changes, they quickly condemn Islam and break away from Muslims.

When Rasūlllāhﷺ migrated to Madīnah, many people accepted Islam only for show, and they actually worked against Islam. It is difficult to know who is a munāfiq because their hypocrisy remains hidden from others.

Munāfiqs are the worst enemies of Islam and Muslims. For this reason, the Qur'ān promises severe punishment for them in the Hereafter.

Give glad tidings to the hypocrites; for them is but a painful punishment. (4:138)

Surely the hypocrites are in the lowest depths of the Fire, and you will never find for them a helper. (4:145)

1. Read āyah 11:50 of the Qur'ān. Who conveyed the message of tawhīd?

   hud

2. Read the translation of the last three verses of Sūrah Al-Hashr (#59). Based on your reading of these verses, list some of the attributes or qualities of Allāh that are unique to Him and, therefore, reflect to tawhīd.

   a. _the all knowing_

   b. _most gracious_

   c. _most rewaring_

   d. _One god_

   e. _most kind_

   f. _most forgiving_

   g. _most generous_

   h. _righteas teacher_

3. Read āyah 25:2 of the Qur'ān. How many partners does Allāh have to rule over the universe?

   god
   he has no partners

4. Read āyah 21:22 of the Qur'ān. What would have happened if there were more than one deity?

   they would have destroyed the
   earth and heavens

5. Read Surah Yūnus āyah 106. Then answer the following two questions:

   a. Why should we not worship anyone except Allāhﷻ?

   Allāh is the only god we worship

   b. What will be the result if someone worships a deity other than Allāhﷻ?

   go to hell and there none belivers

6. What is the meaning of the word nifāq?

   A. A cave.

   B. Theocracy.

   C. Hypocrisy.

   D. Aristocracy.

7. Read āyah 4:168 of the Qur'ān. What would Allāhﷻ not do for those who display and practice kufr?

   A. Pardon and bless.

   B. Honor and reward.

   C. Guide and educate.

   D. Pardon and guide.

8. What is the original meaning of the word kāfir?

   A. Belief in theism.

   B. Dual standards.

   C. Agriculture.

   D. One who covers the truth.

9. Unscramble the following letters to make meaningful words.

   H R S K I   s h i c k

   U K R F   k u f r

Why Should We Worship Allāh﷾?

Objective of the Lesson:

Why do people worship objects, and why do they worship idols? These simple questions do not have simple answers. But we can try to understand why we should worship only Allāh﷾. This lesson explains the reasons in simple terms by using a story about a robot.

Let us travel to an imaginary land where you are a genius scientist who makes robots. In this Roboland, you have created several fancy robots. You have programmed their computer brains, so they can work smoothly. These programs follow the rules of Roboland, so the robots will work without any problems.

Mr. ChefRobo cooks, Mr. GreenRobo tends the garden, and Ms. EduRobo teaches the children. DocRobo works in the hospital fixing the electric wires of other robots, and RuffRobo guards the yard. One day, SillyRobo Jr., who was in charge of turning on the lights, decided not to follow the rules. He assumed there was no need to turn on the switches. Roboland turned dark. JunkRobo, who was a patient in DocRobo's hospital, died as soon as the power failed. ChefRobo's waffles remained uncooked, and GreenRobo's electric lawn-mower smashed into TreeRobo, which fell on Ms. EduRobo's classroom. Your Roboland just turned into a big mess because SillyRobo Jr. refused to obey your rules—the rules of its creator.

Everything needs rules

Just like Roboland, everything in our world also needs rules. A river cannot flow upstream, and a rock cannot float in the air. A lion cannot live in the ocean. An eagle cannot start living underground, and a whale cannot live on top of a tree. The sun cannot take a day off next Sunday. We also need some rules so that we can be the way our Creator had planned.

Meaning of worship

Worship means to show devotion and respect to Allāh‎ﷻ. We can show respect only if we follow the rules created by Allāh‎ﷻ.

Some of these rules are related to routine acts of worship, and some rules are related to daily activities. Examples of routine acts of worship are salāh, sawm (fasting), and sacrifice. Examples of worship through daily activities are how we behave with each other, how we do business, and what we eat. Allāh‎ﷻ has made rules to tell us how to behave with others, how to conduct business transactions, and what food to eat, to name a few. When we follow these rules as prescribed by Allāh‎ﷻ, we are worshipping Him.

Who makes the rules?

In Roboland, you made the rules because you were the creator. SillyRobo Jr. should not have made his own rules, which started the mess. SillyRobo Jr. did not know how his bad decision would affect others. If anyone other than the Creator makes rules to run the world, it will be a disaster. Allāh‎ﷻ said:

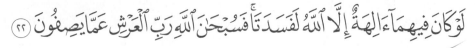

لَوْ كَانَ فِيهِمَا آلِهَةٌ إِلَّا اللَّهُ لَفَسَدَتَا فَسُبْحَانَ اللَّهِ رَبِّ الْعَرْشِ عَمَّا يَصِفُونَ ﴿٢٢﴾

Had there been in them [that is, in the Heaven and on the earth] deities except Allāh, these would surely have been disordered. Therefore, glory be to Allāh, the Author of the Throne, above what they attribute. (al-Anbiya 21:22)

In our world, the rules should also be made by the one who created us. The rules should be made by someone who has full knowledge of everything—knowledge of the past, present, and future. Just as you were the owner of the robots, the owner of this universe is the Creator. We may call this Creator Allāh ﷻ, God, Eloheim, or Ishwar.[17:110] The name of the Creator does not really matter. We use the name Allāh ﷻ because the Creator, Himself, used this name in His Book, the Qur'ān.

قُلِ ٱدْعُوا۟ ٱللَّهَ أَوِ ٱدْعُوا۟ ٱلرَّحْمَٰنَ أَيًّا مَّا تَدْعُوا۟ فَلَهُ ٱلْأَسْمَآءُ ٱلْحُسْنَىٰ

Say, "Call upon as Allāh or call upon as Rahman, by whatever you call, His are the most beautiful names. ... (17:110)

Who benefits from worship?

In Roboland, maybe you benefited when everything followed your rules. However, that is not so in this world. Allāh ﷻ does not need money or food. When we sacrifice an animal during Eid al-Adha, it is part of our worship because we are following Allāh's ﷻ command. But Allāh ﷻ does not need the meat.[22:37]

لَن يَنَالَ ٱللَّهَ لُحُومُهَا وَلَا دِمَآؤُهَا وَلَٰكِن يَنَالُهُ ٱلتَّقْوَىٰ مِنكُمْ

Their flesh never reaches Allāh, nor does their blood, but it is the piety from you that reaches Him ... (22:37)

When we follow the rules of our Creator, the world becomes a better place, and we become successful in our lives. When we follow the rules, we get the benefits of this world.[7:128]

Points to Ponder

God does not need our food, money or sacrifice. None of these benefit Him. He does not even need our worship. But He insists that we worship Him and no one else. So what happens with our worship and who benefits from it?

Can there be any other God?

Instead of worshipping Allāh﷿, can we select someone else to worship? It would be silly to worship a person, who becomes sick and dies. A person cannot have knowledge of everything. He or she will need food to survive. When a bee stings him or her, he or she is hurt. A human being does not have the power to create us because he or she was created by someone else—the Creator.

Along with Allāh﷿, can we worship another god or a group of gods? To be God, one must be the Creator. God must be eternal—one who never dies. God must be all-Powerful. No one, no statue, no powerful person, no one alive or dead, can claim these qualities except the One and Only Allāh﷿.[22:34]

Do we have to worship God?

Is it really necessary to worship Allāh﷿? Can we live by choosing some good values as our guiding rules? If we refuse to worship Allāh﷿, we still remain under His Laws. The problem with making our own rules is that we cannot see the future. What we think is good for us today may prove to be bad tomorrow. When we study history, we find many examples of people who thought their own rules were better than Allāh's﷿ rules. Within a few years, these man-made rules proved to be wrong.

Can we partially worship Allāh﷿?

Would it be acceptable to select some rules from Allāh ﷿ that appear easy for us, and change some other rules that we think are hard? Most likely, our modified rules will turn out to be bad ideas. Governments of every country continue to change their rules and laws

Interesting facts

Examples of silly man-made laws in the USA:

- In California, peeling an orange in your hotel room is banned.
- In Hartford, Connecticut, you cannot cross a street while walking on your hands.
- In Utah, it is against the law to fish on horseback.
- In Kansas, no one may catch fish using their bare hands.
- In Maryland, lions may not be taken to the theater.
- In Alaska, it is illegal to push a live moose out of a moving airplane.
- In Louisiana, it is illegal to rob a bank and then shoot at the bank teller with a water pistol.
- In Oklahoma, you can be fined, arrested, or jailed for making ugly faces at a dog.
- In Kentucky, it is illegal to transport an ice cream cone in your pocket.

because over a period of time, they learn that their rules were not good. The best thing for us would be to follow the rules of the Creator, who knows everything.

Why Islam?

If we call the Creator Allāh﷾, God, Ishwar, or Eloheim, is it acceptable to follow another religion? Many of the religions that exist today were originally from Allāh﷾. However, He gave these religions to small groups of people living in small areas. Their books were not preserved properly. People changed many of these books. This means that people added new rules or removed the rules made by Allāh﷾ in those books. These revised religions are no longer the right religions from Allāh﷾. The Qur'ān is the last divine book, and it has been preserved as it was sent to Rasūlullāhﷺ. No rules have been removed, and no new rules have been added. If we follow the Qur'ān, then we are following the rules made by our Creator who made us.

Time to Review

1. Why should a lawmaker have knowledge of the past, present, and future?
2. Why can we not make our own rules and live happily ever after?
3. Why can we not worship another god along with Allāh﷾?

1. Allāhﷻ created us to do something. Read āyah 51:56 of the Qur'ān and write down what human beings are supposed to do.

I did not create humans for nothing they must warship me

In the same āyah, who else—other than human beings—is required to do the same thing regarding Allāhﷻ?

the jinn

2. In āyah 16:20 of the Qur'ān, two opposite things are mentioned about idols and creations. What are these two things?

1. _created nothing_

2. _created_

3. In āyah 19:42 of the Qur'ān, Ibrāhīm (A) asked his father why he worshipped idols. Ibrāhīm (A) pointed out three things the idols could not do. What are these three things?

1. _Cannot see_

2. _cannot hear_

3. _cannot help_

4. Circle T if the sentence is true about Islam. Circle F if the sentence is false.

A.   The message of Islam is complete and perfect.   (T)   F

B.   Islam provides guidance toward the right path.   (T)   F

C.   Islam is the message for all of mankind.   (T)   F

D.   It is acceptable to partially worship Allāhﷻ.   T   (F)

5. Circle T if the sentence is true about Allāh﷾. Circle F if the sentence is false.

    A.   Allāh﷾ is our ultimate lawmaker.   **(T)**   F

    B.   Allāh's﷾ laws do not change.   **(T)**   F

    C.   Allāh﷾ is the Creator of everything.   **(T)**   F

    D.   Allāh﷾ does not know about the past and the future.   T   **(F)**

    E.   Allāh﷾ is the One and Only, He is Everlasting, and most Knowledgeable. **(T)**   F

6. Why did the Roboland have so much chaos?

    (A.)   Because only one robot makes all the rules.

    B.   Because there were no rules in Roboland.

    C.   Because it was a world of machines.

    (D.)   Because one robot did not follow the rules.

7. Who makes all the rules in the world and in the universe?

    A.   Nature.

    (B.)   Allāh﷾.

    C.   Angels.

    D.   Scientists.

8. What would happen to the world if everybody followed the rules of the Creator?

    (A.)   The world would turn peaceful.

    B.   The world would become very chaotic.

    C.   The world would become unlivable.

    D.   All human beings would die.

9. In order to make perfect rules, what should the rule-maker know? Circle all the correct answers.

    (A.)   Have full knowledge of everything.

    (B.)   Have wisdom.

    (C.)   Have knowledge of the past, present, and future.

    D.   His or her rules should not conflict with each other.

Revelation of the Qur'ān

Objective of the Lesson:

The revelation of the Qur'ān was a long process involving several steps and requiring several years. It was revealed under different circumstances, and in different locations, in order to solve different problems. This lesson introduces students to the process of the revelation of the Qur'ān.

The Qur'ān was revealed to Rasūlullāhﷺ over a 23-year period. It was not revealed in one sitting, or at one time. Sometimes only a few verses were revealed. At other times, an entire sūrah was revealed. These revelations were sent under different circumstances, and in different locations, in order to address different problems and issues.

Concern for people

The revelation of the Qur'ān took place at a time when Muhammadﷺ became increasingly worried and disturbed by the moral and spiritual condition of people in Makkah. He was unhappy about how the rich treated the poor. He was unhappy about people worshipping idols that could not help anybody. He felt these idols could not be God. He would often go to a quiet place to think about the purpose of life and who could be God of the whole world.

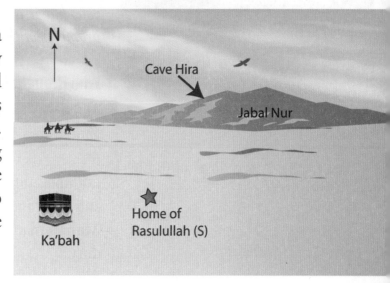

The more Muhammadﷺ thought about people and God, the more he began to experience powerful internal signs. He would dream about darkness breaking apart with the light of the early morning. As a result of these experiences and visions, Muhammadﷺ began to spend more time in isolation—in deep meditation.

Every year in Makkah spiritually minded people would go to quiet places to meditate. Muhammadﷺ also began to spend time in isolation. The best place for uninterrupted meditation was in caves in nearby mountains. Muhammadﷺ began to visit some caves, spending hours and sometimes days in the cave. During this time, Khadījah (ra) brought him food and water.

Faith of Muhammadﷺ

Muhammadﷺ was not a Christian, Jew or pagan worshipper. Before Islam, he did not follow any particular religion. Therefore, his meditation and worshipping in the caves did not have any particular format. The Islamic prayer method had not been established yet. During these long, solitary periods in the caves, Allāhﷻ was actually preparing Muhammadﷺ. But Muhammadﷺ was not aware that he was being prepared. He did not want to become a monk. He did not want to become a priest or find a new religion. He was not hoping to get a divine revelation. He was simply thinking and wondering about the Makkan people. Much later the Qur'ān mentioned that he was not hoping to receive a divine book, but it was sent to him as a mercy from Allāhﷻ.

وَمَا كُنتَ تَرْجُوٓاْ أَن يُلْقَىٰٓ إِلَيْكَ ٱلْكِتَٰبُ إِلَّا رَحْمَةً مِّن رَّبِّكَ فَلَا تَكُونَنَّ ظَهِيرًا لِّلْكَٰفِرِينَ ﴿٨٦﴾

And you did not expect that the Book would be given to you, but it is a mercy from your Rabb. Therefore, never be a promoter of the Unbelievers. (al-Qasas, 28:86)

Who Brought the Revelations?

The time shortly arrived when Allāhﷻ sent revelation to Muhammadﷺ. In the history of mankind, all revelations to messengers were sent through an angel named **Jibril (A)**. For example, angel Jibril brought revelations to Mūsā (A), 'Isā (A), and other messengers. When it was time to send revelations to Muhammadﷺ, Jibril (A) was the only angel chosen for this duty.

The first revelation

The revelation of the Qur'ān began when angel Jibril (A) brought **five āyāt** to Muhammadﷺ. This happened during one of the last ten nights of **Ramadan** in 610 C.E. During that month, Muhammadﷺ went to a cave called **Hira** on **Jabal Nūr** mountain. He went there to think about the purpose of life and the Creator of the world. The cave was a few miles away from his home. When Jibril (A) appeared to Muhammadﷺ with the first five verses of the Qur'ān, Muhammad ﷺ was so terrified that he was not sure what was happening to him. He felt like his entire body was being crushed and squeezed by some power. When he felt relief, an unknown voice asked him to read. He replied that he did not know how to read. Then he felt something squeeze him again so tightly that he could not breathe. Then he felt better, and the feeling of pressure was gone. This happened three times. Each time he heard someone say, "Read!"

سُورَةُ ٱلۡعَلَقِ

ٱقۡرَأۡ بِٱسۡمِ رَبِّكَ ٱلَّذِى خَلَقَ ﴿١﴾

خَلَقَ ٱلۡإِنسَٰنَ مِنۡ عَلَقٍ ﴿٢﴾

ٱقۡرَأۡ وَرَبُّكَ ٱلۡأَكۡرَمُ ﴿٣﴾

ٱلَّذِى عَلَّمَ بِٱلۡقَلَمِ ﴿٤﴾

عَلَّمَ ٱلۡإِنسَٰنَ مَا لَمۡ يَعۡلَمۡ ﴿٥﴾

Sūrah al-'Alaq

1. Read in the name of your Rabb who created

2. He has created man from a clot

3. Read and your Rabb is the most Gracious

4. Who has taught by the pen

5. He has taught man that which he did not know

Finally he felt better and was able to repeat the words after they were recited to him. Muhammadﷺ was terrified by this experience. After the incident, he ran downhill and dashed into his home. Later Muhammadﷺ discussed the incident in the cave with his wife Khadījah (ra). She assured him that the experience in the cave was not caused by an evil spirit, but was divine. The reason she concluded this way was because her husband was a good person, who never harmed anyone and never indulged in wrong things and never worshipped idols.

Time to Review

1. Why would Jibril's (A) duty end after the revelation of the Qur'ān?
2. What were some of the reasons Muhammadﷺ went to caves to meditate?
3. Why was Khadījah convinced that the experience in the cave was not caused by evil spirit?

How revelations reached Rasūlullāhﷺ

After the first revelation to Muhammadﷺ, the second revelation did not come for some time. During the first few years of revelations, Rasūlullāhﷺ felt pain in his body and he would faint. Later, he became accustomed to receiving the divine messages. He would not feel any pain during the process. The messages began to be revealed in his heart. He could tell if something that occurred in his mind was divine or just his own thought.

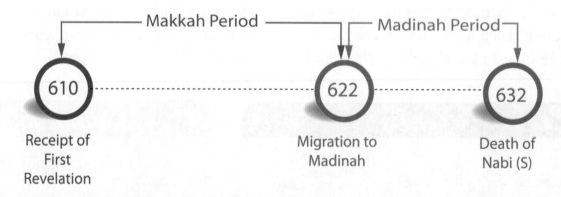

Makkan and Madīnan revelations

All the revelations were revealed either in Makkah or Madīnah. Accordingly, they are categorized as the Makkan or Madīnan revelations. The Makkan revelations are those that were revealed to Rasūlullāhﷺ during the first 13 years of prophethood, when he was in Makkah. During his migration to Madīnah, some verses were revealed. These were categorized as the Madīnan revelations. All the revelations received in and around Madīnah are called the Madīnan revelations. After Rasūlullāhﷺ liberated Makkah in 630 C.E., he continued to receive revelations for another two years. The revelations that he received after the liberation of Makkah are recognized as the Madīnan revelations, even though some of these were received in Makkah. In other words, all revelations prior to 622 C.E. are called the Makkan revelations, and all revelations in 622 C.E. and later are called the Madīnan revelations.

The early Makkan revelations were short, many of which were placed in the second half of the Qur'ān. Juz 30, or Part 30, of the Qur'ān, has some of the well-known short sūrahs. These revelations have a melodic tone. Most of the Makkan sūrahs have some sort of rhyme. Makkan sūrahs are mostly about the Majesty of Allāh, His Oneness, the *akhirat*, and the ultimate fate of human beings. The Makkan revelations did not provide detailed rules and regulations for day-to-day life.

The Madīnan revelations are long sūrahs. Most of the Madīnan revelations were placed in the beginning of the Qur'ān. For example, al-Baqarah is the longest sūrah in the Qur'ān, and it is the second sūrah. The Madīnan revelations provide laws, rules, and regulations. They deal with the problems of life and provide solutions. They also describe people from the past and other messengers.

Compilation of the revelations

The revelations were not compiled in the Qur'ān in the same order they were revealed. The first five revealed verses were placed in sūrah 96. Sūrah al-Fātihah is the first sūrah in the Qur'ān, but it was not the first sūrah to be revealed. The compilation of the verses was done in a proper manner by Rasūlullāh under divine guidance.

Each time a revelation was sent to Rasūlullāh, he would first memorize it attentively and carefully. Next he would tell his companions, who would immediately write it down. There were several companions who were given the duty to write down the revelation and cross-check it with Rasūlullāh. Then they

Points to Ponder

There must be some reason why the Makkan revelations did not provide detailed rules and regulations for day-to-day life, and instead focus on the majesty of Allāh, the Hereafter, and so forth. What could be the reason for not providing rules and regulations first?

would save all the written versions. From time to time, the companions would check the saved documents and verify them with Rasūlullāh. Large number of the companions also memorize   d the revelations. In addition to this procedure, it is reported that each year angel Jibril (A) would review the revelations with Rasūlullāh.

Reaction of the people

When the revelations were given to Rasūlullāh, nobody saw angel Jibril (A). Unless Rasūlullāh told them it was a revelation, people could not say whether something that Rasūlullāh said was a revelation. For this reason, many people thought Rasūlullāh was making up stories. Others said some foreigner was teaching him stories about the past. The Jews once honored angel Jibril (A). But after angel Jibril (A) began bringing divine revelations to Muhammad, the Jews did not like angel Jibril (A) anymore.

Final revelation

The final revelation was sent in the year 10 A.H., or 632 C.E., when Rasūlullāh was performing the Farewell Pilgrimage and delivering the **Farewell Khutba**. During the khutba, Allāh revealed āyah 5:3. A part of this āyah and its translation is as follows:

$$ \text{ٱلْيَوْمَ أَكْمَلْتُ لَكُمْ دِينَكُمْ وَأَتْمَمْتُ عَلَيْكُمْ نِعْمَتِي وَرَضِيتُ لَكُمُ ٱلْإِسْلَٰمَ دِينًا} $$

This day I have perfected for you your religion, and completed upon you My blessing, and have accepted for you ISLAM as the religion. (5:3)

Many scholars consider this āyah to be the last āyah revealed to Rasūlullāh. Thus the Qur'ān was completed. Allāh, Himself, protects the contents of the Qur'ān.

Note: C.E. stands for Common Era. The numbering of years is identical to the A.D. system. Common Era is preferred because it does not use any religious titles referring to Jesus Christ.

1. Which of the following choices about the Makkan revelations is correct?

    A.   All Makkan sūrahs are long.

    B.   All Makkan sūrahs are placed in the first half of the Qur'ān.

    C.   Most of the Makkan sūrahs have rhymes and sound melodic.

    D.   Most of the Makkan sūrahs provide laws and codes of conduct.

2. What are the beginning and ending years of all Makkan revelations?

    Beginning: _____ C.E.   Ending: _____ C.E.

3. Which of the following choices about the compilation and arrangement of the revelations in the Qur'ān is correct?

    A.   The Makkan sūrahs were placed first, and then the Madīnan sūrahs.

    B.   The order of arrangement was from the longest sūrah to the shortest.

    C.   The compilation and arrangement of the sūrahs was done by Abu Bakr (R).

    D.   The sūrahs were not compiled in the order they were revealed.

4. Name two important features of most of the Madīnan revelations.

    1.   _____

    2.   _____

5. Read āyah 16:102 of the Qur'ān. Here angel Jibril (A) is mentioned by a special name. Write the special name.

    _____

6. What are two major themes or topics mentioned in many of the Makkan revelations?

    1.   _____

    2.   _____

7. How many suwar (plural of sūrah) were revealed in Makkah?

    A.   80 suwar.

    B.   114 suwar.

    C.   86 suwar.

    D.   28 suwar.

8. In which year was the famous Farewell Khutba was delivered?

    A.   In 610 C.E.

    B.   In 622 C.E.

    C.   In 630 C.E.

    D.   In 632 C.E.

9. From which year onwards were all the revelations categorized as Madīnan revelations?

    A.   Revelations from 615 C.E. onwards.

    B.   Revelations from 622 C.E. onwards.

    C.   Revelations from 610 C.E. onwards.

    D.   Revelations from 630 C.E. onwards.

10. Unscramble the following letters to make meaningful words. Then rearrange the circled letters to make a secret word.

R E S V E

R I H A

F L N A I

Secret word:

Characteristics of the Messengers

Objective of the Lesson:

The messengers of Islam came during different periods, to different communities, and to solve different problems. Yet all of them showed a similar nature, behavior, and activities. This lesson discusses some of the qualities in common of all messengers and explains why these qualities made them righteous servants of Allāhﷻ

Saleem bought several books from a bookstore. He thought he did not have to go to school anymore because he had all the books that were used in school. Saleem's sister, Salwa, explained that in addition to books, you also need a teacher. A teacher can show you how to do things and corrects you when you make a mistake.

Messenger as a teacher

A messenger is a teacher who is selected by Allāhﷻ. Messengers, or *Nabis*, teach us how to follow the Right Path. A person cannot decide to become a *nabi*. Only Allāhﷻ chooses who can become a *nabi*.[22:75] By sending the Qur'ān, Allāhﷻ has provided the complete written guidance.[5:3] To help us understand and follow this guidance, Allāhﷻ selected Muhammadﷺ as our teacher and guide. The Qur'ān contains complete guidance, so there is no need for us to have any more prophets after Muhammadﷺ. Muhammad ﷺ, therefore, is the Last and Final Messenger.[33:40]

$$ لَّقَدْ كَانَ لَكُمْ فِى رَسُولِ ٱللَّهِ أُسْوَةٌ حَسَنَةٌ لِّمَن كَانَ يَرْجُوا ٱللَّهَ وَٱلْيَوْمَ ٱلْءَاخِرَ وَذَكَرَ ٱللَّهَ كَثِيرًا ۝ $$

Certainly you have in the messenger of Allāh an excellent exemplar for him who is confident of Allāh and the Hereafter, and who remembers Allāh much. (33:21)

Messengers were human beings

All *nabis* were human beings.[14:11] They all lived similar to the way we do. They all needed food and drink for their survival.[21:8] They went to markets to get their food and other necessities.[25:7,20] They were human beings, therefore, they could not live forever. Like us they had to die eventually.

$$ وَمَا جَعَلْنَاهُمْ جَسَدًا لَّا يَأْكُلُونَ ٱلطَّعَامَ وَمَا كَانُوا خَالِدِينَ ۝ $$

And We did not give them bodies not taking food and neither are they abiding. (21:8)

The messengers were not Superman. They were not angels. When they showed their people a sign, it was from Allāh.[13:38] They did things that are possible for human beings to do. Therefore, if they could lead a truthful life, so can we. All the messengers had families and children.[13:38] They set an example of ideal family life, and how to treat members of the family.

It is important to remember that all the messengers were human beings, just like we are. Allāh sent human messengers as examples for us to follow. A computer or a machine can do many things better than we can. We do not compare ourselves to a computer. A bird can fly, a fish can stay underwater all its life, and a cheetah can sprint fast, but we cannot do such acts. We do not compare ourselves to animals. They are not our examples.

If Allāh﷾ had sent an angel or some other non-human creature as a messenger, such a creature would not have been our best example.

إِنَّ إِبْرَٰهِيمَ كَانَ أُمَّةً قَانِتًا لِّلَّهِ حَنِيفًا وَلَمْ يَكُ مِنَ ٱلْمُشْرِكِينَ ۝

Surely Ibrāhīm was a model [person]—obedient to Allāh, upright, and he was not a polytheist. (16:120)

قَدْ كَانَتْ لَكُمْ أُسْوَةٌ حَسَنَةٌ فِىٓ إِبْرَٰهِيمَ

Surely there is a good example for you in Ibrāhīm... (60:4)

Messengers were truthful

All the *nabis* were truthful people. None of them acted badly.[21:27] They did things the way Allāh﷾ wanted. They were honest, humble, and wise. Some of them, such as Dāwūd (A) and Sulaimān (A), were powerful kings. Other messengers, such as Mūsā (A) and Hārūn (A), opposed a cruel ruler. Some of them, such as Ayyub (A), was at one time a very poor and weak person. All of them, whether powerful or weak, were always truthful. They set an example for us to remain truthful in our lives.

The messengers warned their communities of punishment if they did evil things, and they gave them good news of rewards if they did the right things. All of them preached Islam as the only religion.[42:13] The religion of Islam was perfected with the last messenger, Muhammadﷺ. He is the best example for us.

Time to Review

1. Why was it important for the messengers to always be truthful?
2. Why did Allāh﷾ emphasize that messengers needed food and drink for survival?
3. What are some conclusions that we can draw from the fact that the messengers were not Superman?

Messengers spoke local languages

Messengers were sent to every nation of the world.[10:47] It is not necessary that the Qur'ān provide a list of all the messengers. What is true is that these messengers spoke the language of the community.[14:4] If Rasūlullāhﷺ had spoken English or Chinese, he would not have been able to communicate his message. A messenger in Arabia must speak Arabic, and a messenger in China must speak Chinese. We do not know the messengers in China, Greece, Rome, India, or other civilizations. Allāh﷾ did not tell us the names of all the messengers in the Qur'ān.[4:164]

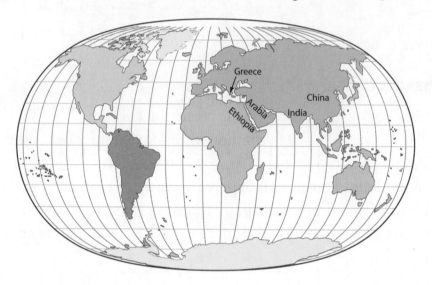

People opposed the messengers

Although the messengers tried to show the right path, their people opposed them.[6:34] Their enemies laughed at them, insulted them, injured them, and even tried to kill them. Later their people changed the true messages of the *nabis*. But Allāh ﷾ protects the messages of the Qur'ān from any changes made by people.

None of the *nabis* ever claimed to be a god. They never told people to worship them.[21:29] They never told people to worship idols or other gods. When people worshipped false gods and did not listen to the right teachings, they were punished by Allāh﷾.

Belief in all the messengers

As Muslims, we believe in all the messengers.[2:4, 136] All the *nabis* belong to the same rank, although Allāh﷾ made some *nabis* become better known than others.[2:253] We do not make any distinctions among the messengers.[2:136] Muhammadﷺ is the *nabi* for the whole world and all generations that followed him. He brought the complete and perfect teachings for mankind. Others were *nabi* only for their own communities. They brought messages suitable for their

Points to Ponder

Many people rejected their messengers because they were human beings. It can be argued that it would have been easier if Allāh﷾ had sent angels as messengers. People probably would have accepted the angels. What might be the reasons angels were not sent as messengers?

own generation, not for all of mankind. Their messages were time-bound, not designed to last for the rest of human life on Earth. Although we believe in all the messengers, it is not enough to follow just one of the past messengers. We must follow the messages that Muhammadﷺ brought to all of mankind.

Messengers brought guidance

All the messengers, or *rasuls*, were given divine guidance, and all of them received books from Allāh﷿.[6:90; 57:25] None of them preached whatever they wanted.[21:27] None of them preached any other book as a divine book from Allāh﷿.[13:38] We know the names of some of the books, but Allāh﷿ did not tell us about other books. The Qur'ān is the last divine book, so Allāh﷿ protects the Qur'ān from changes by human beings.[85:21–22] The role of the messengers was limited to delivering the messages to their people. They did not force people to accept a particular message.

1. Read āyah 2:136 of the Qur'ān. Write the names of some of the *nabis* mentioned in the āyah:

Ibrahim(a) musa(a) isa(a) Yacub(a) Isaac(a)
Ismail(a)

2. In this same āyah (2:136), who seems to be a better messenger? Why?

No one is better because they're all equal

3. Read āyah 6:112 of the Qur'ān, and then answer the following questions:

a. How many *nabis* had enemies? _____all_____

b. What were the two kinds of enemies 1) _human actions_ 2) _jinn_

4. Read āyah 7:65 of the Qur'ān. What did nabi Hūd (A) tell his people? Write the answer in your own words.

"oh my people, worship one good, Aallah(swt)
a) books

5. Read āyah 13:38 of the Qur'ān, and then answer the following questions:

a. What did all the messengers have? _____Wifes_____

b. With Allāh's permission, what did the messengers bring? _children_

6. Read āyah 14:11 of the Qur'ān. In this āyah, one of the important characteristics of all messengers is mentioned. What is the characteristic?

Human itrustworthy

7. Read āyah 10:47 of the Qur'ān. What did Allāh﷾ send to each community?

A messenger

8. Check the box ✓ if the sentence is correct. Mark the box ✗ if the sentence is incorrect.

A. Messengers always forced their people to accept the truth.

B. Some of the messengers were superhuman because they could do amazing things.

C. A few messenger told their people to worship them after they died.

D. All messengers were human beings.

E. All messengers were truthful people.

9. As Muslims, what should we think about the messengers?

A. We make no difference among the messengers.
B. We believe messengers came only in Arabia.
C. If needed, we can worship some messengers for bringing the truth.
D. We only believe in Muhammadﷺ, but not other messengers.

10. Where did Allāh﷾ send all His messengers?

A. In the Middle East only.
B. To the Jewish land and the Arab lands only.
C. In Jerusalem, Makkah and Yemen.
D. To every nation in the world.

Unit 2: The Battles and Other Developments

The second unit focuses on some of the significant battles in the history of Islam. A clear understanding of the reasons for these battles and their outcomes is critical in appreciating how the Muslims handled serious challenges—when they responded properly and when they faltered. The chapter on the Pledge of 'Aqabah explains different negotiation tactics and styles, as well as the importance of taking the necessary steps before making a final decision. The lesson on the Hudaibiyah Treaty shows how apparent failure can turn into a decisive victory. We should realize that with Allāh's help, our own perceived failure could turn into actual success. The battles of Badr, Uhud, and the Trench provide important lessons applicable to us in our daily lives. The Liberation of Makkah chapter highlights a brilliant military strategy that won over the Makkan people without bloodshed, using the power of forgiveness and mercy. These accounts should not be presented as simple historical narrative; they also offer meaningful moral lessons that are still relevant today.

The Battles and Other Developments

Pledges of 'Aqabah: *Invitation to Migrate*

Rasūlullāh's migration to Madīnah was made possible by two pledges that came to be known as the Pledges of 'Aqabah. Who were the people involved and why did they make the pledges? Students will learn about these events and their significance in shaping the history of Islam.

The Battle of Badr: *Allāh Supports the Righteous*

The Battle of Badr was an important event that changed Muslim history. If Muslims had lost this battle, their progress, or even their survival, would have been very difficult. This lesson briefly describes the incidents that led to this battle, and explains how Muslims were successful against a much larger and well-equipped army.

The Battle of Uhud: *Obey Allāh and Obey the Rasūl*

This battle was the second major battle fought by Muslims. They did not win the battle. This lesson discusses the main reasons for not winning the battle. What message did early Muslims learn from this battle? Can we apply the message to our lives today?

The Battle of the Trench: *A Bloodless Battle*

The Battle of the Trench was another significant battle in the history of Islam. This battle was never fought face to face, but it had a lasting impact on the Muslims and the polytheist tribes from all over Arabia. The treachery of the Jewish tribe Banu Qurayzah nearly destroyed the Muslims. Thanks to Allāh, the crisis was averted. This lesson provides a brief overview of the battle and its outcome. .

The Treaty of Hudaibiyah: *A Clear Victory*

The Treaty of Hudaibiyah was largely viewed as a defeat for the Muslims, but soon the treaty turned out to be a major victory for them. The treaty helped shape the future of Islam. This lesson provides a brief account of the treaty and discusses its lasting impact on the history of Islam.

Liberation of Makkah: *A Bloodless Victory*

Within two years of signing the Treaty of Hudaibiyah, the Muslims liberated Makkah in a dramatic event. The lesson provides an overview of the events that led to the bloodless liberation of Makkah from the clutches of idol-worshipping. Instead of punishing the polytheists, Rasūlullāh forgave them, thus making it possible for all of Arabia to accept Islam.

Pledges of 'Aqabah: *Invitation to Migrate*

Objective of the Lesson:

Rasūlullāh'sﷺ migration to Madīnah was made possible by two pledges that came to be known as the Pledges of 'Aqabah. Who were the people involved and why did they make the pledges? Students will learn about these events and their significance in shaping the history of Islam.

After becoming a messenger of Allāhﷻ, Muhammadﷺ lived in Makkah for 13 years. He received the first revelation in 610 C.E. Nine years after he received the first revelation, his uncle Abū Tālib and wife Khadījah (ra) passed away. Our Nabi Muhammad'sﷺ life was already difficult, but after the deaths of his wife and uncle, his life became even more difficult. People in Makkah respected him as a good man, but most of them did not like his teachings. These non-believers were planning to harm him.

Hajj in 620 C.E.

Within a few months of returning from Tā'if, it was time for the annual Hajj. The year was 620 C.E. As before, Rasūlullāhﷺ tried to make the best of the season by contacting as many pilgrims as he could and speak to them about Islam. A key development happened during this Hajj season that changed the history of Islam forever. This development was meaningful contact with a group of people who had traveled from Yathrib.

People of Yathrib

Yathrib would later become famous as Madinatun-Nabi, the City of the Nabi, or simply Madīnah. The city of Yathrib had several tribes; the main tribes were the Jews, the **'Aws,** and the **Khazraj**. The 'Aws and the Khazraj had rivalry between them, and they had been fighting each other for a long time. They also wanted peace between them, but there was no one who could be neutral and settle their rivalry.

During the Hajj in 620 C.E., the people of the Khazraj tribe became interested in Muhammadﷺ. They believed he would be the best person to solve their rivalry. They heard Muhammadﷺ speak of justice, equality, human values, and the importance of worshipping one God. He invited these men from Yathrib to accept Islam. **Six** of them accepted Islam. These six men returned to Yathrib and invited others to accept Islam.

The first pledge

In 621 C.E., **12** people traveled from Yathrib to perform Hajj. Ten of them were from the Khazraj tribe, and two were from the 'Aws tribe. They secretly met with Rasūlullāhﷺ in a place called **al-'Aqabah**, near Makkah, and made an agreement with him. In the history of Islam, this agreement is known as the **First Pledge of al-'Aqabah**. A pledge is a promise or agreement to do something. Rasūlullāhﷺ asked them to make several oaths. Some of the main oaths were:

- To obey none but Allāhﷻ
- Not to steal
- Not to kill their children
- Not to commit any evil acts

Rasūlullāhﷺ told them that if they honored the oaths, Allāhﷻ would be happy with them. Allāhﷻ would reward them with a life in Heaven. After taking the oaths, they finished their Hajj with the rest of the people. Then they went back to Yathrib and told others about Islam. Through them even more people accepted Islam.

The pagan Quraish in Makkah had no clue about this development. During the Hajj, a large number of people gathered and interacted with others. It was impossible for one person to keep an eye on others and learn about any secret deals. The Quraish knew Muhammadﷺ met people and talked to them about Islam. But they had no idea that such a game-changing agreement was being negotiated during Hajj.

Appointing an educator

Simply obeying the pledge might not help these new Muslims. Therefore, Rasūlullāhﷺ also sent a teacher with them. This teacher was Mu'sab ibn 'Umayr. His job was to educate the 'Aws and the Khazraj about Islam, teach them the Qur'ān, and answer any questions these new Muslims might have. Mu'sab stayed in Yathrib for a long time, performing his job with utmost dedication.

The second pledge

The following year, in 622 C.E., **75** people traveled from Yathrib to Makkah to perform Hajj. Among them were two women. During Hajj, they had another secret meeting with Rasūlullāhﷺ in al-'Aqabah. The people from Yathrib took another oath. In the history of Islam, this oath is known as the **Second Pledge of al-'Aqabah**. This oath was similar to the first oath, but it was more detailed.

During these secret meetings, the people of Yathrib learned that Nabi Muhammad'sﷺ life in Makkah was becoming very difficult. They found out that most of the Makkans did not like Islam. They also learned that the top leaders in Makkah opposed Muhammadﷺ or his teachings. These leaders were planning to stop Rasūlullāhﷺ from teaching Islam. They were even ready to kill him to stop him.

An invitation to move

These 75 Muslims from Yathrib invited Nabi Muhammadﷺ to come to Yathrib, live with them, and continue his preaching. **Al-'Abbās**, one of Rasūlullāh'sﷺ uncles, was present during the secret meeting. He was not yet a Muslim, but he loved his nephew. He was concerned for his nephew just as the people from Yathrib were concerned. He explained to the people of Yathrib the danger of having Nabi Muhammadﷺ among them. He told them that the Makkans would not like it and that they might take revenge on the people of Yathrib. He also advised them that if they really wanted Nabi Muhammadﷺ to go with them, they had to protect him at all costs. All 75 people from Yathrib promised to protect Muhammadﷺ. This was the main condition in the Second Pledge of al-'Aqabah.

Points to know

Rasūlullāhﷺ had several uncles, and aunts, most notable among them were Abū Tālib, Hamzah, Abū Lahab, and Al-'Abbās.

Abū Tālib and Abū Lahab never accepted Islam.

Hamzah was the first uncle to accept Islam.

Al-'Abbās did not accept Islam during the early years. But he provided protection to Muslims as needed. His wife accepted Islam.

During the Battle of Badr, Al-'Abbās fought against the Muslims. He was taken as a prisoner of war. Then he was released after he paid a ransom.

Some say he secretly accepted Islam before the battle, but other disagree. He formally accepted Islam in 630 C.E., right before the liberation of Makkah.

Short summary

- In 620 C.E., the first group of people came from Yathrib to Makkah.
- Six of the people in the first group accepted Islam.
- In 621 C.E., 12 people traveled from Yathrib and took the First Pledge of 'Aqabah.
- In 622 C.E., 75 people came from Yathrib, including two women.
- In 622 C.E., the Second Pledge of al-'Aqabah was adopted.
- Al-'Abbās, Rasūlullāh'sﷺ uncle, was present during the signing of the pledge.

The people from Yathrib promised to lead good lives and protect Nabi Muhammadﷺ as they would protect their own women and children. They declared that it would be a duty upon them to protect Muhammadﷺ if anyone from Makkah attacked them.

At the end of Hajj, and after taking the Second Pledge of al-'Aqabah, the 75 people from Yathrib left. Rasūlullāhﷺ stayed in Makkah, waiting for the best opportunity to leave the city.

Despite all the attempts to keep the meeting secret, some of the Makkans finally learned about the pledge. They were furious about it. They asked the people from Yathrib if they really made an agreement with the Muslims. Not all the people made the agreement, and not all of them knew about it. The people who were not involved with the agreement denied that any such agreement was made. It was not a lie because they did not know about it. The 75 people who made the agreement were scattered among the other people from Yathrib. Nobody knew who they were. Nobody asked them directly; therefore they remained silent. The Quraish leaders were led to believe no such agreement took place.

Evil plans of the Makkans

By the time the Quraish leaders collected evidence that a pledge did take place, the Hajj was over, and the people from Yathrib had already left Makkah. The Quraish could not do much about it and they fumed with anger. They began

serious discussions about what to do with Muhammadﷺ. They realized that if Muhammadﷺ went to Yathrib, he might convert the entire city to Islam and create problems for the Makkans. Finally, the idol worshippers of Makkah decided to kill him. One night, several men from the Quraish tribe gathered outside Rasūlullāh'sﷺ home to kill him. However, late in the night, Rasūlullāhﷺ had secretly left his house. 'Ali, Rasūlullāh'sﷺ cousin, took Rasūlullāh'sﷺ place in his bed. Rasūlullāhﷺ went to his friend Abū Bakr's (R) house, and together they headed towards Yathrib. He knew he would be safe in Yathrib.

The Pledges of al-'Aqabah are very important in the history of Islam. Soon after the second pledge, in the year 622 C.E., Rasūlullāhﷺ moved to Yathrib. If the people of Yathrib had not offered help to Muhammadﷺ, he could not have gone there for shelter. He had no other place to go. Without proper shelter, his life would have been in danger. The Pledges of al-'Aqabah provided a new opportunity for Islam. They created a new generation of Muslims who supported Nabi Muhammadﷺ with their lives and wealth.

An example of negotiation skill

Today in the modern world, everybody makes agreements with another party at one time or another. Deals can be made between two individuals, two families, two companies, two organizations or two countries. In some deals, there are lengthy discussions and offers and counter-offers made until an agreement is reached.

The Pledges of al-'Aqabah are beautiful examples of how to make a successful negotiation. Here we see that Nabi Muhammadﷺ took nearly two years to finalize the deal. He did not jump into an agreement all of a sudden. He worked out the strategies and offered his suggestions to the other party. He gave them time to think it over and respond. He maintained their trust, and in return, they kept their promise of secrecy. He made sure the deal was strong and nobody could violate it. He sent a teacher to Yathrib to make sure the people did not abandon Islam. In this way he consolidated his position. Only after making sure the people of Yathrib were fully committed to their oath, did he decide to migrate to Yathrib.

1. How many people from Yathrib took the First Pledge of al-'Aqabah?

   _____

2. How many people from Yathrib took the Second Pledge of al-'Aqabah?

   _____

3. When were the First and Second Pledges of al-'Aqabah taken?

   a. First Pledge in the year: _____

   b. Second Pledge in the year: _____

4. Circle T if the statement is true. Circle F if the statement is false.

Uncle Abū Ṭālib was present for the Pledge of al-'Aqabah.	T	F
Uncle Al-'Abbās was present for the Pledge of al-'Aqabah.	T	F
The Pledge of al-'Aqabah was taken openly in front of the Ka'bah.	T	F
The idol worshippers also signed the Pledges of al-'Aqabah.	T	F
Six men accepted Islam before any pledge of al-'Aqabah was taken.	T	F

5. How long after the Second Pledge of al-'Aqabah did Rasūlullāhﷺ secretly leave Makkah?

   A. Three years after the Second Pledge of al-'Aqabah.

   B. Five years after the Second Pledge of al-'Aqabah.

   C. Shortly after the Second Pledge of al-'Aqabah.

   D. One year before the Second Pledge of al-'Aqabah.

6. What was the main condition of the Second Pledge of al-'Aqabah?

   A. The people of Yathrib would travel for Hajj.

   B. The people of Yathrib would love each other as Muslims.

   C. The people of Yathrib would not give shelter to Muhammadﷺ.

   D. The people of Yathrib would protect Muhammadﷺ at any cost.

7. During the Second Pledge of Aqabah, 75 people came to Makkah. How many of them were women?

    A.   2 women.

    B.   5 women.

    C.   7 women.

    D.   10 women.

8. Unscramble the following letters to make meaningful words.

E M N Y E   __ __ __ __ __

B T E I R   __ __ __ __ __

D G P E L E   __ __ __ __ __ __

S A B A B   __ __ __ __ __

9. Each of the letters below corresponds to a number. In this exercise, find the letter corresponding to the number to solve the puzzle.

A	B	C	D	E	F	G	H	I	J	K	L	M
1	2	3	4	5	6	7	8	9	10	11	12	13

N	O	P	Q	R	S	T	U	V	W	X	Y	Z
14	15	16	17	18	19	20	21	22	23	24	25	26

Find the letters corresponding to the following numbers.

1   17   1   2   1   8

__ __ __ __ __ __

25   1   20   8   18   9   2

__ __ __ __ __ __ __

The Battle of Badr: *Allāh ﷻ Supports the Righteous*

Objective of the Lesson:

The Battle of Badr was an important event that changed Muslim history. If Muslims had lost this battle, their progress, or even their survival, would have been very difficult. The purpose of this lesson is to briefly describe the incidents that led to this battle, and explain how Muslims were successful against a much larger and well-equipped army.

In the year 622 C.E., our Messenger Muhammadﷺ migrated from Makkah to Madīnah to freely teach the message of Islam. The first two years in Madīnah was relatively quiet as Rasūlullāhﷺ focused on making rules and regulations for leading a peaceful life in all communities in Madīnah. But life in Madīnah soon changed as a major battle was fought between the Muslims and the idolaters of Makkah. This battle, fought in the year 624 C.E—two years after the migration—is known as the **Battle of Badr**, named after the location of the battlefield. Sūrah Anfāl discusses the battle and its result.

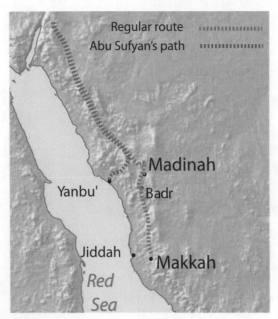

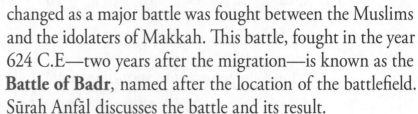

Regular route ::::::::::::::::
Abu Sufyan's path ::::::::::::::::

Madinah
Yanbu'   Badr
Jiddah   Makkah
Red
Sea

The main reasons for the battle

No large-scale battle happens without a reason. The Battle of Badr also did not happen without a reason. Several minor and major events happened within a few months that ultimately led to the battle.

1. The first reason is tension between the Muslims and idolaters in Makkah. The idolaters in Makkah seized the

wealth and properties of the Muslims who had migrated to Madīnah. In āyah 22:39, Allāh﷿ gave permission for the oppressed to fight against the oppressors. With the permission of Allāh﷿, the Muslims decided to recover their lost wealth by conducting small raids on Makkan traders. Traders from various parts of Arabia used to travel through Madīnah to reach their business destination in Syria. Although the raids on the Makkan pagan traders were small-scale incidents, these attacks worried them. They thought that if the Muslims became strong in Madīnah, the traders might not have a safe passage to Syria.

2. The Makkan pagan leaders soon realized Muhammadﷺ was becoming too powerful in Madīnah. His power was causing trouble for them. They wanted to stop the progress of the Muslims and curb the power of Muhammadﷺ.

3. The tension between the Muslims and the Makkan pagans reached a new height after a few Muslims killed a pagan trader named **Amr bin Hadrami**. A small group of Muslims were on a surveillance mission in **Nakhla**. They had an encounter with the Makkan trader group; Hadrami was killed and two other polytheists were taken as prisoners.

4. All these incidents created tension between the Muslims and the pagan Quraish. But the final incident that triggered the battle was an attempt by the Muslims to ambush **Abū Sufyān**'s caravan. A caravan is a group of travelers journeying together. Abu Sufyān was retuning from Syria to Makkah. The caravan was loaded with merchandise. Almost all of the wealthy merchants in Makkah were heavily invested in the trade. The Muslims decided to capture the caravan to recover some of their lost wealth in Makkah. In addition, the Muslims feared that if they did not stop the caravan, the profit from such trades would be used to form a big army to fight against them in the future.

Abū Sufyān's caravan

In the summer of 623 C.E., the Quraish sent a large caravan to Syria to conduct business. The leader of the caravan was Abu Sufyān, who, at that time, was an enemy of the Muslims. His business in Syria was very successful and profitable. He brought camel-loads of goods from Syria to sell in Makkah. While returning home, he realized there was a problem—the road from Syria to Makkah passed alongside Madīnah, where Muslims lived.

Points to Remember

- The Battle of Badr was the first major battle fought by the Muslims.
- The battle was fought two years after the migration of Rasūlullāhﷺ.
- The Muslims had an army of 313 men against a 1,000-man Makkan army.
- The main cause of the battle was a Muslim plan to ambush a Makkan caravan.
- The caravan was returning from Syria with camel-loads of supplies.
- The battle was fought around the wells in Badr.
- The Makkans were totally defeated in the battle.

Points to Ponder

If the Muslims had not conducted smaller raids on the Makkan caravan, and they had not planned to ambush Abū Sufyān's caravan, the Battle of Badr probably would not have happened. In view of the Muslims in exile, how would you justify their plan to raid these caravans?

When Abū Sufyān was near Madīnah, he was tipped off about a possible Muslim ambush on the caravan. In order to protect his caravan from the possible ambush, Abū Sufyān sent for an escort from Makkah. He, himself, led his caravan several miles away from the usual trade route by the seacoast near **Yanbu** (see map). After he ensured the safety of the caravan, Abū Sufyān could have easily traveled to Makkah by following the route by the seacoast. Instead, he waited for the Makkans to arrive with an army. Obviously, Abu Sufyān was preparing for a full-blown battle.

The Makkan army prepares

When the Makkan idolaters learned about the plans of the Muslims, they became furious. Immediately they formed an army of about 1,000 men. They collected many horses and camels for the army. The army was strong and the soldiers were experts in warfare. They marched northbound from Makkah to secure the caravan and to crush the Muslims.

Initial Muslim plan

The initial plan of the Muslims was to ambush Abu Sufyān's caravan. With this intention, a small group secretly moved toward Badr, a place about 80 miles away

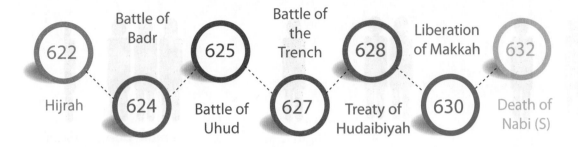

from Madīnah. Due to the presence of a large number of water wells in the area, it was a popular resting place for traders. After the Muslims reached Badr, they realized the caravan had already passed through. Their ambush plan now appeared impossible. This small group of Muslims wanted the easy target—the unarmed caravan. But Allāh wanted something better and bigger for them. That bigger goal is mentioned in āyah 8:7 of the Qur'ān: "to cut off the roots of the unbelievers."

And behold! Allāh promised you that one of the two parties would surely be yours, while you wished that the one which was not possessing arms should be yours; and Allāh wished that the Truth be proved true by His Words, and to cut off the roots of the unbelievers. (8:7)

The Muslim army prepares

Back in Madīnah, Rasūlullāh learned that the ambush plan failed. Now the Muslims were at risk of facing a larger Makkan army. Rasūlullāh convened a *shura* council asking for the companions' advice. The council advised him to prepare for a full-scale battle because they calculated a vast army was not coming merely to rescue the caravan. They were going to wage war against the Muslims.

Rasūlullāh had difficulty forming an army to confront the powerful Makkan army. After a careful search, the Muslims could only mobilize 313 men as their temporary army, which included many youths and elderly men. It was a weak army by all standards. However, Rasūlullāh knew Allāh was on their side. Allāh would help the Muslims.

The battlefield

After reaching Badr, Rasūlullāh camped near the first well they came across. A companion suggested moving forward to the well nearest the enemy so that all the other wells would be behind them, and their enemies could not access any of them. This was a good battle tactic, and Rasūlullāh liked it. This example shows that Rasūlullāh had an open mind to listen to good suggestions from his companions. That very night it rained in Badr.[8:11] It is reported that in the

Actual Strength
3 enemies for 1 Muslim

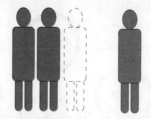

Muslims thought
2 enemies for 1 Muslim

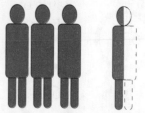

Enemies miscalculated
Small Muslim army

Muslim location of the valley, it rained lightly, just enough to give them relief from heat and thirst. But in the Quraish camp it rained heavily, causing a big mess.

Actual strength not realized

After the Muslims and the Makkan idolaters reached Badr, something strange happened. Neither of the armies could determine the other's strength. The Makkans were scattered around the higher grounds. When the Muslims saw them, they thought their enemies were about twice their number. In reality, the Makkans were about three times larger than the Muslims. When the polytheists saw the Muslims, the Muslims appeared to be few in number.

The Muslims did not realize the actual strength of their enemies, so they thought the battle would not be difficult. On the other hand, the polytheists were confident about their victory because they thought the Muslims were fewer in number. They underestimated the Muslims, thinking they could easily defeat them.

Time to Review

1. Why the location of wells in Badr were strategically important for the Muslims?
2. What could be the reasons the Makkans underestimated the Muslims?
3. Some of the Muslims wanted to ambush the caravan but Allāh had a bigger plan for them. What was the bigger plan?

Actual battle

It was customary at that time that a duel would be fought before actual battle. Three warriors from each groups came forward to fight the duel. Hamzah, 'Ali and 'Ubaydah from the Muslim camp fought the duel and they killed their enemies.

Then the actual battle began. The Muslims began the battle thinking that each of them needed to fight just two enemies because they thought the enemies were only twice their number. They fought bravely. Allāh﷾ helped the Muslims by sending 1,000 angels. The Muslims and the polytheists did not see the angels. The Muslims never thought they could fight so well. With every swing of the sword, an enemy was either hurt or killed. The polytheists were surprised to see a much larger Muslim army than they expected. Their attacks on the Muslims were not effective. The Makkans also realized that too many of their soldiers were getting killed. They lost hope and started running away. The battle had started at noon, and within a few hours, it was over.

Muslim victory

The Muslims won the battle. When they counted their losses, they found that only 14 brave Muslims had died in the battle. The losses of their enemies was much larger. About 70 enemies were killed, and another 70 were taken as prisoners. The Makkan's biggest loss was the death of Abu Jahl—the polytheist leader. He was one of the most notorious enemies of the Muslims.

The Battle of Badr shows that Allāh﷾ always helps those who stand up for His cause. This battle made the Muslims stronger. They realized they were not weak anymore and could protect themselves from their enemies. The non-Muslims in Madīnah began to respect Rasūlullāhﷺ and the Muslims. The Muslims established themselves as a major power in Madīnah.

1. Which sūrah in the Qur'ān discusses the Battle of Badr in detail?

_____

2. Before the Battle of Badr, what was the Muslim plan?

    A.   To go to Syria.

    B.   To send a caravan to Makkah.

    C.   To capture Abu Sufyān's caravan.

    D.   To capture Abu Jahl.

3. Who was the leader of the caravan that went to Syria to conduct business?

    A.   Abu Jahl.

    B.   Abu Sufyān.

    C.   Abu Muslim.

    D.   Abu Dawud.

4. During the Battle of Badr, what was the actual ratio of enemies to Muslims?

    A.   3 enemies to 1 Muslim.

    B.   3 enemies to 2 Muslims.

    C.   1 enemy to 1 Muslim.

    D.   2 enemies to 3 Muslims.

5. Read āyah 8:44 of the Qur'ān. According to the āyah, what did Allāhﷻ make the Muslims see?

_____

6. Read āyah 8:9 of the Qur'ān. How was Allāhﷻ going to help the Muslims?

_____

7. Which famous Makkan leader was killed during the Battle of Badr?

    A.   Abu Jahl.

    B.   Abu Sufyān.

    C.   Abdullah Ibn Ubayy.

    D.   Abu Lahab.

8. How big was the Makkan army of when it came to fight the battle at Badr?

    A.   Army of 313 people.

    B.   Army of 700 people.

    C.   Army of 1,000 people.

    D.   Army of 10,000 people.

9. Towards what city did the Abū Sufyān's caravan move to avoid the Muslim army?

    A.   Towards Yanbu.

    B.   Towards Syria.

    C.   Towards Madīnah.

    D.   Towards Taif.

10. According to the Qur'ān, how many angels did Allāh send into the Battle of Badr to help the Muslims?

    A.   313 angels.

    B.   500 angels.

    C.   1,000 angels.

    D.   1,500 angels.

The Battle of Uhud: *Obey Allāh and Obey the Rasūl*

Objective of the Lesson:

In this chapter, we will learn a brief account of the Battle of Uhud. This battle was the second major battle fought by Muslims. They did not win the battle. This lesson discusses the main reasons for not winning the battle. What message did early Muslims learn from this battle? Can we apply the message to our lives today?

One year after the Muslims won the Battle of Badr, the Makkan pagan people were still very upset about losing the battle. Ever since the defeat, they planned to take revenge. The Quraish knew they would need better preparation and a larger army to defeat the Muslims. After a year-long preparation, they finally fought the Muslims. This battle is known as the **Battle of Uhud**. This battle was fought in 625 C.E. in a valley near Mount Uhud located north of Madīnah. It was the second battle fought by the Muslims. **Sūrah al-e-'Imrān** contains details of the battle.

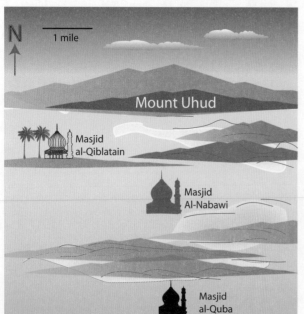

In the previous chapter on the Battle of Badr, we learned that Allāh helps those who struggle on the right path. In order to get Allāh's help, we also have to listen to Allāh and follow Rasūlullāh. In the Battle of Uhud, the Muslims were fighting for a good cause, but they did not win because some of them did not listen to Allāh and did not follow Rasūlullāh. Let us see what happened in this battle.

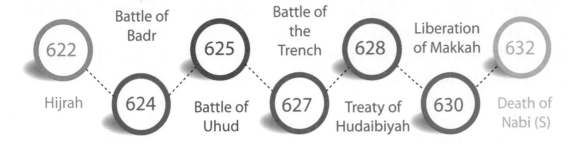

622 — Hijrah
Battle of Badr
624 — Battle of Uhud
625
Battle of the Trench
627 — Treaty of Hudaibiyah
628
Liberation of Makkah
630
632 — Death of Nabi (S)

Makkan preparation

After the Battle of Badr, **Abū Sufyān** became the leader of the Makkan idolaters. Under his leadership, the Makkans began preparations to take revenge for losing the Battle of Badr. The caravan that returned from Syria during the Battle of Badr brought huge profits. The money was used to purchase armor for Makkan the army. Poets were sent to various Arab tribes to recite poems about war. They provoked the sentiment of the people by asking them to rise up and help the Quraish against the Muslims. Soon the Makkans were able to mobilize a large army consisting of 3,000 men, 700 of whom were shielded with metal armor. The army had a large number of riding- and transport-camels and about 200 horses.

Muslim preparation

During the month of Ramadan in 625 C.E., Rasūlullāhﷺ received a letter from his uncle **Al-'Abbās**, who was still in Makkah. The letter warned that the Quraish in Makkah were mobilizing a large army to attack the Muslims.

Initially, Rasūlullāhﷺ wanted to stay in Madīnah and block the attack from the fortified walls of the city. When the Makkan army reached Uhud, Rasūlullāh ﷺ called for a conference of men. This **majlis i-shura,** or council, decided how the battle should be fought. Rasūlullāhﷺ did not decide this on his own. The *shura* council decided to advance to the battlefield. Rasūlullāhﷺ agreed with the decision of the council. The reason to go to the battlefield was to avoid civilian losses and fight a true battle to defeat the enemies.

The Muslim army was mobilized from volunteers, most of whom did not have any experience in battle. About 1,000 men volunteered for the Muslim army, and they were all foot soldiers.

Abdullah ibn Ubayy leaves the Muslims

In Madīnah a person named **Abdullah ibn Ubayy** was the leader of the **hypocrites**. This type of hypocrite is a person who says he or she is a Muslim, but actually works against the Muslims. Before reaching the battleground, Abdullah ibn Ubayy suddenly decided he did not want to fight. He left the Muslim army and took 300 soldiers with him who were loyal to him.[3:155] Rasūlullāhﷺ was left with only 700 soldiers.

Army ratio

Before the battle began, the ratio of enemies to Muslims was 3:1. After Abdullah ibn Ubayy left with 300 men, the strength of the Muslim army dropped to 700. The new army ratio of enemies to Muslims then became 4:1.

Before the Battle
3,000 enemies to 1,000 Muslims
3:1 Ratio

After Abdullah ibn Ubayy left
3,000 enemies to 700 Muslims
4:1 Ratio

Location of Uhud

Uhud is located north of Madīnah on the trade route between Syria and Makkah. Uhud is a mountainous region. The southern part of Uhud is plain, open land. The southern part served as an easy escape route for the Quraish if they needed to run from the battle. There were no palm trees or palm groves in Uhud. Large numbers of palm groves in a region would have hindered a battle. This was another advantage of the location of the battle.

Placing the archers

On the day of the battle, during the early-morning darkness, Rasūlullāhﷺ instructed 50 of his best archers to climb a hill. **Abdullah ibn Jubair** was appointed commander of the archers. Their purpose was to guard the Muslim army from

Time to Review

1. The idea of blocking the Makkan attack from inside the city was not approved. Why not?
2. Why did Abdullah ibn Ubayy leave the Muslims on the battlefield?
3. What example did Rasūlullāhﷺ set when he agreed with the suggestion of the *shura* council to go to the battlefield?

attack from the sides or from the back. They would also shoot arrows at the advancing Makkan army, causing havoc among them. Their position high on the hill seemed to provide them with a key advantage to accomplish the mission. Rasūlullāhﷺ gave them one other very important strategic instruction—never leave their positions, no matter what happened during the battle.

Actual battle

When the battle started, the Muslims fought like great warriors. The archers on top of the hill shot arrows and caused major damage to the enemy. The Muslims realized they would win the battle if they continued this strategy. Halfway through the battle, the idolaters realized they were losing the battle. At one point, many started running away from the battleground. They left behind all of their supplies and other items brought for the battle. The Muslims found discarded items scattered all over the battleground. Some of them started collecting these items. The archers on the hill noticed this, and they thought they might miss out if they did not collect the items, too. They forgot Rasūlullāh'sﷺ instruction not to leave the hill at any time. Most of the archers left the hill to collect the items left behind by the enemy.

Turning point

The turning point in the battle came when most of the archers left the hill to collect the items left behind. At that point, some members of the Makkan army attacked the Muslims from the side of the hill. In the beginning of the battle, this group of the army did not participate in the battle because the archers were shooting

arrows at them. They were waiting for their chance. Finally, they had a chance. They attacked the Muslims and started killing them. Due to the sudden attack, the Muslims began to run away without even looking sideways at anyone.[3:153] Rasūlullāhﷺ called them, but they did not listen. As a result, they suffered heavy losses. Finally, they listened to him and began fighting again. But by that time the damage was already done. Many of the Muslims died. Even Rasūlullāhﷺ fell down unconscious when a sword hit his helmet.[3:144] People thought he had passed away.

When the polytheists heard that Muhammadﷺ died, they thought there was nothing else to do. The battle was over, so they left. A little later, Rasūlullāhﷺ regained consciousness. The battle was over and the Muslims had suffered a great loss. The polytheists thought they won the battle. Actually, they did not win because they had not completed their task. They did not kill our Nabi Muhammadﷺ and stop the progress of Islam.

Lesson learned

The Muslims learned an important lesson from this battle. Rasūlullāhﷺ had told the archers not to leave the hill under any circumstance. If the archers had listened to him, they would have won the battle. It was due to their carelessness that they lost the battle.

We can learn a valuable lesson from the history of this battle. If we do not listen to Rasūlullāh'sﷺ advice, we will also suffer losses. In the Qur'ān, Allāhﷻ tells us: *obey Allāh and obey the Messenger*.[3:32; 3:132; 4:59; 8:20] It is our duty to always listen to and follow the guidance and teachings of Rasūlullāhﷺ. Let us memorize the following āyah and its meaning.

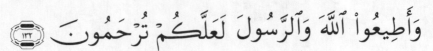

And obey Allāh and the rasul so that you may be shown mercy. (3:132)

1. How many years after the Battle of Badr was the Battle of Uhud fought?

    A.   After ten years.

    B.   After five years.

    C.   After one year.

    D.   After one month.

2. Right before the Battle of Uhud, who walked away with 300 soldiers?

    A.   Abū Jahl.

    B.   Abdullah ibn Ubayy.

    C.   Adbullah ibn Muttalib.

    D.   Abū Sufyān.

3. What did Rasūlullāhﷺ tell the archers not to do in the Battle of Uhud?

_____

4. Read āyah 3:125 of the Qur'ān. What two things did Allāhﷻ tell the Muslims to observe when the enemy came rushing toward them?

    1.   _____

    2.   _____

5. Read āyah 3:153 of the Qur'ān. Who do you think was running away without casting a sideways glance at anyone?

_____

Based on the same āyah, what did Allāhﷻ give to the same people who were running away?

_____

6. What was the biggest turning point in the Battle of Uhud, which led to Muslim losses?

    A.   When 300 soldiers left the Muslim army.

    B.   When Makkan Quraish camped in the valley.

    C.   When Rasūlullāhﷺ fell down unconscious.

    D.   When the archers left their positions on the hill.

7. If you are standing in Madīnah, in which direction is Uhud located?

    A.   South of Madīnah.

    B.   East of Madīnah.

    C.   West of Madīnah.

    D.   North of Madīnah.

8. What was the ratio of Quraish enemies and Muslims in the Battle of Uhud after Abdullah ibn Ubayy left?

    A.   3:1

    B.   4:1

    C.   7:2

    D.   1:1

9. What was the main reason the archers left their positions on the hill?

    A.   They were attacked from the other side of the hill.

    B.   They wanted to drink water from the well.

    C.   They wanted to protect Nabi Muhammadﷺ when he fell down.

    D.   They wanted to collect the supplies left behind by the fleeing Quraish.

10. The Muslims started with a 1,000-man army before the Battle of Uhud. How many men remained when the actual battle started?

    A.   500.

    B.   700.

    C.   900.

    D.   313.

The Battle of the Trench: *A Bloodless Battle*

Objective of the Lesson:

The Battle of the Trench was another significant battle in the history of Islam. This battle was never fought face to face, but it had a lasting impact on the Muslims and the polytheist tribes from all over Arabia. The treachery of the Jewish tribe Banu Qurayzah nearly destroyed the Muslims. Thanks to Allāhﷻ, the crisis was averted. This lesson provides a brief overview of the battle and its outcome.

In the previous two lessons, we studied two major battles fought by the Muslims. Two years after the Battle of Uhud, in the year 627 C.E., the Muslims faced yet another battle, the **Battle of the Trench**. It is named after a trench, or a ditch, dug by the Muslims to prevent the Makkans from reaching the territories of Madīnah. It is also known as the **Battle of the Confederates** because a large number of tribes teamed up to fight the Muslims. The battle is also known as the **Battle of Khandaq** and the **Battle of Ahzāb**. *Khandaq* means trench, and *Ahzāb* means confederates or partners. In the Qur'ān, **sūrah al-Ahzāb** discusses the details of the battle.

Reason for the battle

Life in Madīnah was not entirely peaceful. The enemies of Islam continued to plot secretly against the Muslims and Rasūlullāhﷺ. One of the enemies was the Jewish tribe **Banu Nadīr**. Shortly after the Battle of Uhud, Banu Nadīr was expelled from Madīnah for conspiring to assassinate Rasūlullāhﷺ and for collaborating with

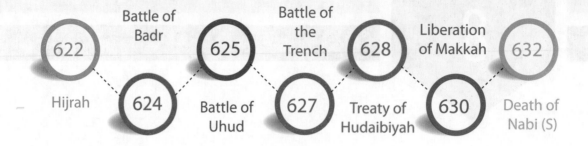

the Makkan Quraish. The tribe left Madīnah and settled near **Khaibar**, north of Madīnah.

From Khaibar they began making plans to destroy the Muslims. They contacted the Makkans, and together, they hatched plans to take revenge upon the Muslims. They decided to assemble as large an army as possible. They reached out to many tribes in Arabia for support. Many of them promised to give support.

March to Madīnah

During the month of Shawwal, the coalition army marched towards Madīnah under their commander-in-chief, Abū Sufyān. As the army moved towards Madīnah, other Arab tribes joined them. By the time they were near Madīnah, they had an army of 10,000 men. The army also consisted of thousands of camels and several hundred horses.

Muslim preparation

As with all other battles, Rasūlullāh received secret information about the Makkan preparations. Due to this advance information, the Muslims had time to prepare. Rasūlullāh discussed a suitable battle strategy with his companions. One of his companions, **Salman al-Farsi,** suggested a very innovative battle plan. He suggested digging a deep ditch along the outer border of the city of Madīnah. This unusual battle tactic was unheard of in Arabia, but it was a tested and successful strategy in Persia. The ditch would provide several strategic advantages to the Muslims. For example:

1. A massive assault by the enemy army would be prevented,
2. A charge by the Quraish cavalry would be foiled,
3. Face-to-face battle with a larger and mightier Quraish army would be avoided,
4. Foot soldiers trying to cross over the deep ditch would be obstructed, and
5. Above all, the morale of the Quraish coalition would be weakened.

Rasūlullāhﷺ agreed to follow the advice of Salman al-Farsi. Madīnah was naturally protected on three sides—west, east, and south—by large plantations of date palms, volcanic rocky plains, and granite hills. Muslims had to dig a trench only on the open side of the city. Every able-bodied man engaged in the task of digging the trench. The entire length of the corridor was divided into several equal parts, and groups of ten men were assigned to dig part of the corridor. Rasūlullāhﷺ himself dug a part of the trench along with his other companions. The dirt removed from digging raised the edge of the trench even higher, thereby making the trench even deeper.

Surprise In Madīnah

When 10,000 enemies arrived near Madīnah, they were surprised to see the trench. They did not understand the purpose of the trench. It was a new battle plan they had never seen. The army tried to cross over the trench, but they could not. The Muslims on the other side shot arrows and prevented them from crossing over. The enemies did not know what to do; they camped outside the trench and waited. They planned what to do next. They could not attack the Muslims from the other side of Madīnah, as the mountain was too high. As days passed, their wait became longer and longer. Soon they became bored.

The Makkan secret plot

As the Makkans could not cross the trench, they decided on another plot to destroy the Muslims. They contacted a Jewish tribe named **Banu Qurayzah**. This tribe lived inside the boundaries of Madīnah. The tribe had a treaty of keeping peace with the Muslims and not supporting the enemies of the Muslims. The Quraish told Banu Qurayzah to attack the Muslims inside Madīnah. Initially Banu Qurayzah hesitated to attack the Muslims because they were under a treaty.

If the Muslims could dig the trench, the large Makkan army could have undone the trench by filling in any one part of the trench. This would have paved a way for them to cross to the other side. What prevented them from doing it? Even if they had tried it, why do you think this strategy would have failed?

Also, they feared that if the Muslims won the battle, they would punish them as they had punished Banu Nadir. The Quraish promised to help them. After a lot of hesitation, the leaders of Banu Qurayzah decided to attack the Muslims.

When this news reached the Muslim camp, they became very disappointed and alarmed. Rasūlullāhﷺ immediately contacted them to prevent them from defecting. But it did not work.

Arrival of Nuaym ibn Masud

Just when the members of Banu Qurayzah decided to break their peace agreement with the Muslims, a key development happened. A person named **Nuaym**, from **Banu Ghatafān** tribe, secretly accepted Islam. He decided to create a misunderstanding between the Quraish and Banu Qurayzah.

First, Nuaym went to Banu Qurayzah's camp as a good friend. They did not know that Nuaym had already embraced Islam. They listened to him attentively. After the discussion with Nuaym, they were afraid that the Quraish might abandon them during or after the battle. Nuaym advised them to hold a few important Quraish men as friendly hostages to make sure the Quraish would not abandon them.

Then Nuaym went to the Quraish camp and told Abū Sufyān that Banu Qurayzah was sorry that they called off their treaty with the Muslims. They had re-established the treaty with the Muslims, and as proof of their good intentions, they agreed to hand over a few Quraish men to them.

Abū Sufyān wanted to verify the facts. When he asked Banu Qurayzah if they really wanted to take friendly hostages, they replied yes. On hearing this, Abū Sufyān became furious, thinking that Banu Qurayzah cheated them. The Quraish refused to send friendly hostages, and without friendly hostages, Banu Qurayzah did not dare attack the Muslims.

Allāh's help arrives

Before Banu Qurayzah could attack the Muslims, the situation changed. The misunderstanding that occurred between the Quraish and Banu Qurayzah was help from Allāh. At the same time, the weather suddenly changed. This was also Allāh's help. Strong, dusty winds started to blow. The clouds became darker. A heavy storm began with thunder and pouring rain. The Makkan camp was totally destroyed. The camels and horses freed themselves and ran away. The tents were uprooted and blown away. The Makkans were already bored during their long wait, and the storm made their lives extremely miserable. They decided to give up and leave. They left behind all of their belongings and returned to Makkah. Although there was no fighting, the Muslims won the battle because they successfully foiled the Makkan plan.

Points to Remember

- The Battle of Khandaq was fought three years after the Battle of Badr.
- The battle was fought in 627 C.E., or 5 A.H.
- Salmān al-Fārisī advised the Muslims to dig a deep trench, or a ditch, around Madīnah.
- The Jewish tribe Banu Nadir conspired to start the battle.
- The Jewish tribe Banu Qurayzah wanted to attack the Muslims inside Madīnah.
- A fierce storm destroyed the Makkan camp.
- Banu Qurayzah was punished according to Jewish law.

71

Time to Review

1. Why did Banu Qurayza want a few friendly hostages from the Makkan army?
2. How did the trench work as an excellent battle strategy for the Muslims?
3. What natural event enhanced defeat of the Makkan army?

Fate of Banu Qurayzah

After the battle, the Muslims decided to deal with Banu Qurayzah for their treachery. The members of the tribe took shelter in their territory. Muslims did not let them come out of their territory for three weeks. No food or water was allowed inside their territory. All this time the tribe hoped to receive help from the outside. They hoped that if help arrived, they would fight the Muslims. After about 25 days, when no help reached them, they decided to surrender. They asked their friend, a leader of the 'Aws tribe, to be the judge in their trial. The judge decided to punish them according to Jewish law.

Lesson for us

No matter how strong and powerful the enemy, Allāh always helps the believers. During the Battle of the Trench, an army of 10,000 men could not harm the Muslims. Even enemies within Madīnah could not do any harm. The reason for this is the Muslims were righteous, and they believed in Allāh.

As long as we believe in Allāh and keep doing what Allāh commands us to do, we should have no fear.

...but there can be no harm to them at all without Allāh's permission. Therefore, upon Allāh should the believers rely. (58:10)

1. Write down three different names for the Battle of the Trench.

   1.   _____

   2.   _____

   3.   _____

2. Which sūrah in the Qur'ān discusses details about the Battle of the Trench?

   A.   Sūrah Anfal.
   B.   Sūrah Al-e-'Imrān.
   C.   Sūrah al-Ahzāb.
   D.   Sūrah Ankabut.

3. Who advised Rasūlullāh to dig a deep trench around Madīnah to prevent the attack?

   A.   Abū Sufyān.
   B.   Salmān al-Fārisī.
   C.   Abdullah ibn Ubayy.
   D.   Abū Bakr.

4. Which Jewish tribe encouraged the Makkan polytheists to launch the attack on Madīnah that led to the Battle of the Trench?

   A.   Banu Qaynuka.
   B.   Banu Nadir.
   C.   Banu Qurayzah.
   D.   Banu Israel.

5. The Makkan polytheists made a pact with Banu Qurayzah to attack the Muslims, but Banu Qurayzah did not attack. What was the reason? Select the best choice.

   A.   Muslims gave them 100 camels for not attacking them.
   B.   Banu Qurayzah did not want to break their peace agreement with the Muslims.
   C.   Banu Qurayzah had a misunderstanding with the Quraish polytheists.
   D.   Banu Qurayzah was afraid of Jewish law about treachery.

6. Unscramble the following letters to make meaningful words.

MNSALA ☐☐☐☐☐☐

NECTHR ☐☐☐☐☐☐

7. Circle T if the sentence is true. Circle F if the sentence is false.

A. During the Battle of Khandaq, Banu Qurayzah strongly supported the   T   F
Muslims.

B. The Battle of Khandaq started at the instigation of Banu Qurayzah.   T   F

C. The Battle of the Trench ended when a fierce storm destroyed the Makkan   T   F
camp.

D. During the Battle of Khandaq, some of the archers left the hill to collect   T   F
the leftover valuables.

E. Islamic law was applied to punish Banu Qurayzah for their treachery.   T   F

8. After how many days of a blockade did Banu Qurayzah come out of their dwellings and
surrender to the Muslims?

A. After 15 days.
B. After 20 days.
C. After 25 days.
D. After 35 days.

9. What is the name of the place where Banu Nadir settled and from that place conspired to
attack the Muslims?

A. Khandaq.
B. Khaibar.
C. Kandahar.
D. Karbala.

The Treaty of Hudaibiyah: *A Clear Victory*

Objective of the Lesson:

The Treaty of Hudaibiyah was largely viewed as a defeat for the Muslims, but soon the treaty turned out to be a major victory for them. The treaty helped shape the future of Islam. This lesson provides a brief account of the treaty and discusses its lasting impact on the history of Islam.

It is reported that one year after the Battle of the Trench, our Messenger Muhammadﷺ dreamt that he entered Makkah with his companions and performed **'Umrah**, or a short pilgrimage. It was the sixth year of hijrah corresponding to 628 C.E.

When Rasūlullāhﷺ told his companions about the dream, they considered it a divine instruction to perform 'Umrah. After consultation with his companions, Rasūlullāhﷺ began preparations for the shorter pilgrimage. In the month of Dhul Qadha, he began his journey with 1,400 companions. The pilgrims wore pilgrim clothes and were in the state of *ihrām*. They had 70 camels with them to sacrifice at the end of pilgrimage.

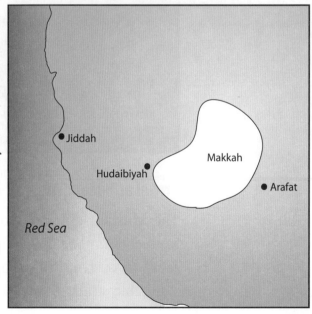

During every major mission, Rasūlullāhﷺ always took one of his wives with him. This time, **Umm Salama** was selected to accompany him.

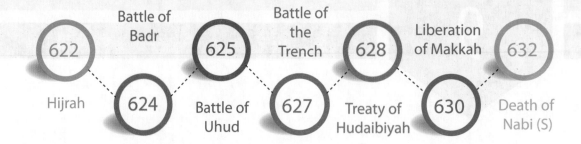

622 — Hijrah

624 — Battle of Badr

625 — Battle of Uhud

627 — Battle of the Trench

628 — Treaty of Hudaibiyah

630 — Liberation of Makkah

632 — Death of Nabi (S)

Makkans became careful

When Rasūlullāhﷺ started his journey with 1,400 of his companions to Makkah, word spread quickly. The idol worshippers learned that the Muslims were not carrying any weapons with them. The pilgrimage attempt by Nabi Muhammadﷺ and his followers became an issue for the Makkans. If they allowed Muhammadﷺ to perform the pilgrimage, it would mean defeat for them, because they allowed their enemy to enter Makkah unopposed. They decided to stop Muhammadﷺ from entering Makkah. They sent two of their most famous warriors, **Khālid Ibn Walīd** and 'Ikrimah, to watch the movement of the Muslims and stop them from entering Makkah.

Arrival at Hudaibiyah

The Muslims quickly found out that the Makkans were planning to stop them from entering the city. They also learned that the Makkans had assembled a large army to obstruct their journey. Rasūlullāhﷺ consulted his companions about a suitable strategy whereby they could avoid facing the army, yet get closer to

Makkah. After consulting, they decided to take a different route—a route usually not taken by travelers. They chose a rough, rocky route that remained unnoticed by the Quraish or the advancing army of Khālid Ibn Walīd. Thus, they reached Hudaibiyah, a place very close to Makkah.

Investigating Muslim intentions

Khālid Ibn Walīd returned to Makkah to update the Quraish about the Muslim escape by a different road. The Quraish sent a few people to find out more about the pilgrims and their intentions. Someone noticed that the Muslims were wearing ihrām. This indicated they were eager to perform a pilgrimage, not fight. He also noticed a large number of camels were brought for the purpose of sacrifice. At the end of a pilgrimage, the camels are slaughtered to mark the completion of Hajj or 'Umrah. This also indicated that the Muslims had come for peaceful reasons.

'Uthman sent to negotiate

The Muslims did not want to proceed unless their safety could be assured. In order to ensure their safety, Rasūlullāhﷺ asked 'Umar to go to Makkah and persuade the Makkan chiefs to let them perform 'Umrah. 'Umar suggested that he was not the right candidate as the Makkans did not respect him very much, and his presence might complicate the situation. Upon further consultation, everyone decided to send 'Uthmān bin Affān, because he had more tribal connections with many of the chiefs and they liked him for his gentle demeanor.

The Makkans allowed 'Uthmān to perform the duties of 'Umrah. However, he refused to perform these duties without Rasūlullāhﷺ by his side. After hearing this, the Makkans became angry. 'Uthmān stayed in Makkah for a few days to continue negotiations.

Bai'ah al-Ridwān

In the meantime, the Muslim camp was eagerly waiting for 'Uthmān to return. When he did not return and more time passed, a rumor spread that he had been killed. Rasūlullāhﷺ vowed that he would not return without getting revenge for 'Uthmān's murder. A battle seemed inevitable. At that time, Rasūlullāhﷺ sat down under a tree and took an oath from all his companions. They promised that they would fight, not flee from battle, and protect Rasūlullāhﷺ under any circumstance. This oath came to be known as the **Bai'ah al-Ridwān**. The Qur'ān mentions the oath as follows:

$$ \text{۞لَّقَدْ رَضِيَ ٱللَّهُ عَنِ ٱلْمُؤْمِنِينَ إِذْ يُبَايِعُونَكَ تَحْتَ ٱلشَّجَرَةِ فَعَلِمَ مَا فِي قُلُوبِهِمْ فَأَنزَلَ ٱلسَّكِينَةَ عَلَيْهِمْ وَأَثَـٰبَهُمْ فَتْحًا قَرِيبًا ۝} $$

Now Allāh indeed was satisfied with the Believers when they swore allegiance to you under the tree, then He knew what was in their hearts, therefore He sent down Sekinah upon them, and He rewarded them with a Near Victory. (48:18)

Later, 'Uthmān safely returned from the Makkan camp. It was a relief for the Muslims to see him alive. The possibility of a battle had been averted.

Quraish compromise

The Quraish wanted to avoid a fight with the Muslims near the Ka'bah because it would look bad to other Arab tribes. At the same time, they wanted to save their honor by not giving in to Muslim pressure. The Muslims also showed interest in peace, not fighting. The Makkans sent **Suhail Ibn Amr** to negotiate a deal with the Muslims. He mentioned the terms of the treaty to Rasūlullāhﷺ, and Rasūlullāhﷺ agreed to them.

Points to Ponder

On several occasions the Quraish marched all the way to Madīnah to fight the Muslims. But when the Muslims came near Makkah, they were an easy target for the Quraish. Why did the Makkans not take this opportunity to fight the Muslims and destroy them once and for all?

Rasūlullāhﷺ asked 'Ali to draft the agreement. 'Ali wrote "Bismillāhir Rahmānir Rahim." Suhail objected to the opening words. He said that they did not recognize "Rahmān." Instead, he told them simply to write *Bismika Allāhumma*, which means, "in your name, O Allāh." Then 'Ali wrote the first sentence: "This is an agreement between Muhammad, rasūlullāh." At this point, Suhail objected again. He said that if they believed Muhammad was rasūlullāh, there would not have been any dispute. They did not accept Muhammad as rasūlullāh, therefore, they should write "Muhammad Ibn Abdullah." Rasūlullāhﷺ asked 'Ali to erase the part that said "rasulullāh," but 'Ali said he could not do that. Then Rasūlullāhﷺ asked 'Ali to show him where the word was written, then he erased the word.

Treaty of Hudaibiyah:

The treaty contained five major points. These points were:

1. The Muslims would return home that year, but the following year they could perform 'Umrah and remain in Makkah for only three days.

2. The treaty would remain valid for ten years. During that period, no one from either side would attack the other side.

3. Each tribe would have the right to enter into an agreement with any party of their choice, but everybody would follow the terms of the treaty.

4. If anyone from the Quraish tribe went to Rasūlullāhﷺ without the permission of his guardian, he would be returned. But if anyone from Rasūlullāh's side went to the Quraish, the Quraish were not bound to return him.

5. Each party would neutral in the event of a war with a third party.

Time to Review

1. Why was 'Uthmān considered a suitable envoy to negotiate with the Makkans?
2. What pledge was taken at Bai'ah al-Ridwān?
3. According to the terms of the treaty, how many days would the Muslims be allowed to stay in Makkah the following year?

Clear victory

The Muslims returned home without performing the pilgrimage. They thought that the Hudaibiyah Treaty was a defeat for the Muslims. Rasūlullāhﷺ believed that the treaty was not a defeat, and Allāhﷻ would make the effect of the treaty a good one. In **sūrah al-Fath**, Allāhﷻ declared that the Hudaibiyah Treaty was a clear victory.[48:1]

$$إِنَّا فَتَحْنَا لَكَ فَتْحًا مُّبِينًا ۝$$

Surely, We have given a victory to you—a Clear Victory. (48:1)

Main Conditions of the Treaty

- The Muslims would not perform 'Umrah that year.
- The next year the Muslims could perform 'Umrah and stay in Makkah for three days.
- The Muslims and the Quraish would maintain peace for ten years.
- The Muslims and the Quraish would not kill each other.
- Each party would remain neutral in the event of war with a third party.

As a result of the treaty, for the first time, Muslims were relieved from fighting any more battles. They were able to concentrate on spreading Islam. A large number of people were happy to see peace in the region. Many people who did not accept Islam before now began to accept Islam. The number of Muslims continued to rise. Rasūlullāhﷺ sent the message of Islam to various countries. People from far-away places learned about Islam and many of them accepted the religion. Soon Islam became a way of life for a large number of people in Arabia. Although in the beginning it appeared that the treaty was a defeat, Allāhﷻ had bigger plans for the Muslims. The perceived defeat turned into a victory—a clear victory.

1. When did Rasūlullāhﷺ march to Makkah to perform the shorter pilgrimage that ended in signing the Treaty of Hudaibiyah?

    A. 610 C.E.

    B. 622 C.E.

    C. 625 C.E.

    D. 628 C.E.

2. During the march to Makkah to perform ʿUmrah, how many Muslims accompanied Rasūlullāhﷺ?

    A. 50.

    B. 500.

    C. 1,000.

    D. 1,400.

3. The Quraish did not want the Muslims to perform the pilgrimage. Why did they not allow the Muslims to perform the pilgrimage?

_____

4. What was the main condition of the Hudaibiyah Treaty that the Muslims agreed to?

_____

_____

5. Read the first āyah of sūrah al-Fath. In this āyah, Allāhﷻ says He gave Muslims something. What did He give them?

_____

6. In the Treaty of Hudaibiyah, the Muslims and the Quraish agreed to maintain peace. How many years of peace did they agree upon?

_____

7. Which of the following was a condition of the Treaty of Hudaibiyah?
   A.   Peace to be maintained forever.
   B.   All Quraish would accept Islam after five years.
   C.   All Muslims would perform 'Umrah in three years.
   D.   The next year, Muslims could perform 'Umrah and stay in Makkah for three days.

8. What was the initial reaction of the Quraish in Makkah when the Messengerﷺ reached Hudaibiyah?

   A.   They sent him gifts and camels.
   B.   They opposed his intention to perform 'Umrah.
   C.   They opposed his intention to sign a treaty.
   D.   They allowed him to perform 'Umrah alone.

9. How many years of peace were agreed to in the Treaty of Hudaibiyah?

   A.   Two years of peace.
   B.   Five years of peace.
   C.   Eight years of peace.
   D.   Ten years of peace.

10. Unscramble the following letters to make meaningful words.

   YETTAR   ☐☐☐☐☐☐

   RMUHA   ☐☐☐☐☐

   CIYVTRO   ☐☐☐☐☐☐☐

Liberation of Makkah: *A Bloodless Victory*

Objective of the Lesson:

Within two years of signing the Treaty of Hudaibiyah, the Muslims liberated Makkah in a dramatic event. The lesson provides an overview of the events that led to the bloodless liberation of Makkah from the clutches of idol-worshipping. Instead of punishing the polytheists, Rasūlullāh ﷺ forgave them, thus making it possible for all of Arabia to accept Islam.

In the previous lesson, we learned about the Treaty of Hudaibiyah. Most Muslims at that time thought the treaty was a defeat for them, but Allāh ﷻ sent a revelation that said the treaty was not only a victory, but a Clear Victory.[48:1]

إِنَّا فَتَحْنَا لَكَ فَتْحًا مُّبِينًا ١

Surely, We have given a victory to you—a Clear Victory. (48:1)

In this context we might remember a Qur'ānic āyah that says sometimes we dislike something, but the thing that we dislike actually has some good for us in it. Similarly, sometimes we may love something, but it is actually bad for us.

وَعَسَىٰ أَن تَكْرَهُوا۟ شَيْـًٔا وَهُوَ خَيْرٌ لَّكُمْ ۖ وَعَسَىٰٓ أَن تُحِبُّوا۟ شَيْـًٔا وَهُوَ شَرٌّ لَّكُمْ ۗ وَٱللَّهُ يَعْلَمُ وَأَنتُمْ لَا تَعْلَمُونَ ٢١٦

... You may dislike something although it is good for you, or like something although it is bad for you. God knows, but you do not. (2:216)

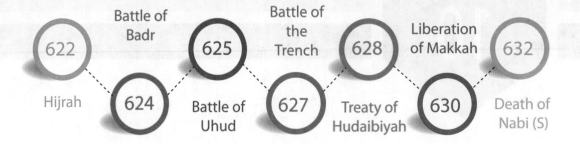

Most of the Muslims who attended the Hudaibiyah agreement thought the treaty was bad for them. But through the treaty Allāhﷻ brought tremendous benefit to the Muslims. In order to realize how beneficial it was for them and how it could be a clear victory, the Muslims had to wait a few more years.

The immediate benefit

The immediate benefit of the treaty was that peace began to prevail in the region. Due to the peaceful conditions, a large number of people came forward to accept Islam. They were not afraid of suffering anymore at the hands of non-Muslims. The Muslim population continued to increase. During this time, one of the staunch enemies of Islam, **Khālid Ibn Walīd**, accepted Islam. He had fought against the Muslims in the Battle of Uhud. Many other warriors also accepted Islam. Many of the tribes who had opposed Islam now became friendly to Muslims and many accepted Islam.

Clash between two tribes

Two peaceful years passed after signing the treaty. Peace prevailed throughout Arabia. Under the Treaty of Hudaibiyah, supporters of the Muslims or the Quraish were not supposed to attack or kill each other.

During this peaceful period, a tribe named **Banū Khuzāʻah** became friendly with the Muslims. Another tribe named **Banū Bakr** was friendly with the Quraish in Makkah. In the year 630 C.E., some men from Banū Bakr broke the conditions of the peace treaty. One night they attacked a Banū Khuzāʻah camp, killed some of their people, and looted their belongings.

Points to Ponder

If there was a single incident that enabled the uninterrupted spread of Islam to other areas of Arabia, it was the Treaty of Hudaibiyah. How did the treaty help to spread Islam?

Rasūlullāh was not happy

The chief of Banū Khuzā‘ah reported this incident to Rasūlullāh in Madīnah. Rasūlullāh was very disappointed to learn about the incident. He immediately sent a message to the Makkan leaders with three conditions:

1. Banū Bakr must pay blood money to Banū Khuzā‘ah for their losses.
2. The Makkans should withdraw their support for Banū Bakr.
3. The Makkans should declare that the Hudaibiyah Treaty had been cancelled.

Initial Makkan response

The Makkans were unhappy to see the Muslims making major progress during the peaceful period. They had been waiting for an opportunity to break the treaty. They thought the attack by Banū Bakr gave them the opportunity. The success of Banū Bakr reminded them of their old enmity against the Muslims. They refused to agree to Rasūlullāh's first two conditions. However, they agreed to the third condition because that was what they wanted. They declared that the Treaty of Hudaibiyah had been cancelled.

> **Definition**
>
> **Blood money:** Money paid in compensation to the family of someone who has been killed. In return for the receipt of blood money, the family of the deceased would forgive the killer.

Fear grips Makkah

Shortly after that, the Quraish realized it had been a great mistake to kill people when they were under a peace treaty. They became nervous. In response to this violation, if the Muslims decided to attack Makkah to take revenge, would the

Makkans fight? They had already lost many battles against the Muslims. They did not dare fight a battle in Makkah. All the Makkan leaders decided to make up with the Muslims and reestablish the peace treaty. The Quraish decided to send one of their leaders, Abū Sufyān, to Madīnah to say they were sorry for killing the friends of Muslims and to promise to follow the treaty.

Abū Sufyān visits Madinah

After reaching Madīnah, Abū Sufyān decided to seek support from Rasūlullāh's ﷺ own household before seeking support from others. Abū Sufyān's daughter, Ramlah, better known as Umm Habiba, was Rasūlullāh's ﷺ wife. But Umm Habiba decided not to help a non-Muslim family member, even if he was her father. The reason was her father had fought so many battles against the Muslims and hated the Muslims.

Abū Sufyān met with Rasūlullāh ﷺ to tell him the Makkan Quraish were sorry for the killings. He also assured Rasūlullāh ﷺ that they would follow the treaty. But knowing the enmity of the Makkans, there was no guarantee that they would follow the treaty. Therefore, Rasūlullāh ﷺ did not listen to Abū Sufyān. Then Abū Sufyān met with Abū Bakr (R) and 'Umar (R) to try to convince them. But they were not convinced. He tried to convince 'Ali (R), and he, too, was not interested. When all attempts failed, Abū Sufyān returned to Makkah. He was very worried.

Rasūlullāh'S ﷺ response

When Rasūlullāh ﷺ found out about the Makkan response, he realized that the time had come for him to take a major step. The major step would be to travel to and liberate Makkah. He began preparations. In the meantime, the Makkans realized they had made a big mistake. Makkan leader Abū Sufyān personally went to Madīnah and begged the Muslims to make the treaty valid again. Rasūlullāh ﷺ refused to see him. Abū Sufyān became even more worried. He knew that the situation was serious. He went to Abū Bakr, 'Umar, 'Ali, Fāṭimah, and Habiba—his own daughter. She was married to Rasūlullāh ﷺ. All of them refused to help him. Abū Sufyān returned to Makkah knowing very well that something bad would happen.

Muslims march to Makkah

On the tenth of Ramadan in the year of the eighth Hijrah, Rasūlullāh ﷺ began his journey to Makkah with an army of 10,000 men and women. The army included people from many neighboring Arab tribes.

Once Rasūlullāh ﷺ was outside of Madīnah, and some distance had already been covered, he asked for a jug of water. When it was brought to him, he raised it high so that everybody could see it. He drank the water in clear sight of everyone. He wanted his companions to follow his example and not fast during traveling. He did not fast for several days, until he reached Makkah. This was in accordance with the Qur'ānic teaching about not fasting during travel.

$$ فَمَن شَهِدَ مِنكُمُ الشَّهْرَ فَلْيَصُمْهُ ۖ وَمَن كَانَ مَرِيضًا أَوْ عَلَىٰ سَفَرٍ فَعِدَّةٌ مِّنْ أَيَّامٍ أُخَرَ $$

...So, whoever among you witnesses the month, he will then observe Sawm therein. But whoever is sick or on a journey, there is then counting of other days... (2:185)

After proceeding quite a distance, the Muslims met Abū Sufyān, who had come to meet them in advance. He was desperate to persuade the Muslims not to attack Makkah. He was nervous about the fate of the Makkans. During the course of the meeting, Rasūlullāh ﷺ repeated a āyah from sūrah Yūsuf about Yūsuf (A) pardoning his brothers.

$$ قَالَ لَا تَثْرِيبَ عَلَيْكُمُ الْيَوْمَ ۖ يَغْفِرُ اللَّهُ لَكُمْ ۖ وَهُوَ أَرْحَمُ الرَّاحِمِينَ ﴿٩٢﴾ $$

No blame be on you this day; Allāh may forgive you, for He is the most Rewarding of those who show mercy. (12:92)

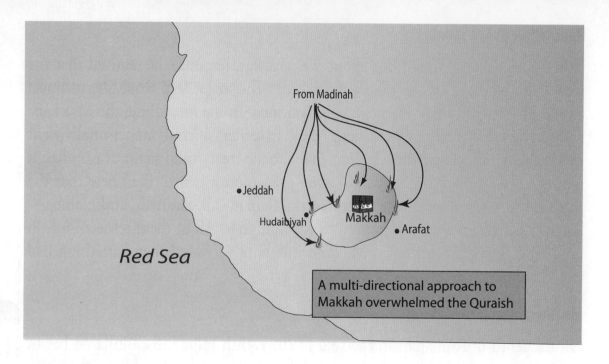

A multi-directional approach to Makkah overwhelmed the Quraish

Campfire strategy

The Muslims reached a place not very far from Makkah in the evening. Rasūlullāhﷺ ordered each companion to light a campfire a short distance from each other. In the darkness of night, these campfires would give the impression that an unusually large number of people had assembled there. Rasūlullāhﷺ chose this strategy because he was still not sure about the Makkan's plans. The big question was whether they would fight a full-scale battle or surrender.

Abū Sufyān accepts Islam

All night long, the Makkans were restless, worried, and eager to avert a battle. The next morning, Abū Sufyān went to the Muslim camp. He said that had there been other deities besides Allāh, they would have helped the Makkans by now. This indicated that he believed in the oneness of God. When he was asked whether he believed Muhammadﷺ was the messenger of God, he was unsure. Upon hearing this, 'Umar almost wanted to kill him, but others stopped him. Al-'Abbās, Rasūlullāh'sﷺ uncle, persuaded Abū Sufyān to declare his full faith in Islam. Finally he declared that there is no god but Allāhﷻ, and Muhammadﷺ is the messenger of Allāh.

Safety assured to all in Makkah

After Abū Sufyān accepted Islam, Rasūlullāhﷺ declared that anyone near the Ka'bah, or in their house, or in the house of Abū Sufyān, would be safe. Rasūlullāhﷺ wanted to make sure that nobody would revolt or confront the Muslims as they entered the city.

Time to Review

1. Why did Umm Habiba refuse to help her own father when he sought her help?
2. What event led to the breakdown of Hudaibiyah Treaty?
3. In the night prior to entering Makkah, what strategy did Rasūlullāh adopt to give the impression that unusually large force assembled outside of Makkah?

Muslims liberate Makkah

On the morning the Muslims prepared to enter Makkah, Rasūlullāh split the procession into four divisions. Each division would enter the city from a different direction so that the entire city could be taken in one incident. Nobody resisted the Muslims. Only a few people came forward to protest or resist the entry of the Muslims, but they soon gave up. Makkah was liberated without any bloodshed.

Rasūlullāh forgives everybody

After entering Makkah, Rasūlullāh first went to the Ka'bah. One by one, he and other Muslims removed all the idols. The Makkans were very nervous. They thought Rasūlullāh and the Muslims would take revenge against them. But Rasūlullāh declared that no one would be punished—everybody was forgiven. All the Makkans were safe!

The people in Makkah could not believe this. They could not understand why Muhammad pardoned them. This act of forgiveness overwhelmed them. Many of them cried to express their relief. Many of them accepted Islam then and there. Many others accepted Islam shortly thereafter. Within several days, almost everyone in Makkah had accepted Islam. Two years after the liberation of Makkah, Rasūlullāh passed away.

1. Who accepted Islam soon after the Treaty of Hudaibiyah, but before the liberation of Makkah?

    A.   Abū Jahl.

    B.   Abū Sufyān.

    C.   Banū Bakr.

    D.   Khālid Ibn Walīd.

2. After Banū Bakr attacked Banū Khuzāʻah, Rasūlullāhﷺ sent three conditions to the Makkans. How many conditions did they accept?

    A.   Only one condition.

    B.   Only two conditions.

    C.   All three conditions.

    D.   They did not agree to any conditions.

3. When did Abū Sufyān accept Islam?

    A.   After he went to Madīnah.

    B.   After all the idols in Makkah were broken.

    C.   In the morning of the day Makkah was liberated.

    D.   The night after Makkah was liberated.

4. What event cancelled the Treaty of Hudaibiyah?

_____

_____

5. How many years after the Hijrah did Rasūlullāhﷺ return to liberate Makkah?

_____

6. How many years after the Treaty of Hudaibiyah did the Makkans violate the treaty?

_____

7. How many years after the Treaty of Hudaibiyah was Makkah finally liberated?

   A.   Two years.

   B.   Four years.

   C.   Five years.

   D.   Ten years.

8. When Rasūlullāhﷺ was liberating Makkah, what did he say would happen to people who were in Abu Sufyān's house?

   A.   They would be taken prisoner.

   B.   They would be punished.

   C.   They would be made slaves.

   D.   They would be safe.

9. How many years after the liberation of Makkah, did Rasūlullāhﷺ pass away?

   A.   He passed away the same year.

   B.   He passed away two years later.

   C.   He passed away four years later.

   D.   He passed away five years later.

10. The night before entering Makkah, why did the Muslims start many camp fires near Makkah?

   A.   To keep them warm in the winter night.

   B.   To prevent any disease.

   C.   To roast a large number of camels.

   D.   To give the impression that all of Makkah was surrounded.

Unit 3: Stories of the Messengers of Allāh

Throughout the Weekend Learning curriculum, students will learn about the lives and major activities of the messengers. This unit presents the engaging stories of some of the illustrious messengers of Islam. The goal is to capture the imagination of young readers. Whether the lesson focuses on the entire life of a messenger or a specific incident in the messenger's life, these accounts present the narrative true to the Qur'an. The story of Ādam's (A) is covered in several grades because there are many moral issues surrounding his trials and triumphs. Two lessons on Ibrāhīm (A) show his resolve to educate people, and to convince them to give up polytheism and worship One God. Luqmān's (A) account highlights many Islamic values that are as relevant today as they were during his lifetime. Each of the three chapters on Yūsuf (A) discusses one particular phase of his life. The story of Nabi Ayyūb (A) teaches us the important values of patience and perseverance. The final lesson, on Zakariyyāh (A) and Yahyā (A), explains Allāh's 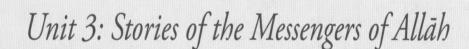 mercy and blessings for the prominent father and son messengers.

Lesson 11: **Ādam (A):** *The Creation of Human Beings*

Lesson 12: **Ibrāhīm (A):** *His Debate with the Polytheists*

Lesson 13: **Ibrāhīm (A):** *His Plan Against the Idols*

Lesson 14: **Luqmān (A):** *A Wise Man's Lifelong Advice*

Lesson 15: **Yūsuf (A):** *His Childhood and Life in Aziz's Home*

Lesson 16: **Yūsuf (A):** *Standing Up for Righteousness*

Lesson 17: **Yūsuf (A):** *Childhood Dream Comes True*

Lesson 18: **Ayyūb (A):** *Example of Patience and Perseverance*

Lesson 19: **Zakariyyāh (A) and Yahyā (A)**

Stories of the Messengers of Allāh

Ādam (A): *The Creation of Human Beings*

Before and after the creation of human beings, the angels and Iblīs talked with Allāh﷾ about human beings and their status. The angels obeyed Allāh﷾, but Iblīs refused to obey Allāh﷾. This resulted in an eternal clash between human beings and Shaitān. This lesson provides an overview of the creation of Ādam (A) and his interactions with Iblīs.

Ibrāhīm (A): *His Debate with the Polytheists*

Nabi Ibrāhīm (A) was known to debate with people to make them realize there is one God and to encourage them to worship God. His debates not only helped many people understand the oneness of Allāh﷾, but also created enemies for him. This lesson discusses some of Ibrāhīm's (A) debates.

Ibrāhīm (A): *His Plan Against the Idols*

Ibrāhīm (A) once broke several idols in a temple to help people understand that idol-worshipping is useless. Some people understood the message, but many others became angry with him. This entire incident was very dramatic. This lesson provides a summary of the this event.

Luqmān (A): *A Wise Man's Lifelong Advice*

The advice Luqmān (A) gave to his son contains great lessons for us. The Qur'ān has given much importance to Luqmān's (A) teachings. In fact, a sūrah is named after him. This lesson provides a summary of Luqmān's (A) teachings along with a brief account of the life of this important man.

Yūsuf (A): *His Childhood and Life in Aziz's Home*

In this lesson, we will learn the key events during Yūsuf's (A) childhood. We will also learn about a dream that he had as a child. There is a great lesson to learn from the incidents in Yūsuf's (A) life.

Yūsuf (A): *Standing Up for Righteousness*

Yūsuf (A) was thrown into prison even though he was not guilty. He remained in prison until the truth was established. This lesson provides a summary of events of his time in and after prison. This lesson also demonstrates how patience ultimately pays off in the long run.

Yūsuf (A): *Childhood Dream Comes True*

Yūsuf's (A) half-brothers wanted to kill him, but he was saved due to Allāh's﷾ grace. Eventually he was reunited with his father. His childhood dream about stars, the sun, and the moon prostrating was fulfilled. The lesson provides a summary of these events.   .

Ayyūb (A): *Example of Patience and Perseverance*

Sometimes Allāh﷾ gives people everything and then takes it away to test them. People who persevere and have faith in Allāh﷾ ultimately become successful. The story of Ayyūb (A) shows how he lost everything, but never lost trust in Allāh﷾. He persevered and ultimately received many blessings. There is a great moral to learn from this lesson.

Zakariyyāh (A) and Yahyā (A)

Zakariyyāh (A) and Yahyā (A) were the last father-and-son messengers in Islam. The Qur'ān mentions them briefly. They lived around the same time as 'Isā (A). The purpose of the lesson is to introduce their story as narrated in the Qur'ān.

Ādam (A): *The Creation of Human Beings*

Objective of the Lesson:

The Qur'ān contains a fascinating account of the creation of Ādam (A). Before and after the creation of human beings, the angels and Iblīs talked with Allāhﷻ about human beings and their status. The angels obeyed Allāh ﷻ, but Iblīs refused to obey Allāhﷻ. This resulted in an eternal clash between human beings and Shaitān. This lesson provides an overview of the creation of Ādam (A) and his interactions with Iblīs.

The Qur'ān narrates a beautiful account of the creation of Ādam (A). He was the first human being Allāhﷻ created. The story of Ādam (A) shows us the struggle of human beings against falsehood and their will to become successful. Let us read more about him as narrated in the Qur'ān.

The plan of creation

In sūrah al-Baqarah, Allāhﷻ tells us He decided to create human beings on earth. These human beings would be **khalīfahs**.

وَإِذْ قَالَ رَبُّكَ لِلْمَلَـٰٓئِكَةِ إِنِّى جَاعِلٌ فِى ٱلْأَرْضِ خَلِيفَةً

And behold! your Rabb said to the angels, "Certainly I am going to place on the earth a vicegerent." (2:30)

The simple meaning of khalīfah is "one who inherits." The word is generally translated as "vicegerent," which means, "a person exercising power on behalf of a sovereign or ruler." As khalīfahs on earth, human beings would inherit, or take over, the earth and rule it as representatives of God. Human beings would represent Allāh's﷿ qualities and values, and pass them on generation after generation.

Upon hearing this announcement, the angels thought human beings would create trouble on earth and kill each other. Allāh﷿ told the angels He knows what the angels do not know.

$$قَالُوٓاْ أَتَجْعَلُ فِيهَا مَن يُفْسِدُ فِيهَا وَيَسْفِكُ ٱلدِّمَآءَ وَنَحْنُ نُسَبِّحُ بِحَمْدِكَ وَنُقَدِّسُ لَكَ قَالَ إِنِّيٓ أَعْلَمُ مَا لَا تَعْلَمُونَ ٣٠$$

They said: "Are You going to place thereon one who would make mischief on it and shed blood; while we celebrate Your praise, and we glorify Your holiness?" He said: "I surely know which you do not know." (2:30)

Interesting Facts

Modern scientists are finding that clay was an essential part of the formation of the earliest cells and RNA processing. (*Science* 2003, 302:618–622.)

Clay is an important component of fertile soil. It maintains potassium, iron, calcium, and other essential elements for plant growth.

A wet mass of clay can be given any shape. When dried, the clay maintains the same shape.

Ancient Egyptians and Persians 5,000 years ago were experts in using a potter's wheel.

Allāh creates Ādam (A)

Allāh﷿ created Ādam (A) from the ingredients, or components, of clay. This clay is similar to a potter's clay.[55:14] Clay has all the necessary chemicals that can nourish life. After creating Ādam (A), Allāh﷿ blew divine *rūh* into him and made him a human being. Then Allāh﷿ taught Ādam (A) the names of everything to prove that Ādam (A) was superior. By teaching Ādam (A) the names of everything, Allāh﷿ gave him power over the things he learned.

$$وَعَلَّمَ ءَادَمَ ٱلْأَسْمَآءَ كُلَّهَا$$

And He taught Adam the names—all of them... (2:31)

Angel's level of knowledge

Allāh﷿ tells us that Ādam (A) learned the names and functions of everything. Then Allāh﷿ asked all the angels to name all the things in the garden. The angels realized they did not know everything. They only knew what Allāh﷿ told them. They replied:

$$قَالُواْ سُبْحَٰنَكَ لَا عِلْمَ لَنَآ إِلَّا مَا عَلَّمْتَنَآ إِنَّكَ أَنتَ ٱلْعَلِيمُ ٱلْحَكِيمُ ٣٢$$

Glory be to You! We do not have any knowledge other than what You have taught us. You indeed, You are the all-Knowing, most-Wise. (2:32)

When Ādam (A) could name everything, the angels realized that their position was lower than the human beings. Allāhﷻ commanded the angels and Iblīs to bow down to Ādam (A).[2:34] All of the angels bowed down to Ādam (A), except Iblīs. Iblīs was one of the invisible creatures called jinn.

Pride of Iblīs

Iblīs was proud and he refused to bow down to Ādam (A). Iblīs was created from fire. He thought fire was a better ingredient than clay, from which Ādam (A) was created. It was a false idea and he had faulty pride. Faulty pride is bad, and to boast about faulty pride is even worse. When Allāhﷻ asked Iblīs why he did not bow down, he boasted:

قَالَ أَنَا۠ خَيْرٌ مِّنْهُ خَلَقْتَنِي مِن نَّارٍ وَخَلَقْتَهُ مِن طِينٍ ﴿١٢﴾ ،

I am better than he; You have created me of fire, while You created him of clay. (7:12)

Allāhﷻ then rejected Iblis. Now that Iblīs was rejected, he did not give up his pride, and he continued his rebellion. He was sure he could mislead human beings from the right path. Allāhﷻ gave him the opportunity, until the end of time, to try to mislead human beings. Allāhﷻ also made it clear that Iblīs would not be

Time to Review

1. What is the one thing that determined human beings are superior to angels?
2. What was the underlying reason for Iblīs's pride?
3. When the angels were told about the creation of human beings, what did the angels think human beings would do on the earth?

able to mislead the righteous people.[15:42] Iblīs, himself, agreed that he would have no authority over the righteous people.

Life in the Garden of Eden

Allāh﷾ told Ādam (A) and his wife to live in the Garden, but not to go near a particular tree or they would be wrongdoers.[2:35] Shaitān wanted to make Ādam (A) a wrongdoer and prove that Ādam (A) was not better than him. One day he sneaked up on Ādam (A) and tempted him with sin. He knew Ādam (A) could not be tempted, but if he lied to him and showed him bad things are very attractive, he might be successful. He told Ādam (A) that if he ate from the tree, he could become an angel or live forever.[20:120] Ādam (A) forgot about Allāh's﷾ caution.[20:115] He thought he had great promise ahead of him—he would live forever or become an angel! It sounded like a very attractive offer. He and his wife ate from the tree.[20:121]

Ādam (A) realizes his mistake

As soon as Ādam (A) and his wife ate from the tree, Shaitān's objective was fulfilled. He had wanted them to disobey Allāh﷾, and he was successful. Shaitān was happy because he showed his power to fool people. Ādam (A) realized his mistake. He understood that he did not become an angel, nor did he become immortal. Instead, he had disobeyed Allāh﷾! He realized his mistake and became ashamed of his conduct. In order to cover their shame, Ādam and his wife began to cover themselves with the leaves of a tree. They realized Shaitān was not their friend, but their enemy.

Allāh﷾ was disappointed with Ādam (A)

As punishment for their mistake, Allāh﷾ told Ādam (A) and his wife to leave the Garden of Eden. Ādam (A) learned a prayer of forgiveness and prayed to Allāh﷾

Points to Ponder

How did Shaitān react after Ādam (A) ate from the tree? Based on the way Shaitān reacted, what precaution can we take when Shaitān approaches us with his tempting suggestions?

to forgive him and his wife. Allāhﷻ forgave them. This was probably the very first du'ā made by a human being. Ādam (A) and his wife prayed:

$$رَبَّنَا ظَلَمْنَا أَنفُسَنَا وَإِن لَّمْ تَغْفِرْ لَنَا وَتَرْحَمْنَا لَنَكُونَنَّ مِنَ الْخَاسِرِينَ ٢٣$$

Our Rabb! we have done wrong to ourselves; and if You do not forgive us and have mercy on us, we shall surely become of the losers (7:23).

Lesson for us to learn

Every day we commit various sins, knowingly or unknowingly. We must learn the du'ā and pray to Allāhﷻ for forgiveness. If Allāhﷻ does not forgive us, then we will become sinner. If Allāhﷻ forgives us, then we will become better people. What lesson have we learned from the incident with Ādam (A) and his wife? Let us think about how we can apply the moral of the story to our daily lives.

1. Disobedience of Allāh'sﷻ instructions can cause serious problems in our lives.

2. Allāhﷻ always guides us. Shaitān always misguides us.

3. We should not challenge Allāh'sﷻ authority.

4. False pride, arrogance, and rebellion against Allāhﷻ are harmful.

5. Shaitān tempts us by showing us the wrong things as highly attractive. He also makes us think the good things are boring.

6. The consequence of listening to Shaitān's temptations will be very bad.

7. Sometimes we may fall into Shaitān's trap, but as soon as we realize it, we must repent and pray to Allāhﷻ for forgiveness.

8. In order to avoid Shaitān's temptations, we must remain careful.

9. Always listen to Allāhﷻ and remember Him. This will keep Shaitān away from us.

10. Allāhﷻ is merciful. If we commit a sin, we should express repentance and ask for forgiveness.

1. Memorize the du'ā made by Ādam (A) and his wife, as provided in the lesson. Memorize the meaning. Why should we pray to Allāhﷻ using this du'ā?

We can ask for forgivness

2. What are the two things that Shaitān promised Ādam (A) to make him eat from the tree?

1. become an angel   2. living forever

3. What will happen to us if we listen to Shaitān's tempting words? Circle the correct answer below.

    A.   We will become successful.

    B.   We will be happy.

    C.   We will live forever.

    (D)   We will suffer loss.

4. In order to avoid Shaitān's temptations, what should we do? Circle all correct answers.

    A.   Follow only good advice from Shaitān.

    B.   We cannot do anything. Shaitān is very powerful.

    C.   Follow Allāh'sﷻ command.

    D.   Remain careful to avoid Shaitān's whisperings.

    E.   Shaitān will always guide us to goodness if we do something wrong.

    F.   Make friendships with good people.

    G.   Whenever in doubt about what is right or wrong, check with a teacher or your parents.

5. After Allāh ﷻ told the angels about His plans to create human beings, how did the angels respond?

A. They were very sad.
B. They were very happy to know about it.
C. They were afraid that human beings would be superior.
D. They were afraid that human beings would shed blood and create trouble.

6. Why did Shaitan refuse to bow down to Adam (A)?

A. He thought Ādam (A) was not a prophet.
B. He thought Ādam (A) did not know anything.
C. He thought he was better than Ādam (A).
D. He thought Ādam (A) was an angel.

7. Shaitan has no authority over what type of people?

A. The righteous people.
B. The people who do not kill.
C. The educated people.
D. The Muslim people.

8. After listening to Shaitan, Ādam (A) realized he made a mistake. He felt ashamed. What did he use to cover himself?

A. Some leaves.
B. Skins of animals.
C. Mud.
D. Paper.

Ibrāhīm (A): *His Debate with the Polytheists*

Objective of the Lesson:

Nabi Ibrāhīm (A) was known to debate with people to make them realize there is one God and to encourage them to worship God. His intelligent debates not only helped many people understand the oneness of Allāhﷻ, but also created many enemies for him. This lesson discusses some of Ibrāhīm's (A) debates.

Changing the mindset of people is difficult. It usually requires years of teaching, convincing, and showing proof and examples. Even then, most people refuse to accept a new thought, particularly if it relates to religion and lifestyle. People who do not believe in one Allāhﷻ have a type of mindset that prevents them from believing that He exists or that He is the only One. To tell people who have such a mindset about the oneness of Allāhﷻ is not an easy job. If you try to tell them about Allāhﷻ, many people would not be interested. Many people worship idols, objects, animals, planets, or other human beings. Many people believe there are many gods. They make images of gods and worship these images. Thousands of years ago, it was the same story—people made images of gods and worshipped the images.

Allāhﷻ sent messengers to teach people about one God, and explain the reasons they should worship none but Him. But most people did not want to hear about Allāhﷻ. Still, the messengers did not give up. They used various examples and arguments to help people understand that Allāhﷻ is the only One. Today, we will learn about one such messenger who taught the oneness of Allāhﷻ by using various examples. He is Nabi Ibrāhīm (A).

Ibrāhīm (A) received guidance

When Ibrāhīm (A) was a youth, Allāhﷻ gave him wisdom and knowledge to understand the operations of the heavens and the earth[6:75] Allāhﷻ also gave him guidance and made him a nabi.

$$۞ وَلَقَدْ ءَاتَيْنَآ إِبْرَٰهِيمَ رُشْدَهُۥ مِن قَبْلُ وَكُنَّا بِهِۦ عَٰلِمِينَ ۝$$

And certainly We gave Ibrāhīm his guidance before, and We were well-Aware of him. (21:51)

People worshipped idols

Messenger Ibrāhīm (A) fully understood that man-made objects—such as idols —or natural objects—the sun, the moon, the plants, the trees, and so forth cannot be God. As he observed at the practices of people, he wondered why they worshipped idols. Idols are statues made of stone, clay, wood or metal. Idols are lifeless objects—they have no power whatsoever. They cannot see, hear, speak, listen or answer prayers.

People did not understand that these lifeless idols could not be gods. They thought that the idols were images of gods. God never told people to make these images, but many people made idols and worshipped them.

Ibrāhīm (A) lived in a place called **Ur** in ancient Iraq. Most of the people in Ur worshipped idols. The leaders worshipped idols. Even Ibrāhīm's (A) forefathers worshipped idols. They would make idols and sell them to people. The ruler of the country made people believe that he was a god.

Ibrāhīm (A) reasons with his father

Ibrāhīm (A) was sorry to see that his father worshipped idols. He was under the influence of Shaitān.[19:44] Ibrāhīm (A) wanted to make his father a good person. One day he asked his father why he worshipped idols.

إِذْ قَالَ لِأَبِيهِ يَٰٓأَبَتِ لِمَ تَعْبُدُ مَا لَا يَسْمَعُ وَلَا يُبْصِرُ وَلَا يُغْنِى عَنكَ شَيْـًٔا ۞

Behold! he said to his father, "Why do you worship things that cannot hear and cannot see, and that cannot help you at all?" (19:42)

He thought his father would understand that idols were figures made of clay. They do not hear, could not speak, or could not do anything. So why worship them? We should worship Allāh ﷻ because He hears, He speaks, and He does everything. Ibrāhīm (A) wanted his father to listen to him, but his father would not listen. Instead he became angry. He wanted Ibrāhīm (A) to leave the house for not respecting the idols.[19:46] Eventually Ibrāhīm (A) had to leave. He cut off his relationship with his father.

Ibrāhīm (A) reasons with people

During Ibrāhīm's (A) time, many people worshipped idols, the moon, the sun, and the stars in the sky. Even today, many people in the world think the sun is a god. Ibrāhīm (A) was not like his people. He told them that if the stars set, these cannot be gods. He said he did not like things that set. He told them that

Time to Review

1. Who influenced Ibrāhīm's (A) father to worship idols?
2. What are some of the faculties none of the idols have?
3. What drama did Ibrāhīm (A) do with the people during the nighttime and daytime?

the moon could not be a god as it also disappears! Some people still did not understand. Then Ibrāhīm (A) said, "Can the biggest one, the sun, be my god? The big one sets, too! How can these be gods?" Some people understood Ibrāhīm's (A) arguments, but most people did not want to understand.

Ibrāhīm (A) debates with a king

Life for Ibrāhīm (A) became very difficult in his native city, Ur. To continue his mission, he moved to another city. The king of that city was **Nimrod**. He was king and had all the power, so he began to think that he was God. When Nimrod heard about a young man named Ibrāhīm (A) speaking about One God, he summoned him to find out more. During the course of the discussion, Ibrāhīm (A) told him about God in this manner:

إِذْ قَالَ إِبْرَاهِـمُ رَبِّيَ ٱلَّذِى يُحْيِ ۦ وَيُمِيتُ

My Rabb is He who causes life and Who causes death. (2:258)

Nimrod thought that giving life or causing death was easy. A king has the power to punish a person with death or let him live. He though there was nothing special about God. In order to make him understand, Ibrāhīm (A) challenged him in a different way. He said:

قَالَ إِبْرَاهِـمُ فَإِنَّ ٱللَّهَ يَأْتِي بِٱلشَّمْسِ مِنَ ٱلْمَشْرِقِ فَأْتِ بِهَا مِنَ ٱلْمَغْرِبِ

Allāh brings out the sun from the east. So, you bring it from the west? (2:258)

Nimrod realized that he could not bring out the sun from the west. Thus, Nimrod was defeated in the argument. As human beings, we have certain power, but that does not make us God. Almighty God has absolute power to do anything and everything. He is the One who created the heavens, the earth, and all living creatures. He causes rain and thunder. In realization of this, people should worship none but one God.

How to discuss the truth

The Qur'ān and the sunnah of Rasūlullāhﷺ teaches us how to discuss or debate the truth. The Islamic way to discuss or debate truth or any other matter is to be gentle and respectful.

The Qur'ān tells us to speak gently and politely when we talk about the truth. The purpose of argument is to listen to the opinion of both sides, and then speak about your beliefs. Argument does not mean we should shout or call someone names. All we have to do is tell the truth without being afraid or nervous. If people start ridiculing or laughing at your argument, the Qur'ān teaches us to simply walk away. There is no point discussing anything with people who do not apply wisdom. Allāhﷻ does not guide the unjust people.

Ibrāhīm (A) did not shout at his father, at his people, or at the king. He told them the truth in a gentle manner without being afraid. His father shouted at Ibrāhīm (A). This is unIslamic. When Mūsā (A) spoke to Fir'awn in Egypt, Allāh ﷻ advised him to speak in a gentle manner.

$$فَقُولَا لَهُ قَوْلًا لَّيِّنًا لَّعَلَّهُ يَتَذَكَّرُ أَوْ يَخْشَىٰ ٤٤$$

Then you speak to him a gentle speech, perhaps he may mind or he may fear. (20:44)

Whenever we speak about religion or any matter, we should always talk in a gentle manner. The Qur'ān also teaches us to speak to people with wisdom and in civil manner.

$$ٱدْعُ إِلَىٰ سَبِيلِ رَبِّكَ بِٱلْحِكْمَةِ وَٱلْمَوْعِظَةِ ٱلْحَسَنَةِ وَجَٰدِلْهُم بِٱلَّتِي هِيَ أَحْسَنُ$$

You call towards the way of your Rabb with wisdom and goodly exhortation, and argue with them in a manner which is the best. Surely your Rabb, He knows best who strays from His path, and He knows best the guided. (16:125)

Points to Ponder

People do not often change their beliefs and mindset. They tend to remain faithful to their belief system and choose not to apply reason. Under such circumstances how should a person engage in discussions about religion, politics, or any other sensitive issue?

1. Read āyah 19:44 of the Qur'ān. What did Ibrāhīm (A) tell his father not to worship?

~~Not~~ devils

2. Read āyah 6:76 of the Qur'ān. What did Ibrāhīm (A) say he did not worship?

planets, moon and sun

3. Read āyah 27:24 of the Qur'ān. This āyah says people worshipped something. What did they worship?

the sun

4. Read āyah 29:16 of the Qur'ān. Ibrāhīm (A) told his people to do something. What did he tell them to do?

he did not warship any planets

5. What was the name of the city where Ibrāhīm (A) was born and lived during his childhood?

A. Yanbu.

B. Ukraine.

C. Ur.

D. Ural.

6. When we argue with people, what is the best way to speak to them?

Gentle and respectful

7. According to the Qur'ān, who in Ibrāhīm (A)'s house did not believe in Allāh?

A. His wife.

B. His son.

C. His uncle.

D. His father.

8. What specific thing did Ibrāhīm (A) say to his people about the sun, moon, and stars?

    A.   He did not like the things that set.

    B.   He did not believe in the sun, moon, and stars.

    C.   He did not think the sun, moon, and stars could create.

    D.   He did not think the sun, moon, and stars could speak.

9. What was the name of the king in Iraq that argued with Ibrāhīm (A)?

    A.   Fir'awn.

    B.   King of Saba.

    C.   Nimrod.

    D.   Negus.

10. Ibrāhīm (A) asked the king in Iraq to do something that he could not do. Thus, the king was defeated in the debate. What did Ibrāhīm (A) ask him to do?

    A.   He should give life.

    B.   Make the sun rise from the west.

    C.   Create a fly.

    D.   Build a palace.

Ibrāhīm (A): *His Plan Against the Idols*

Objective of the Lesson:

Ibrāhīm (A) once broke several idols in a temple to help people understand that idol-worshipping is useless. Some people understood the message, but many others became angry with him. This entire incident was very dramatic. This lesson provides a summary of the this event.

In the previous lesson, we learned how Ibrāhīm (A) tried to convince his people to give up idol-worshipping. He talked about his beliefs and tried to make people think meaningfully, so they could realize the truth. At times, it was difficult to help people understand the truth because they would not give up their faith. At other times, some people listened to him and understood his explanations.

In this lesson, we will study a dramatic event involving Ibrāhīm (A) and the idols. Ibrāhīm (A) tried to prove to his people that idol-worshipping was meaningless. This event is mentioned in detail in sūrah **al-Anbiyā**, sūrah number 21.

Ibrāhīm (A) argues with his father

Sūrah al-Anbiyā says Ibrāhīm (A) tried his best to convince his father and other people to give up idol-worshipping. He asked them a straightforward question.

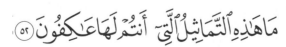

مَا هَٰذِهِ ٱلتَّمَاثِيلُ ٱلَّتِىٓ أَنتُمْ لَهَا عَٰكِفُونَ ٥٢

What are these images to which you are so devoted? (21:52)

The people had no good reason for worshipping idols. They were surprised because nobody had asked them such a question before. They worshipped these idols without thinking and without knowing if it was right to worship them. They were simply imitating the ways of worship from their ancestors, even though their ancestors did not know right from wrong. They replied:

وَجَدْنَآ ءَابَآءَنَا لَهَا عَٰبِدِينَ ۝

"We have found our forefathers worshipping them." (21:53)

Ibrāhīm (A) knew that was not a valid reason. If the forefathers were wrong, the people should not keep doing the wrong thing. Ibrāhīm (A) tried to make them understand. He said:

قَالَ لَقَدْ كُنتُمْ أَنتُمْ وَءَابَآؤُكُمْ فِى ضَلَٰلٍ مُّبِينٍ ۝

"Surely you have been, you and your forefathers, in manifest error." (21:54)

Ibrāhīm (A) continued to explain his point, but the people did not want to understand this simple point. Finally, Ibrāhīm (A) announced that he would plan a drama about the idols after the people left the temple site.[21:57]

Ibrāhīm (A) breaks the idols

After everyone left the temple, Ibrāhīm (A) broke all the idols in the temple except the biggest one. Later, when people returned to the temple, they were shocked to see broken idols all over the place. They asked:

قَالُوا مَن فَعَلَ هَٰذَا بِـَٔالِهَتِنَآ إِنَّهُۥ لَمِنَ ٱلظَّٰلِمِينَ ۝

They said, "Who has done this to our gods? He is surely of the wrongdoers." 21:59

They had no sense of right and wrong. But they determined that whoever had broken their gods was a wrongdoer. Obviously they were furious and wanted to punish the person. They wanted someone to tell them who might have done such a bad thing to their gods.

Points to Ponder

Superstitions are blind beliefs in some odd event or in the causes of the event. Black cats or "knock on wood" and so forth are common superstitions. Why do people believe in superstitions? How is idol-worshipping part of superstition?

Some of the people remembered very well that Ibrāhīm (A) had talked against the idols and also that he had planned a drama about the idols. But nobody saw him break the idols, therefore, nobody could be sure. They said:

$$ سَمِعْنَا فَتًى يَذْكُرُهُمْ يُقَالُ لَهُ إِبْرَاهِيمُ ۝ $$

"We heard a young man talking against them. His name is Ibrāhīm." (21:60)

Ibrāhīm (A) appears for questioning

The angry priests of the temple called Ibrāhīm (A) to come forward for questioning. They asked him:

$$ ءَأَنتَ فَعَلْتَ هَٰذَا بِءَالِهَتِنَا يَٰإِبْرَاهِيمُ ۝ $$

"Is it you who has done this to our gods, O Ibrahim?" (21:62)

Ibrāhīm (A) had waited for this opportunity. He wanted the people to realize the idols could not do anything, and they have no power to do any good or harm. He wanted people to see that if idols could not protect themselves, how could they protect human beings? He did not break the biggest idol because he wanted people to realize that even the largest idol had no power to protect the smaller ones. The large idol was helpless when the destruction occurred right in front of it!

Now the situation was serious. Ibrāhīm (A) faced an angry group of people. He was not a coward, and he would not lie to save himself. Why should he lie? Allāh repeatedly says that Ibrahim (A) was a **Hanīf**—an upright person.[3:67, 3:95,]

Definition

Hanīf: One who is inclined to truth, being upright and always righteous in every aspect of life. The Qur'ān uses the term Hanīf in connection with Ibrāhīm (A).

4:125, 6:161, 16:120 A Hanīf is someone who is always truthful and avoids falsehood. Allāh﷿ had selected him to be the Imām, or the leader, for mankind.²:¹²⁴ He would not lie or falsify to establish the Truth! However, he was not willing to answer all the questions of the priests. His purpose was to make people realize the uselessness of idol-worshipping. He answered cleverly, saying that Surely someone did it. But your chief idol is still around. Ask him if he had seen anything, and why he did not try to stop this destruction. Ask him to speak up, if he can. Maybe you want to ask your broken idols, who did this terrible thing to them. The Qur'ān says:

قَالَ بَلْ فَعَلَهُۥ كَبِيرُهُمْ هَٰذَا فَسْـَٔلُوهُمْ إِن كَانُوا۟ يَنطِقُونَ ۝

He said, "Surely someone has done it. This is the big one, ask them if they can speak." (21:63)

Points to Ponder

Sometime we read that Ibrāhīm (A) replied "no" when asked whether he broke the idols, and he pointed to the big idol, saying, "The big one did it." Why it is impossible that Ibrāhīm (A) lied and put the blame on one who did not do it?

The plan worked well

The priests knew the idols could not speak. They turned to each other and realized that they were wrong.²¹:⁶⁴ They realized that if the idols could not protect themselves from being broken, how could they bring good fortune or a good harvest to the people? One of the priests said:

"Surely you know that they do not speak." (21:65)

Ibrāhīm (A) noticed the priests were ashamed. Hoping they finally understood their mistake, Ibrāhīm (A) pointed out the Truth:

"Do you then worship besides Allāh things that can neither profit you nor harm you? Shame upon you and upon that which you worship besides Allāh!" (21:66–67)

Hatred increases

Although the priests realized idol-worshipping was meaningless, they would not accept defeat. They felt they had been insulted by a young man. They had to protect their honor in front of the common people. They became furious. A fire of hatred increased everywhere. People wanted to burn Ibrāhīm (A) in a fire. When the situation was out of control, Allāh﷿ said:

يَٰنَارُ كُونِى بَرْدًا وَسَلَٰمًا عَلَىٰٓ إِبْرَٰهِيمَ ۝

"O fire! be cool and peaceful on Ibrāhīm." (21:69)

The people wanted to harm Ibrāhīm (A), but Allāh﷿ showed that they were the wrongdoers. Ibrāhīm's (A) struggle to establish the truth shows us that we can win over people through careful and proper discussion. The path to establish the truth is always difficult, but Allāh﷿ says that when truth arrives, falsehood vanishes. Falsehood is sure to vanish.

وَقُلْ جَآءَ ٱلْحَقُّ وَزَهَقَ ٱلْبَٰطِلُ إِنَّ ٱلْبَٰطِلَ كَانَ زَهُوقًا ۝

And you say, "The Truth has come and falsehood has vanished. Surely the falsehood does ever vanish away." (17:81)

1. In the story of Ibrāhīm (A), what reason did people give for worshipping idols?

    A.   They worshipped idols because idols gave them food.

    B.   They worshipped idols because idols protected them from danger.

    (C.)   They worshipped idols because their forefathers worshipped them.

    D.   They worshipped idols because they did not know about Allāh.

2. Which sūrah describes the incident of Ibrāhīm (A) breaking the idols?

surah anbiya

3. Read āyah 21:56 of the Qur'ān. What did Ibrāhīm (A) mention about the Lord (or Rabb) to his father?

that he is the lord of the heaven and earth

4. Read āyah 21:65 of the Qur'ān. When Ibrāhīm (A) told his people to ask their idols who had broken them, what was their reply?

sarely you know not to speak

5. Read āyah 21:70 of the Qur'ān. What happened to the people who wanted to harm Ibrāhīm (A)?

allah made those the worest losers

6. When the priests asked Ibrāhīm (A) if he broke the idols, how did he reply?

    A.   He lied to avoid the anger of the priests.

    (B.)   He told the truth, but in a clever way.

    C.   He and his father ran away from the temple.

    D.   He became angry and walked away to a fire pit.

7. Based on the lesson, write the meaning of the word Hanīf.

true deliever

8. In the story of Ibrāhīm (A), what was the explanation people gave as to their reason for worshipping idols ?

    A.   They believed idols can speak, hear, and respond to their calls.
    B.   They worshipped idols because their forefathers worshipped them.
    C.   They worshipped idols because idols have power.
    D.   They worshipped idols because idols told them to do so.

9. Which idol did Ibrāhīm (A) not break in the temple?

    A.   The most powerful one.
    B.   The biggest one.
    C.   The one that sent them food.
    D.   The smallest one.

10. How many people saw Ibrāhīm (A) break the idols in the temple?

    A.   Only three people.
    B.   Only the main priest of the temple.
    C.   Only the biggest idol.
    D.   Nobody saw him break the idols.

11. When the priests asked Ibrāhīm (A) if he broke the idols, what did he do?

    A.   He ran away to Madyan.
    B.   He lied to them.
    C.   He spoke the truth.
    D.   He blamed someone else.

Luqmān (A): *A Wise Man's Lifelong Advice*

Objective of the Lesson:

The advice Luqmān (A) gave to his son contains great lessons for us. The Qur'ān has given much importance to Luqmān's (A) teachings. In fact, a sūrah is named after him. This lesson provides a summary of Luqmān's (A) teachings along with a brief account of the life of this important man.

The Qur'ān tells a beautiful story about a wise person named Luqmān (A). A sūrah in the Qur'ān, sūrah number 31, is named after him. Thousands of years ago, Luqmān (A) lived in a country called **Ethiopia**. His knowledge and wisdom were so vast that people from all over the country and the region knew about him. His name and reputation spread across the land. People in Arabia, ancient Europe, and Persia knew about him. Many stories and fables were told about him and his wisdom.

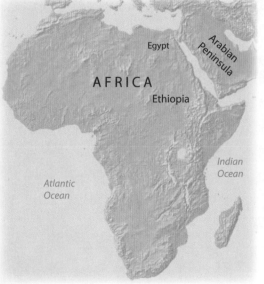

Some Western scholars think the renowned Greek man known as Aesop is none other than Luqmān (A). We do not know that for sure, though in Greek literature, Aesop is mentioned as a slave who probably came from Ethiopia. The name Aesop may have originated from the word "Ethiopia." Aesop told many fables, and many of these teachings agree with Islamic teachings.

Was he a rasūl?

Some Muslim scholars believe Luqmān (A) was not a rasūl, but a wise person. One reason for this conclusion is he is not an Israelite messenger and he does not have any link to the ancient Palestine region. Other than in sūrah 31, there is no mention of Luqmān (A) in any other sūrah. The Qur'ān frequently mentions the name and activities of many Israelite messengers. But other than the names of non-Israelite messengers and non-Arab messengers, there seems to be no mention of the names of messengers appearing in other regions of the world. The second reason scholars of Islam do not consider Luqmān (A) a messenger is they do not find a reference to him in the Bible.

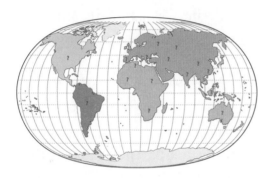

List of Known Messengers

Non-Israelite Nabi	Israelite Nabi
• Adam (A)	• Yaqub (A)
• Idris (A)	• Yusuf (A)
• Nuh (A)	• Ayyub (A)
• Ibrahim (A)	• Shuaib (A)
• Lut (A)	• Musa (A)
• Ishaq (A)	• Harun (A)
• Ismail (A)	• Dawud (A)
• Dhul-Kifl (A)	• Sulaiman (A)
	• Ilyas (A)
	• Alyasa (A)
Arab Nabi	• Yunus (A)
• Hud (A)	• Zakariyyah (A)
• Salih (A)	• Yahya (A)
• Muhammad ﷺ	• 'Isa (A)

Luqmān (A) is known in Islamic writings as **Luqmān al-Hakīm**, or Luqmān the Wise Man. Allāh ﷻ gave him *hikmah*, or wisdom, and knowledge about religion.[31:12] Allāh ﷻ gave *hikmah* to all the messengers, such as Yūsuf (A),[12:22] 'Isā (A),[3:48] Lūt (A),[21:74] and Sulaimān (A).[21:79] Allāh ﷻ also sent messengers to all communities and all nations. Some of the messengers are mentioned in the Qur'ān, but many others are not.[4:164; 40:78]

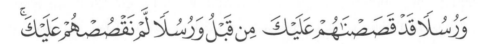

And messengers We have indeed mentioned them to you before, and messengers We have not mentioned them to you. (4:164)

Luqmān (A) very well could have been a messenger, but we do not know that for sure. He was a righteous individual, a servant of Allāh ﷻ, and a wise person.

Luqmān (A) teaches his son

In the Qur'ān, āyāt 31:12–19 describe Luqmān's (A) teachings. Although he taught his son thousands of years ago, his message is still relevant for us today. Luqmān (A) taught his son at least **twelve values** and principles. These values and principles are mentioned in eight verses in the Qur'ān. These values are highly

وَلَقَدْ ءَاتَيْنَا لُقْمَـٰنَ الْحِكْمَةَ أَنِ اشْكُرْ لِلَّهِ ۚ وَمَن يَشْكُرْ فَإِنَّمَا يَشْكُرُ لِنَفْسِهِ ۖ وَمَن كَفَرَ فَإِنَّ اللَّهَ غَنِيٌّ حَمِيدٌ ﴿١٢﴾

12. And certainly We gave wisdom to Luqmān, saying: "Give thanks to Allāh. And whoever gives thanks, he gives thanks for his own soul; and whosoever shows ungratefulness then surely Allāh is Self-sufficient, Praised."

وَإِذْ قَالَ لُقْمَـٰنُ لِابْنِهِ وَهُوَ يَعِظُهُ يَـٰبُنَىَّ لَا تُشْرِكْ بِاللَّهِ ۖ إِنَّ الشِّرْكَ لَظُلْمٌ عَظِيمٌ ﴿١٣﴾

13. And behold! Luqmān said to his son, while he was exhorting him: "O my son! do not associate with Allāh. Surely polytheism is indeed a grievous wrongdoing."

وَوَصَّيْنَا الْإِنسَـٰنَ بِوَٰلِدَيْهِ حَمَلَتْهُ أُمُّهُ وَهْنًا عَلَىٰ وَهْنٍ وَفِصَـٰلُهُ فِى عَامَيْنِ أَنِ اشْكُرْ لِى وَلِوَٰلِدَيْكَ إِلَىَّ الْمَصِيرُ ﴿١٤﴾

14. And We have enjoined on people concerning his parents—his mother carries him with fainting upon fainting, and his weaning is in two years—saying: "Give thanks to Me and to your parents. Towards Me is the return.

وَإِن جَـٰهَدَاكَ عَلَىٰٓ أَن تُشْرِكَ بِى مَا لَيْسَ لَكَ بِهِ عِلْمٌ فَلَا تُطِعْهُمَا ۖ وَصَاحِبْهُمَا فِى الدُّنْيَا مَعْرُوفًا ۖ وَاتَّبِعْ سَبِيلَ مَنْ أَنَابَ إِلَىَّ ۚ ثُمَّ إِلَىَّ مَرْجِعُكُمْ فَأُنَبِّئُكُم بِمَا كُنتُمْ تَعْمَلُونَ ﴿١٥﴾

15. "But if they strive against you that you should associate with Me about which you do not have any knowledge, then do not obey them; yet keep company with them with fairness in this world. And follow the path of him who bends towards Me, and then towards Me is your return, so I shall inform you as to what you used to do."

يَـٰبُنَىَّ إِنَّهَا إِن تَكُ مِثْقَالَ حَبَّةٍ مِّنْ خَرْدَلٍ فَتَكُن فِى صَخْرَةٍ أَوْ فِى السَّمَـٰوَٰتِ أَوْ فِى الْأَرْضِ يَأْتِ بِهَا اللَّهُ ۚ إِنَّ اللَّهَ لَطِيفٌ خَبِيرٌ ﴿١٦﴾

16. "O my son! surely if there be the weight of a grain of mustard-seed, then be it inside a stone, or in the heavens, or in the earth, Allāh will bring it forth. Certainly Allāh is Subtle, Aware.

يَـٰبُنَىَّ أَقِمِ الصَّلَوٰةَ وَأْمُرْ بِالْمَعْرُوفِ وَانْهَ عَنِ الْمُنكَرِ وَاصْبِرْ عَلَىٰ مَا أَصَابَكَ ۖ إِنَّ ذَٰلِكَ مِنْ عَزْمِ الْأُمُورِ ﴿١٧﴾

17. "O my son! establish the Salāt, and bid the good things and forbid the evil things, and persevere upon whatever falls upon you. Truly these are out of the affairs of great determination.

وَلَا تُصَعِّرْ خَدَّكَ لِلنَّاسِ وَلَا تَمْشِ فِي الْأَرْضِ مَرَحًا إِنَّ اللَّهَ لَا يُحِبُّ كُلَّ مُخْتَالٍ فَخُورٍ ۝

18. "And do not turn your cheek towards men, and do not walk in the earth haughtily. Surely Allāh does not love every arrogant boaster.

وَاقْصِدْ فِي مَشْيِكَ وَاغْضُضْ مِن صَوْتِكَ إِنَّ أَنكَرَ الْأَصْوَاتِ لَصَوْتُ الْحَمِيرِ ۝

19. "Rather adopt the right course in your going about, and lower the tone in your voice. Surely the most hateful of voices is undoubtedly the braying of a donkey."

recommended for all of us to learn and follow in our lives. Following only one or two teachings and ignoring the rest will not make us good Muslims. Here is a summary of Luqmān's (A) teachings:

1. Worship Allāh (āyah 13)
2. Give thanks to Allāh (verses 12, 14)
3. Do not associate others with Allāh (āyah 13)
4. Be aware of Allāh's presence and knowledge (āyah 16)
5. Be dutiful to parents (verses 14, 15)
6. Repent to Allāh and be obedient (āyah 15)
7. Establish salāt (āyah 17)
8. Command what is good (āyah 17)
9. Forbid what is bad (āyah 17)
10. Show patience and perseverance (āyah 17)
11. Avoid pride, be humble (āyah 18)
12. Be moderate in action (āyah 19)

Luqmān's (A) teachings about Allāh:

Although Luqmān (A) gave this advice to his son, the message applies to all periods of time. We have to worship Allāh because He is the only deity in the entire universe. Allāh has created us to worship Him.

وَمَا خَلَقْتُ الْجِنَّ وَالْإِنسَ إِلَّا لِيَعْبُدُونِ ۝

And I have not created the jinn and mankind but they should worship me. (51:56)

All Muslims worship Allāh ﷻ and Luqmān (A) also worshipped Allāh ﷻ. The problem is sometimes people worship Allāh ﷻ and simultaneously show devotion to other powers or objects. For example, visiting shrines of Muslim saints and praying to those saints is shirk. Wearing gemstones believing that the gemstones

can bring good luck or prevent harm is also shirk. There are many examples available that show Muslims worship Allāh ﷻ but make the mistake of associating other powers with Allāh ﷻ. For this reason, Luqmān (A) twice cautioned his son not to associate with Allāh ﷻ—first in āyah 13 and then in āyah 15. He tells his son that associating anything or anybody with Allāh ﷻ is a monstrous sin.

We also have to give thanks to Allāh ﷻ. When we give thanks, it makes us acknowledge that everything comes from Allāh ﷻ. He provides, controls, and sustains. Everything He does is for our own good, even if we do not realize it. When we give thanks, we offer it for our own good. Giving thanks makes us humble and aware of Allāh ﷻ. The importance of giving thanks to Allāh ﷻ is mentioned again and again in the Qur'ān. Here is one example:

فَٱذْكُرُونِىٓ أَذْكُرْكُمْ وَٱشْكُرُواْ لِى وَلَا تَكْفُرُونِ ﴿١٥٢﴾

Therefore remember Me, I shall remember you; and give thanks to Me, and do not defy Me. (2:152)

Allāh ﷻ has knowledge of everything. We should remember that we cannot hide anything from Him. Allāh ﷻ knows everything, even if it is equal to the weight of a grain of mustard seed. Our smallest action—good or bad—will be disclosed, and Allāh ﷻ knows everything. We should be careful before we do anything bad behind the backs of our parents, teachers, or anybody else.

Luqmān's (A) advice about duties toward parents

Luqmān (A) taught his son to be dutiful to his parents. We should give thanks to our parents for all the sacrifices they make in raising us from the time of our birth, during our childhood, and beyond. In many verses in the Qur'ān, Allāh ﷻ says that obeying parents is the next most important thing after worshipping Allāh ﷻ.[17:23; 46:15] For example, the following āyah teaches us not to worship anyone except Allāh ﷻ, and to do good to our parents and never say hurtful things to them or scold them.

And your Rabb has commanded that you do not worship anyone except Him alone; and doing good to the parents. If one of them or both of them reach old age in your presence, even then do not say to them "Ugh," and do not scold them and speak to them a generous speech. (17:23)

Luqmān's (A) advice about self-development

Luqmān (A) also taught his son some of the important techniques that can make any person a better individual. One of the techniques is to repent to Allāh﷾ for all his or her sins. Repentance makes us realize our sin and, in turn, encourages us not to commit the same sin again. If we repent, Allāh﷾ forgives us. Unless we earn Allāh's﷾ forgiveness, we will be in deep trouble.

The second technique of self development is to establish salāt. Establishing salāt means to perform your own salāt and, at the same time, encourage others to perform salāt. If there is no place to perform salāt, set up a good place for salāt. Establishing salāt also means to make salāt on time and to make it a priority in your life.

The third technique is to persevere no matter what happens. During normal times it is easy to speak about patience and perseverance. But when difficulty strikes, sometimes people give up hope and become depressed. Sometimes people begin doing the wrong things to overcome their difficulties. They cut a few corners, such as cheating, lying, or stealing so that they can overcome the difficulties quickly. We should learn to practice perseverance and keep doing hard work. Only then Allāh﷾ will help us overcome the crisis and become successful. Through patience, we hope for the best and learn not to complain. Through perseverance, we learn to do our best to overcome the difficulties in life.

Luqmān's (A) advice about social conduct

Salāt is a tool for self development. Salāt also has a social implication. The first social conduct encouraged by Luqmān (A) is performing salāt in a group. When we perform salāt in a group, it helps build social relationships. We learn to interact with people from all walks of life. We learn to establish a sense of closeness with other members of society.

Time to Review

1. If we forget a sin committed years ago, why will Allāh﷾ not forget the sin?
2. What are the finer differences between patience and perseverance?
3. What is the deeper meaning of "establishing" salāt?

A second important tool of good social conduct is to encourage each other to do good deeds and to avoid evil things. Due to its importance, this teaching is mentioned in many sūrah in the Qur'ān.[3:110; 9:71]

كُنتُمْ خَيْرَ أُمَّةٍ أُخْرِجَتْ لِلنَّاسِ تَأْمُرُونَ بِالْمَعْرُوفِ وَتَنْهَوْنَ عَنِ الْمُنكَرِ وَتُؤْمِنُونَ بِاللَّهِ وَلَوْ ءَامَنَ أَهْلُ الْكِتَبِ لَكَانَ خَيْرًا لَّهُمْ مِّنْهُمُ الْمُؤْمِنُونَ وَأَكْثَرُهُمُ

You are the best community raised up for mankind; you bid doing right and forbid from doing wrong, and you believe in Allāh... (3:110)

If we do good things and stay away from bad things, our family, neighborhood, and community will benefit from these good deeds..

A third tool of good social behavior is not turn your cheek toward others. This means you do not put yourself in harm's way. You do not let yourself be oppressed or tortured. If needed, you leave the place of oppression or protest.

A fourth tool of good social conduct is not to behave arrogantly or proudly. The reason is Allāh﷿ does not like arrogant boasters. Arrogance and extreme pride is a sign of Shaitān. We should not behave like Shaitān.

A fifth tool of good social behavior taught by Luqmān (A) is to be moderate in our actions. Being moderate means to be reasonable, sensible, modest, and balanced in everything. Think about what would happen if you played all day and did not study. Think about what would happen if you ate all day, slept all the time, or sat idle all the time. Everything should be done in a balanced manner. We should show moderation in the way we walk and in the way we talk. For example, Luqmān (A) taught us to lower our voice when we speak. A rising voice or speaking in a disrespectful manner is a sign of bad social behavior. He compared a loud voice with the braying of a donkey. Nobody likes it if a person yells or speaks in loud voice.

All of Luqmān's (A) teachings are magnificent. If we follow his teachings, we will become good Muslims. We must remember what Luqmān (A) said Allāh﷿ sees our every conduct—nothing remains hidden from Him—*if there be the weight of a grain of mustard-seed, then be it inside a stone, or in the heavens, or in the earth, Allāh will bring it forth.*

1. Write down three things you can do to express thanks to your parents.

    1. _____

    2. _____

    3. _____

2. What is the second most important thing we should do other than worshipping Allāh ﷻ?

_____

3. Why is it important to give thanks to Allāh ﷻ?

_____

_____

4. How many of Luqmān's (A) teachings should we follow if we live in North America, Europe or Australia?

_____

5. Read āyah 31:13 of the Qur'ān. What is mentioned in the āyah as a great *zūlm*, or wrongdoing?

_____

6. Read āyah 31:16 of the Qur'ān. How small of an item can Allāh ﷻ bring out, even if it is hidden beneath a rock or anywhere in the universe?

_____

7. Solve the crossword puzzle using the clues below.

Across:

1. Earliest sin in history, avoid this, it is bad trait.

5. Next to Allāh, they deserve the most respect.

6. Luqmān (A) spoke to him.

7. Always give this to Allāh.

11. Luqmān's (A) native place.

Down:

2. Do this before it is too late.

3. Number of Luqmān's (A) teachings minus one.

4. Throw food neglectfully, Allāh does not like it.

8. He may have been Luqmān (A).

9. Lower your voice when you do this.

10. We should always follow the right ____.

Yūsuf (A): *His Childhood and Life in Aziz's Home*

Objective of the Lesson:

Yūsuf's (A) childhood was as eventful as his adult life. His brothers wanted to kill him, but Allāhﷻ saved him and gave him shelter in a wealthy household. In this lesson, we will learn the key events during his childhood. We will also learn about a meaningful dream that he had as a child. There is a great lesson to learn from the incidents in Yūsuf's (A) life.

Thousands of years ago, in a region near Egypt, there lived a messenger named Yūsuf (A). His father Ya'qūb (A), was also a messenger. Ya'qūb's (A) father Ishāq (A), was also a messenger. Ishāq's (A) father was Ibrāhīm (A).

The Qur'ān contains a sūrah with a beautiful description of Yūsuf's (A) life. This sūrah is also named Yūsuf. The Qur'ān refers to this description as *"ahsan al-qasas,"* meaning "most-beautiful narration." The word *ashsan* means "beautiful," "pure," or "best." The beautiful narrative of the sūrah refers to the manner in which it is told and to the content of the narrative.

Today, we will learn about Yūsuf's (A) childhood. Even in childhood, his life had many twists and turns of events. Some of the events almost seemed to destroy him, but somehow, at the right moment, something happened to help him overcome the challenges. Allāhﷻ says that we can surely learn a lot from the life of Yūsuf (A) and his brothers.[12:7]

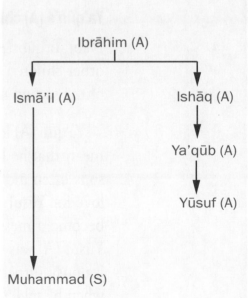

Ibrāhīm (A)

Ismā'īl (A)　　　　Ishāq (A)

Ya'qūb (A)

Yūsuf (A)

Muhammad (S)

$$\text{* لَقَدْ كَانَ فِى يُوسُفَ وَإِخْوَتِهِ ءَايَتٌ لِّلسَّآئِلِينَ ٧}$$

Most surely in Yūsuf and his brothers, there are signs for the inquirers. (12:7)

Yūsuf's (A) dream

When Yūsuf (A) was a child, he had a strange dream. In the dream, he saw the sun, the moon, and 11 stars bowing down and prostrating. The next morning he told his father, Ya'qūb (A), about the dream. His father was a messenger and a wise person. He realized that the dream had a deeper meaning. He told Yūsuf (A) two things:

1. Not to tell any of his brothers the dream,

2. Allāh﷿ had chosen him to teach the meaning of dreams, and to grant His favor upon him and upon the children of Ya'qūb (A).[12:6]

Yūsuf's (A) brothers were jealous of him and Ya'qūb (A) knew this. He did not want the brothers to make evil plots against Yūsuf (A). While using words of caution, Ya'qūb (A) stated a very important fact that we all should always remember. He said:

$$\text{إِنَّ الشَّيْطَنَ لِلْإِنسَنِ عَدُوٌّ مُّبِينٌ ٥}$$

Surely Shaitān is an open enemy to mankind. (12:5)

Ya'qūb's (A) children

Nabi Ya'qūb (A) had twelve children. Ten of them had the same mother. Two other children had different mother. Yūsuf (A) and **Binyamin** were the children of the second mother.

Ya'qūb (A) loved his two younger sons, Yūsuf (A) and Binyamin. This does not mean that he loved his ten sons from his first wife any less. He knew his other sons often did bad things. But despite all this, he loved them, too. The father's love for Yūsuf (A) was stronger because he knew Yūsuf (A) would grow up and become a messenger like him. The ten brothers thought their father's love for Yūsuf (A) was unfair. Their jealousy of him increased by the day. Gradually their jealousy turned into hatred for Yūsuf (A). That is what Ya'qūb (A) was afraid of when he told Yūsuf (A) not to mention the dream to his brothers.

Brothers make a plan

One day the ten brothers hatched a plan to kill Yūsuf (A) or send him secretly to a distant land. They thought that if Yūsuf (A) was gone, their father would start loving them. They did not realize that their father loved them as well. One of the brothers told the other brothers not to kill Yūsuf (A), but to drop him in a well. Some travelers might pick him up and take him with them. The ten brothers agreed on this plan.

After the brothers made their plan, they went to see their father. They wanted to show him that they cared about Yūsuf (A). They asked their father to give them permission to take Yūsuf (A) to a game the next day.[12:11, 12] They pretended that they loved Yūsuf (A) very much.

Their father knew something bad might happen to Yūsuf (A). He told them:

$$قَالَ إِنِّي لَيَحْزُنُنِي أَن تَذْهَبُواْ بِهِ وَأَخَافُ أَن يَأْكُلَهُ ٱلذِّئْبُ وَأَنتُمْ عَنْهُ غَٰفِلُونَ ﴿١٣﴾$$

It hurts me to think that you want to take him away, and I fear that a wolf might eat him when you become busy in play. (12:13)

Wolves usually attack small and weak targets. Yūsuf (A) was a young boy, so he could have easily become wolves' prey. The brothers told their father not to worry. They said they were a strong group. They insisted that if a wolf appeared, they could chase it away. If something really bad happened to Yūsuf (A), then it would be a great loss for them, too.[12:14]

After hearing this, their elderly father gave them permission, although he still had a feeling that something bad might happen.

Yūsuf (A) thrown in a well

The next day, the ten brothers left home with Yūsuf (A). They did not take Binyamin with them; he was too little. Their main hatred was for Yūsuf (A). They went to an area far away from their neighborhood. There were no other people around. In that remote area, they found a natural well used by travelers. They dropped him in a well. Yūsuf (A) was too young to save himself from his ten brothers.

Although the brothers had wanted to harm Yūsuf (A), Allāh﷿ had a different plan. Allāh﷿ had already chosen him to be a nabi when he grew up. Allāh﷿ revealed to him:

$$ لَتُنَبِّئَنَّهُم بِأَمْرِهِمْ هَـٰذَا وَهُمْ لَا يَشْعُرُونَ $$

You will certainly inform them of this act, but they will not recognize you. (12:15)

Yūsuf (A) realized Allāh﷿ would protect him and would not let him die.

Brothers return home

In the evening when it was time to return home, the brothers made another plan. They stained Yūsuf's (A) shirt with blood some animal. Then they returned home, crying. They said:

"O father! We were racing with one another, and we left Yūsuf near our supplies. While we were gone, a wolf ate him. You must believe us. We are telling the truth." (12:17)

The fact that as a young boy, Yūsuf (A) could count up to 11 stars indicates he had some basic education and knew numbers and counting.

During that period, wealthy men wore a single outer garment—a long shirt and nothing underneath. Poor men usually did not wear a shirt.

The brothers brought home Yūsuf's (A) blood stained shirt. This indicates that before dropping him in the well, they took his shirt off, and made him naked. But the Qur'ān does not mention it to show respect to him.

The fact that the shirt was stained with blood indicates the brothers killed an animal along the way. This act also shows how cruel they were.

Their father, Ya'qūb (A), did not believe them. He knew they were lying to him. How did he know? Remember, Ya'qūb (A) had told his sons that he was worried that a wolf might attack Yūsuf (A). Now the sons told him the same story. A wise father like him saw through their lies. He saw that the shirt was not torn. If a wolf ate Yūsuf (A), his shirt would have been torn. A wise person like Ya'qūb (A) probably knew that wolves usually attack in a pack and at night. The sons did not know that wolves usually hunt at night. Ya'qūb (A) clearly saw that their story was false. He simply said:

"Patience is good."

He then asked for Allāh's help regarding what his sons had told him.

Yūsuf (A) rescued

Sometime later a caravan of travelers came upon the well. One of the men dropped his bucket in the well to fetch water. Guess what! Instead of water, a boy came up in the bucket. The men hid the boy with their supplies. They brought him to Egypt and sold him to a wealthy person for a little money.

The wealthy person was named Aziz. He brought Yūsuf (A) to his home and told his wife to take care of the boy. He said that they might adopt the boy as their son, or the boy

Interesting Facts

Wolves are of two types: gray or timber wolves, and red wolves. Only a small number of wild, red wolves exist now.

Wolves are not fast runners, but they can run for a long time.

Wolves are social animals—usually living in groups of 5–11 wolves. Their groups are called a pack.

Wolves usually hunt small animals, but if their pack is large, they may attack animals as big as a moose. Unless wolves are desperate for food, they do not usually attack people.

Wolves howl to locate their members or to alert others if there is danger.

Wolves are a common motif in legends, mythology, and folklore. *Little Red Riding Hood* is one of the most famous fairy tales involving a wolf.

might be of some use one day.[12:21] The brothers had wanted to harm Yūsuf (A), but with Allāh'sﷻ blessing, he was rescued. Not only that, but Yūsuf (A) found a good place to live in Egypt.

Moral of the story

We can learn many lessons from Yūsuf's (A) life. If we remain good and sincere to Allāhﷻ, He will help us even if people want to harm us. Allāhﷻ can overcome all the evil plans of human beings. Sometimes bad things happen in our lives, and we may lose all hope. We may forget that Allāhﷻ can turn a bad situation into a good one. We have to always trust Allāhﷻ and pray to Him. Although the evil brothers wanted to harm Yūsuf (A), Allāhﷻ rewarded him.[12:22]

We also learned that when we experience bad times, we have to be patient. We should remember what Ya'qūb (A) said: "Patience is good."

Time to Review

1. How do wolves typically hunt?
2. What were some of the reasons that Ya'qūb (A) did not believe that a wolf ate his son Yūsuf (A)?
3. At what time of day did the brothers return home after dropping Yūsuf (A) in the well?

Points to Ponder

The brothers dropped Yūsuf (A) in a well during the daytime. They might have heard him cry or shout for help. Did they respond? What does this tell about the brothers? Then they retuned home at night. Why at night? Could it be because they were afraid that during daylight their facial expressions would give away the secret? Was it because they wanted to hide something in the darkness of night? What does all this tell us about these brothers?

1. Write down the names of Yūsuf's (A) forefathers, starting with his ancestor Ibrāhīm (A).

   Ibrāhīm (A), _____, _____, _____.

2. Read āyah 12:9 of the Qur'ān. What were the two ways the brothers wanted to harm Yūsuf (A)?

   1. _____

   2. _____

3. Read āyah 12:18 of the Qur'ān. What did Ya'qūb (A) say in response to the bad news about Yūsuf (A)?

   _____

   _____

4. Allāhﷻ says He will remember us as long as we do something. Read āyah 2:152 of the Qur'ān. What should we do so that Allāhﷻ remembers us?

   _____

5. Read āyah 12:20 of the Qur'ān. For how much money was Yūsuf (A) sold in Egypt? What currency did they use?

   _____

6. What lesson can we learn from Yūsuf's (A) childhood? Mention one lesson that you learned.

   _____

   _____

7. What did Yūsuf (A) see in his childhood dream?

    A.   Seven fat cows and seven lean cows.

    B.   Seven green ears of corn.

    C.   Seven stars, the moon and the sun.

    D.   The sun, the moon and 11 stars prostrating.

8. After Yūsuf (A) told his father about the dream, what did his father advise?

    A.   To forget about the dream.

    B.   Not to tell his brothers about the dream.

    C.   To work hard to fulfill the dream.

    D.   To go out with the brothers to a playground.

9. What was the final plan of the brothers to get rid of Yūsuf (A)?

    A.   To kill him.

    B.   To send him to a far-off place.

    C.   To drop him in a well.

    D.   To bury him alive.

10. According to the brothers, which animal ate Yūsuf (A)?

    A.   Hyena.

    B.   Lion.

    C.   Bear.

    D.   Wolf.

11. After dropping Yūsuf (A) in the well, what proof did the brothers bring to prove that he was dead?

    A.   A blood-covered blanket.

    B.   A blood-covered shirt.

    C.   Torn pajamas.

    D.   A blood-covered woolen cap.

Yūsuf (A): *Standing Up for Righteousness*

Objective of the Lesson:

Yūsuf (A) was thrown into prison even though he was not guilty. He remained in prison until the truth was established. In the meantime, something happened in prison that determined the future course of his life. This lesson provides a summary of events of his time in and after prison. This lesson also demonstrates how patience ultimately pays off in the long run.

In the previous lesson, we learned about the childhood of Nabi Yūsuf (A). Due to a cruel act of his brothers, Yūsuf (A) was separated from his parents. He was sold in the slave market. Just when things seemed to have taken a wrong turn, Allāhﷻ brought new hope to his life. Then life took another difficult turn. Due to an unfortunate series of events, Yūsuf (A) was thrown in prison.

Yūsuf (A) in prison

After Yūsuf (A) was sold in the slave market, his life took a different turn. A rich Egyptian man bought him and thought of raising him as an adopted son. He grew up in the household and became a young man. Life was good for him. But then things turned bad in the household. The woman of the house blamed him for wrongdoing. She and her friends plotted against Yūsuf (A) to send him to prison. We will study the reasons they blamed him in the 7th grade, insha-Allāh.

Yūsuf (A) thought prison would be better than living in a house where the environment was bad.[12:33] Life in prison was difficult for him, but he managed not to get upset. He was a righteous person and obeyed Allāh. He showed patience. He knew Allāh would help him and set him free. He wanted freedom, but only after proving that he was innocent.

Yūsuf (A) meets the prisoners

While in prison, Yūsuf (A) became friendly with two other prisoners. They found out that Yūsuf (A) could explain the meaning of dreams. One day, one of the prisoners told him about a dream that he had. He saw in his dream that he was pressing wine. The other prisoner said he also had a dream. He dreamt that he was carrying bread on his head and birds were eating the bread.

Yūsuf (A) realized the meaning of the dreams. The meaning of the dream about pressing wine was the man would be set free. He would go and pour wine for the king. The meaning of the dream about carrying bread was the man would be found guilty. He would be crucified, and birds would peck on his head.

Yūsuf (A) told the man who would press wine not to forget him. This man would serve drinks to the king, so he would be very close to the king. He would have a chance to speak to the king. Yūsuf (A) told him to mention him to the king. He hoped the king would give an order to bring his case to court and release him if they found him not guilty.

Sometime later this man was released from prison. He began serving drinks to the king. Unfortunately, the man forgot about his prison-friend Yūsuf (A). The man began to enjoy his free life. He felt he was special—after all, he was the king's servant. The Qur'ān says he became influenced by Shaitān, otherwise how could he forget about his prison-friend?[12:42] As a result, Yūsuf (A) remained in prison for a few more years.

The king dreams about cows

Time passed. One night the king had a dream about cows. The next day he told his servants about the dream. In the dream, the king saw seven fat cows and seven thin cows. The thin cows were eating the fat cows. He also saw seven green ears of corn and seven dried ears of corn.[12:43] The entire dream confused him. The king asked if anyone could explain the meaning of this dream. Nobody had clue about its meaning.

The servant, who had been released from prison, heard about the king's dream. Then he remembered his prison-friend who was good at explaining dreams. He went to the prison and asked Yūsuf (A) about the dream.[12:46]

The meaning of the dream

Yūsuf (A) explained the meaning of the dream. He said that people should grow crops for seven years. After the harvest of the crop, most of it should be left on the ear, or stalk, of the crop. Only what

Points to Ponder

Throughout sūrah Yūsuf, dreams are the main accelerator of the story. First, as a child, Yūsuf (A) dreamt about 11 stars, the sun and the moon. Second, the prisoners had dreams about the future course of their lives. Third, the king dreamt about cows and corn, which shaped the future course of Yūsuf's (A) life.

was needed for eating should be processed further. Then seven years of famine would begin. During these seven years, people would eat the grain that they had saved in the earlier years. However, they would continue to preserve some grain for future cultivation. At the end of the famine, better times would follow. There would be abundant rain and crops would grow again. People would be happy and press wine and oil from corn again.[12:47–49]

The king likes the meaning

When the man returned and explained the meaning of the dream, the king was very happy. He realized that such a reasonable explanation must have come from a person who had a lot of knowledge and wisdom. He wanted to see Yūsuf (A), who was still in prison.

Yūsuf (A) said he would not leave the prison until he was declared not guilty. He wanted to remind the king about the women who plotted to send him to prison.

The king asked the women to tell the truth. The women were impressed by Yūsuf's (A) good character, honesty, and righteousness. Finally, they confessed their sins and admitted that Yūsuf (A) was innocent.[12:51] When the women confessed, the truth became established. Yūsuf (A) was declared not guilty and released from the prison.

Yūsuf (A) receives a high position

The king offered Yūsuf (A) a high-ranking job. Yūsuf (A) knew that a job in the agriculture and food department of the kingdom would be best for him. He

Time to Review

1. Why did the prisoner who was released forget to mention Yūsuf (A) to the king?
2. About how many years did Yūsuf (A) remain in prison?
3. At what point did the women admit that Yūsuf (A) was not blameworthy?

would be able to produce and store extra food during good times, and divide the food wisely during famine. The king appointed him chief of the agriculture department. He had full power over the department in the kingdom. Allāh﷿ made this happen because He wanted to show mercy upon him. He wanted to reward him for his good deeds as well as for being patient during his time in prison.

Moral of the story

From this story, we learn that even when bad things happen in our lives, we should never lose hope of receiving Allāh's﷿ blessing. Yūsuf (A) remained in prison for 12 to 13 years. Ultimately, he was released from prison and rewarded with a high-ranking job.

Allāh﷿ says He never forgets to reward the righteous people. Our lives will not always be happy and good. Sometimes we will face difficulties, hardships and suffering. During these difficult times, we have to show patience and dedication to Allāh﷿. We must remain righteous and truthful.

1. Who plotted to send Yūsuf (A) to prison?

   the women and her friend

2. Which prisoner-friend of Yūsuf (A) became free?

   A.   One who carried bread.

   B.   One who pressed wine.

   C.   One who fed the cows.

   D.   One who prepared grain.

3. Read āyah 12:42 of the Qur'ān. The servant forgot to mention Yūsuf (A) to the king. Who made the servant forget?

   Shatan

4. What did Yūsuf (A) tell people to do based on the king's dream about thin cows eating fat cows?

   A.   They should raise seven fat cows during seven years of drought.

   B.   They should sacrifice seven fat cows during seven years of drought.

   C.   They should let cows eat the corn left on the stalk when it did not rain.

   D.   They should grow crops for seven years and save most of the grain, and use the grain for the subsequent seven years of drought.

5. Why did Yūsuf (A) first refuse to leave the prison when the king wanted to see him?

   he wanted to not be gulity

6. Read āyah 12:57 of the Qur'ān. In order to receive a reward from Allāhﷻ, we have to do two things. What are the two things mentioned in the āyah?

1. _to be constant_

2. _to belive in rightiuoes_

7. What plan did the women make against Yūsuf (A)?

    A.   They planned to kill him.
    B.   They planned to send him to a far-off place.
    C.   They planned to poison him.
    D.   They planned to send him to prison.

8. How long did Yūsuf (A) remain in prison?

    A.   A few months.
    B.   Two years.
    C.   Several years.
    D.   Fifty years.

9. Who dreamt about the fat cows, lean cows, and ears of corn?

    A.   One of the two prisoners.
    B.   Yūsuf (A).
    C.   Eleven brothers.
    D.   The king.

10. In the dream about the cows, what were the cows doing?

    A.   The lean cows were eating the fat cows.
    B.   The fat cows were grazing on the corn.
    C.   The lean cows were milking the fat cows.
    D.   The fat cows were eating the lean cows.

Yūsuf (A): *A Childhood Dream Comes True*

Objective of the Lesson:

Yūsuf's (A) half-brothers wanted to kill him, but he was saved due to Allāh's ﷻ grace. Later he became a chief officer in Egypt. In an interesting turn of events, the same brothers who wanted to kill Yūsuf (A) came to seek his help. Yūsuf (A) helped them through a series of dramatic developments. Eventually he was reunited with his father. His childhood dream about stars, the sun, and the moon prostrating was fulfilled. The lesson provides a summary of these events.

In the previous two lessons, we learned about the childhood of messenger Yūsuf (A) and his life in prison in Egypt. In this lesson, we will learn about the period in his life when he was appointed chief of the agriculture department in Egypt. His strategies not only saved the lives of thousands of people, but they also paved the way for him to reunite with his parents.

Yūsuf (A) begins his work

We already read about the king's dream and its meaning. In the dream, he saw seven thin cows eating seven fat cows. The seven fat cows meant seven years of good harvest. The seven thin cows meant seven years of famine. When Yūsuf (A) became a senior officer in the country, his main responsibility was to make sure the country grew enough grain during each of the seven years. Then he saved the extra grain in warehouses as a reserve for the famine years.

Famine begins

As the king had dream, a famine started after seven years of good harvest. The reasons for the famine is not known but we can speculate on them. In ancient Egypt, agriculture was dependent on the annual flood of the Nile River. Probably due to low rainfall for a number of years, the river could not enrich the lands around it. As a result, people could not cultivate crops anymore. This, in turn, affected supply of food. Everybody was hungry. They began to depend upon the government to provide them with grain. Yūsuf's (A) brothers lived in Canaan, a place not far from Egypt. They, too, were affected by the famine. They found out that Egypt had large stocks of grain. They decided to go to Egypt to get a supply of food.

Brothers get food

Yūsuf's (A) ten brothers went to Egypt with some money to buy grain. They approached Yūsuf (A) but did not recognize him. How could they? Many years before they had dropped little Yūsuf (A) in a well and thought he died or had taken away. They had no idea that Yūsuf (A) survived and was now a senior officer in Egypt! Even though the brothers did not recognize Yūsuf (A), he recognized them.[12:58] He showed them the usual hospitality and casually inquired about their family. He learned about the well being of his parents and his youngest brother. When it was time to give them the grain, Yūsuf (A) told them that if they needed more grain, they should bring their youngest brother the next time. If they did not bring their brother, they would not receive any more grain.[12:60]

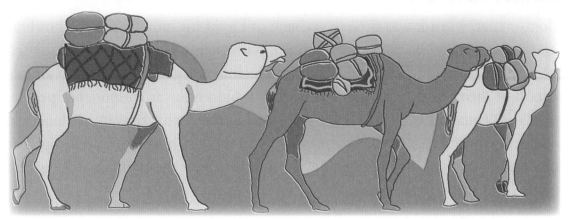

Yūsuf (A) wanted to give them a good reason to return to Egypt with their brother. Therefore, he told his servants to hide the money his brothers had used to buy the grain in their sacks, so they could find it when they went home.[12:62]

Terms about Binyamin

With all the supplies in their caravan, the brothers returned home. As is normal after any journey, the brothers shared their experiences in Egypt with their father Ya'qūb (A). They told him that unless Binyamin went with them, they would not get any more food. This strange condition put a lot of pressure on the father. The family needed food, but Ya'qūb (A) could not risk sending his youngest son in harm's way. The father was reluctant to send Binyamin because he could not trust his other sons after what had happened with Yūsuf (A) long ago.[12:64] The brothers continued to ask their father to agree to the condition.

Then the brothers opened their sacks and found their money had been returned to them. Now they were even more encouraged to return to Egypt for more grain. Ya'qūb (A) said he would let Binyamin go only if they promised they would bring him back.[12:66] After they swore in the name of Allāhﷻ to bring him back, their father agreed to let Binyamin go with them.

Brothers return to Egypt

Months later, when it was time to go back to Egypt for more grain, the brothers brought their younger brother, Binyamin, with them. Their father had advised them to split up and enter the city through different gates.[12:68] It was a simple request of their father, who wanted them to avoid undue attention from people. After they entered Egypt, Yūsuf (A) managed to meet with Binyamin alone. He identified himself as Yūsuf (A), and the two long-lost brothers stayed together for a few days. Nobody suspected anything. The rest of the brothers still did not know Yūsuf's (A) true identity.

Time to Review

1. Why was the money used to purchase grain secretly returned to the brothers?
2. What did Ya'qūb (A) tell his sons to do when they entered Egypt?
3. What did Yūsuf (A) do to improve agriculture in Egypt?

Incident with the king's cup

When it was time for the brothers to return home, Yūsuf (A) gave them their grain. Somehow the king's cup was placed in Binyamin's bag. Commentators have different opinions as to who placed the cup there. But let us continue the story.

As the caravan began to depart, one of the king's servants realized the cup was missing. The servant immediately assumed one of the brothers stole the cup. He called out, *"O you caravan! You are most surely thieves."* (12:70)

The brothers were surprised by the accusation. They turned around and asked, *"What is it that you miss?"* (12:71)

The servant replied, *"We miss the king's drinking cup, and whoever produces it will have the load of a camel, and I am responsible for it."* (12:72)

The brothers swore that they did not steal it.[12:73] Then they were asked what punishment should be given if the cup was found with them. They replied that if the cup was found in one of their bags, the brother in whose bag it was found would be kept prisoner in Egypt.

Everybody agreed to the condition. Then the servants began to search the bags. The cup was found in Binyamin's bag. Therefore, he would be held prisoner in Egypt. The brothers blamed Binyamin for stealing. One of the brothers refused to return home because he swore to his father, in the name of Allāh﷿, that he would bring Binyamin back. This brother stayed in Egypt while the other brothers returned home.

Ya'qūb (A) sends a search team

Ya'qūb (A) became extremely sad when his son, Binyamin, did not return with his brothers. First he lost Yūsuf (A), and now he lost Binyamin. Not only that, but another son stayed behind in Egypt because he would not return without Binyamin. The father cried every day. Ultimately, he told his nine sons to search for Yūsuf (A), Binyamin, and the brother who stayed behind. The sons went to Egypt for the third time. They begged for mercy from Yūsuf (A). They told him about the difficulties in the family and that they did not have enough money to buy grain. At that point, Yūsuf (A) disclosed his identity to his brothers.[12:90] They were sorry for leaving him in the well. The brothers admitted, *"By Allāh! Allāh has certainly preferred you above us, and we were surely the sinners."* On hearing this, Yūsuf (A) said:

$$ لَاتَثْرِيبَ عَلَيْكُمُ ٱلْيَوْمَ يَغْفِرُ ٱللَّهُ لَكُمْ وَهُوَ أَرْحَمُ ٱلرَّاحِمِينَ ﴿٩٢﴾ $$

"No blame be on you this day. Allāh may forgive you, for He is the most Rewarding of those who grant reward." (12:92)

Greatness of Yūsuf (A)

In his reply, we can see Yūsuf (A) was amazingly merciful and great. He had the opportunity to punish the brothers for their sin, but he chose to overlook their past crime and ask of Allāh's﷿ forgiveness.

Meaning of the childhood dream

Yūsuf (A) sent his brothers to Canaan to bring his parents to Egypt. He sent his royal shirt with them, so his father could see it and realize that Yūsuf (A) was still alive.[12:93] When his parents arrived in Egypt, they were all united as one big family. In response to the kindness shown to them by Allāh﷿, all eleven brothers, and their father and mother, fell down in prostration to Allāh. Yūsuf (A) realized that his childhood vision[12:4] of eleven stars, and the sun, and the moon prostrating was finally fulfilled.

1. Read āyah 12:60 of the Qur'ān. What condition did Yūsuf (A) place on his brothers in order to get grain the next time?

_____

2. Read āyah 12:65 of the Qur'ān. Why were the brothers so happy?

_____

_____

3. Read āyah 12:83 of the Qur'ān. What did Ya'qūb (A) say was better for him?

_____

4. How many brothers returned to Egypt for the third time in order to look for Yūsuf (A) and Binyamin?

_____

5. Ya'qūb (A) became convinced that Yūsuf (A) was alive after seeing what item?

    A.   Money returned in bags of grain.

    B.   A shirt covered with blood stains.

    C.   A Yūsuf's (A) royal shirt.

    D.   The king's cup.

6. Read āyah 12:90 of the Qur'ān. In order to receive a reward from Allāhﷻ, the righteous should do something. What are three things mentioned in the āyah?

    1.   _____

    2.   _____

    3.   _____

7. What was Ya'qūb's (A) advice to his sons before they left to collect grain the second time?

   A.   To enter the palace through different gates.

   B.   To enter the city through different gates.

   C.   To enter the city through the main gate, one after another.

   D.   To make sure Binyamin stayed with Yūsuf (A).

8. When the brothers returned from Egypt the first time, they found something in their grain sacs that surprised them. What surprised them?

   A.   A bag full of rare metals.

   B.   Yūsuf's (A) royal shirt.

   C.   The king's cup.

   D.   Their own money.

9. On what condition did Ya'qūb (A) agree to allow Binyamin to go to Egypt?

   A.   The brothers would not kill him.

   B.   The brothers would bring him back.

   C.   Binyamin should stay with Yūsuf (A).

   D.   The brothers should get double the amount of grains.

10. Unscramble the following letters to make meaningful words.

   G E T Y P   ☐☐☐☐☐

   R M D E A   ☐☐☐☐☐

   V C A R A N A   ☐☐☐☐☐☐☐

Ayyūb (A): *Example of Patience and Perseverance*

Objective of the Lesson:

Sometimes Allāh ﷻ gives people everything and then takes it away to test them. People who persevere and have faith in Allāh ﷻ ultimately become successful. The story of Ayyūb (A) shows how he lost everything, but never lost trust in Allāh ﷻ. He persevered and ultimately received many blessings. There is a great moral to learn from this lesson.

The Qur'ān mentions very little about some of the messengers; we should remember that it is not a storybook. For example, the Qur'ān says Nabi Idrīs (A) was a truthful man.[19:56] You cannot find any more details about him in the Qur'ān. Similarly, very little is mentioned about other messengers, such as Al-Yas'a (A) and Iliyās (A). sūrah an-Nisā' says:

وَرُسُلًا قَدْ قَصَصْنَٰهُمْ عَلَيْكَ مِن قَبْلُ وَرُسُلًا لَّمْ نَقْصُصْهُمْ عَلَيْكَ

And messengers We have indeed mentioned to you before, and messengers We have not mentioned to you... (4:164)

It is understandable that the Qur'ān does not mention the names and details of all messengers. Many messengers went to different parts of the world. However, we can get a bit more information about Nabi Ayyūb (A) in the Qur'ān. We can also learn a great moral lesson from the details of his life. Details about his life can be found in ahādīth. The account of Ayyūb's (A) life lesson is based on the Qur'ān and ahādīth.

Who was Ayyūb (A)?

When the Qur'ān was revealed, people in Arabia knew about nabi Ayyūb (A). He was a descendant of Ibrāhīm (A) and Ishāq (A). He lived in the ancient Palestine region. He was a chosen messenger[6:87] and a righteous servant of Allāh. He received revelations and taught people about One God, Allāh, and the importance of worshipping Him alone.

Nabi Ayyūb (A) was wealthy

Nabi Ayyūb (A) was a very wealthy man. He owned a large area of farmland, a large number of cattle, and had a big family. His wealth did not make him proud. He used his wealth for good causes. He often gave to charity and helped the needy. He was a very humble man and always remembered Allāh. His strongest qualities were his faith in Allāh and his patience.

Allāh tests righteous servants

Allāh often tests His righteous servants in many ways. In sūrah al-Baqarah, Allāh says He will test all of us with fear, hunger, and loss of wealth, life, and crops that we grow. But He will reward those who are the most patient.[2:155]

$$\text{وَلَنَبْلُوَنَّكُم بِشَىْءٍ مِّنَ الْخَوْفِ وَالْجُوعِ وَنَقْصٍ مِّنَ الْأَمْوَالِ وَالْأَنفُسِ وَالثَّمَرَاتِ ۗ وَبَشِّرِ الصَّابِرِينَ ﴿١٥٥﴾}$$

And We shall certainly test you with something of fear, and hunger, and loss of property and lives, and of fruits. And give glad tidings to those who persevere. (2:155)

In another āyah Allāhﷻ says people should not think that they will be allowed to avoid some kind of test, even if they happen to be messengers.

أَحَسِبَ ٱلنَّاسُ أَن يُتۡرَكُوٓاْ أَن يَقُولُوٓاْ ءَامَنَّا وَهُمۡ لَا يُفۡتَنُونَ ٢

Do men think that they will be left alone on saying: "We believe," and that they will not be tested? (29:2)

وَلَقَدۡ فَتَنَّا ٱلَّذِينَ مِن قَبۡلِهِمۡۖ فَلَيَعۡلَمَنَّ ٱللَّهُ ٱلَّذِينَ صَدَقُواْ وَلَيَعۡلَمَنَّ ٱلۡكَٰذِبِينَ ٣

And indeed We have already tested those before them, so that Allāh will distinguish those who act truthfully, and He will distinguish the liars. (29:3)

There are several examples in the Qur'ān that show us past messengers were tested. The story of nabi Ayyūb (A) demonstrates an excellent example.

Tests begins

Allāhﷻ tested nabi Ayyūb (A) with all the difficulties mentioned in āyah 2:155 and more. During his life, Ayyūb (A) suffered from many tragedies. Before he could recover from one tragedy, another tragedy struck him. However, he did not complain, lose hope, or stray from Allāhﷻ. He maintained his patience and showed devotion to Allāhﷻ.

For years, Ayyūb (A) had an abundant harvest. However, a time came when the crops on his farmland were destroyed. He lost his livelihood. Then some of his livestock became sick. The disease spread to the other livestock, and soon all of the animals on his farm died. These were terrible losses. Then one day his house collapsed while his children were still inside. It was very sad for a father to lose all

his children. Still he did not lose hope and did not give up worshipping Allāhﷻ. He showed perseverance and continued to worship Allāhﷻ with greater dedication.

With his food sources gone, Nabi Ayyūb (A) had to rely upon his saved money to buy food. Before long, his savings were gone, too. He became very poor. At that time, a skin disease appeared on his body, and his flesh began to rot. People in the community were horrified to see his condition. They thought they would get the same disease if he stayed with them in the same neighborhood. So they forced him to leave the neighborhood. During this period of hardship, his wife stayed with him and supported him. Sometimes she would become frustrated by his poor health and poverty.

Ayyūb (A) prays to Allāhﷻ

Praying to Allāhﷻ is not equal to complaining to Him. Du'ā give us strength and support. Du'ā help us find the right direction. Allāhﷻ wants us to pray to Him always. Allāhﷻ listens to all our prayers.[2:186] Nabi Ayyūb (A) continued to show patience. He did not complain and he did not forget to pray to Allāhﷻ. In the Qur'ān, Allāhﷻ mentions Nabi Ayyūb's (A) two prayers.

$$ أَنِّي مَسَّنِيَ ٱلضُّرُّ وَأَنتَ أَرْحَمُ ٱلرَّٰحِمِينَ ۝ $$

Surely distress has touched me, and You are the most merciful of the merciful ones. (21:83)

$$ أَنِّي مَسَّنِيَ ٱلشَّيْطَٰنُ بِنُصْبٍ وَعَذَابٍ ۝ $$

Certainly the Devil has touched me with fatigue and agony. (38:41)

We should memorize these two du'ā and use them to pray to Allāhﷻ. Many of us suffer from various problems every day. Our sufferings may not be as bad as Nabi Ayyūb's (A) sufferings. But what if something bad happens in our lives? Without Allāh'sﷻ help, we cannot overcome our sufferings. The best way to pray to Allāhﷻ is to use the same words He taught us in the Qur'ān.

How did Allāhﷻ listen to the prayers?

While facing terrible misery, Ayyūb (A) prayed sincerely to Allāhﷻ. The Qur'ān tells us how Allāhﷻ responded to his prayers. Immediately after the du'ā in 21:83, the next āyah says:

$$\text{فَٱسْتَجَبْنَا لَهُۥ فَكَشَفْنَا مَا بِهِۦ مِن ضُرٍّ ۖ وَءَاتَيْنَٰهُ أَهْلَهُۥ وَمِثْلَهُم مَّعَهُمْ رَحْمَةً مِّنْ عِندِنَا وَذِكْرَىٰ لِلْعَٰبِدِينَ ۝}$$

So We responded to him and removed the distress which he had, and We gave him his family circle and the like of them to him—a mercy from Ourselves and a reminder for the worshippers. (21:84)

After Ayyūb (A) had made the second du'ā, he was very tired and thirsty. Immediately after the du'ā in 38:41, the next two verses say:

"Strike with your foot; this is a cool bathing-place and a drink." (38:42)

And We gave him his family, and the like of them to him—as a mercy from Us, and as a reminder to the possessors of understanding. (38:43)

Ayyūb (A) recovers his losses

Allāh﷿ answered Nabi Ayyūb's (A) du'ā and restored his losses. Soon Ayyūb (A) recovered from his illness and regained his health. He was able to work again, thus his financial condition began to improve. His farmlands began to produce good crops. He was able to purchase new livestock and they reproduced. Gradually the number of his livestock increased. In the meantime, his wife gave birth to a child. Over the following years, they were blessed with more children.

The life of Nabi Ayyūb (A) shows us that those who remain patient under difficult conditions, and those who persevere under all circumstances, are the ultimate winners. They always receive rewards from Allāh﷿.

Time to Review

1. What was the first of Nabi Ayyūb's (A) two prayers mentioned in this lesson?
2. In response to Nabi Ayyūb's (A) prayer, what did Allāh﷿ give him?
3. What are the five things mentioned in āyah 2:155 with which Allāh﷿ tests us?

1. Memorize the two du'ā made by nabi Ayyūb (A) that are mentioned in the lesson. Be ready to recite these two du'ā in front of your teacher next week.

2. Nabi Ayyūb (A) suffered many losses in his life. Name five major losses.

   1. _____

   2. _____

   3. _____

   4. _____

   5. _____

3. Read verses 12:18 and 12:83 of the Qur'ān. These verses do not relate to nabi Ayyūb (A), but the message is important. Both verses say that something is excellent. What is said to be excellent?

_____

4. What were two of nabi Ayyūb's (A) strongest qualities?

   1. _____   2. _____

5. Circle T if the sentence is true. Circle F if the sentence is false.

   Allāhﷻ tested nabi Ayyūb (A) because he became proud after gaining wealth.   T   F

   Nabi Ayyūb (A) gave up all hope after he lost everything.   T   F

   Nabi Ayyūb (A) never forgot to pray to Allāhﷻ.   T   F

   Nabi Ayyūb's (A) wife supported him during the difficult times.   T   F

6. Find the following words in the word search puzzle.

AYYUB   WEALTHY   TEST   DISEASE   PATIENCE
DISTRESS   ILLNESS   HEALTH   REWARD

N	U	J	O	H	S	H	P	X	N	Q	A	Q
Y	C	W	Y	W	E	E	T	T	E	Z	P	S
D	E	C	X	Y	U	A	P	H	N	E	R	N
D	J	R	E	V	V	A	L	F	A	B	P	I
A	W	E	A	L	T	H	Y	T	G	J	D	R
D	O	W	L	I	L	S	I	N	H	H	I	S
R	H	X	E	S	M	N	L	W	J	V	S	D
A	S	N	T	P	Z	B	L	I	X	E	E	B
W	C	V	A	D	U	P	N	D	R	T	A	N
E	F	V	N	Y	T	L	E	T	Z	S	S	C
R	P	N	Y	J	O	G	S	V	M	E	E	R
K	C	A	Z	X	A	I	S	D	C	T	T	N
E	P	B	A	N	D	X	C	R	M	C	L	Y

7. Why did Allahﷻ remove Ayyūb's (A) hardship ?

   A.   As a mercy and reminder for the worshippers.

   B.   As a way of saying thanks.

   C.   As a way of rewarding him.

   D.   To set an example of disobedience.

Zakariyyāh (A) and Yahyā (A)

Objective of the Lesson:

Zakariyyāh (A) and Yahyā (A) were the last father-and-son messengers in Islam. The Qur'ān mentions them briefly. They lived around the same time as 'Isā (A). The purpose of the lesson is to introduce their story as narrated in the Qur'ān.

The Qur'ān tells us about several father-and-son messengers. These include Dāwūd (A) and Sulaimān (A). Prior to this, Ibrāhim (A) and Ismā'īl (A), Ibrāhīm (A) and Ishāq (A), Ishāq (A) and Ya'qūb (A), and Ya'qūb (A) and Yūsuf (A) were father-and-son messengers of Allāh. The last father-and-son messengers were Zakariyyāh (A) and Yahyā (A). There may have been more such messengers, but the Qur'ān does not mention all the messenger's name.

In this lesson, we will learn about messengers Zakariyyāh (A) and Yahyā (A) as mentioned in the Qur'ān. They were the messengers of Bani Isrā'īl, or the Children of Israel. Their biblical names are Zechariah and John. They lived a few years before the time of 'Isā (A), or Jesus. We know 'Isā (A) lived about 600 years before our Nabi Muhammad. Zakariyyāh (A) and Yahyā (A) also lived about 600 years before our Messenger Muhammad. At that time, the Roman ruler in Jerusalem was King **Herod**. All of Jerusalem and Palestine were under Roman rule.

Faith of Bani Isrā'īl

The people of Bani Isrā'īl were suffering from moral and spiritual difficulties. Their faith in Allāhﷻ became weak. Corruption spread throughout their faith and religious practice. They broke many of Allāh'sﷻ commands and refused to obey their teachings. Therefore, Allāhﷻ sent Zakariyyāh (A), Yahyā (A), and 'Isā (A) to revive their faith and make them righteous people again.

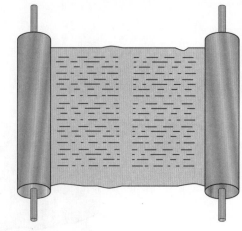

The prophetic mission

The Qur'ān does not mention the prophetic mission of Zakariyyāh (A) or Yahyā (A). Instead, it focuses on their personal struggle, social interactions, and unbending faith in Allāhﷻ.

Zakariyyāh (A) wished to have a child

Zakariyyāh (A) was a priest in a Jewish temple. He was old and did not have any children. The thought of having a child occurred to Zakariyyāh (A) when he saw young Maryam (ra). Maryam's mother placed her under Zakarriyah's (A) care during her childhood.[3:37] Young Maryam worked at the temple. Every time Zakariyyāh (A) saw Maryam in the temple, he was impressed by her piety and quality of service. He also noted plenty of food offerings for her. Wondering who brought the food to her, he asked:

$$قَالَ يَٰمَرْيَمُ أَنَّىٰ لَكِ هَٰذَا ۖ قَالَتْ هُوَ مِنْ عِندِ ٱللَّهِ ۖ إِنَّ ٱللَّهَ يَرْزُقُ مَن يَشَآءُ بِغَيْرِ حِسَابٍ ﴿٣٧﴾$$

"O Maryam! where did this provision come from?" She said: "It is from Allāh." Surely Allāh provides sustenance to whom He pleases without reckoning. (3:37)

On hearing this reply, nabi Zakariyyāh (A) wished to have a child just like Maryam, who would show such piety for Allāhﷻ.[3:38; 21:89] The reason for nabi Zakariyyāh's (A) prayer was not for food, but for guidance, as we will see below.

Zakariyyāh (A) prays for a child

Nabi Zakariyyāh (A) prayed to Allāhﷻ for a child. In sūrah al-i-'Imran and sūrah Maryam, his prayer is mentioned.

$$هُنَالِكَ دَعَا زَكَرِيَّا رَبَّهُ ۖ قَالَ رَبِّ هَبْ لِي مِن لَّدُنكَ ذُرِّيَّةً طَيِّبَةً ۖ إِنَّكَ سَمِيعُ ٱلدُّعَآءِ ﴿٣٨﴾$$

Thereafter Zakariyyāh called to his Rabb; he said: "My Rabb! give me from Yourself a pure offspring. You are indeed Hearer of prayer." (3:38)

However, this prayer was not a request for food, but for guidance. Zakariyyāh (A) was worried that unless he had a child, there would be nobody to inherit the tradition of his ancestors. His ancestors were nabis, including Yaʿqūb (A), the grandson of Ibrāhīm (A).[19:6] Zakariyyāh (A) also feared that without a suitable religious leader, Bani Isrāʾīl would become misguided. He prayed to Allāh﷿, hoping for the best. He was too old to have a child. He knew his wife was not able to give birth to a child. However, he trusted that Allāh﷿ always answered his prayers.[19:4] He knew that if Allāh﷿ wanted, his wife could give birth to a child.

He said: "My Rabb! surely the bones in me are weakened, and the head flares with hoariness, and my Rabb! never have I been unsuccessful in my prayer to You. (19:4)

And surely I fear for my relations after me, and my wife is barren, therefore grant me from Yourself a trustee, (19:5)

who should inherit me, and inherit from the children of Yaʿqūb, and make him, my Rabb! well-pleased." (19:6)

Allāh﷿ responds to the prayer

In the Qurʾān, Allāh﷿ says He always responds to a good and sincere prayer whether it is from a messenger, a righteous person, or even a sinner.[2:186; 3:194]

وَإِذَا سَأَلَكَ عِبَادِى عَنِّى فَإِنِّى قَرِيبٌ أُجِيبُ دَعْوَةَ ٱلدَّاعِ إِذَا دَعَانِ فَلْيَسْتَجِيبُوا۟ لِى وَلْيُؤْمِنُوا۟ بِى لَعَلَّهُمْ يَرْشُدُونَ ﴿١٨٦﴾

And when My servants ask you concerning Me, "Lo! I am near indeed." I respond to the call of the caller when he calls Me. Therefore, they should respond to Me and believe in Me, so that they may walk along the right way. (2:186)

In response to Nabi Zakariyyāh's (A) prayer, Allāh ﷻ sent him the good news that he would have a son. Allāh ﷻ even told him that his son's name would be Yahyā. The meaning of "Yahyā" is "he lives." Nobody in his family had such a beautiful name.

After receiving the good news, Nabi Zakariyyāh (A) could not believe it. He wondered how he could have a son when his wife was not able to bear a child, and he was so old that his hair had turned gray.

In response, Allāh ﷻ said:

قَالَ كَذَٰلِكَ قَالَ رَبُّكَ هُوَ عَلَيَّ هَيِّنٌ وَقَدْ خَلَقْتُكَ مِن قَبْلُ وَلَمْ تَكُ شَيْئًا ﴿٩﴾

"He said: "Likewise; your Rabb says— it is easy for Me, certainly I created you before when you were nothing." (19:9)

Allāh ﷻ has the power to do things that we cannot even imagine. Allāh ﷻ mentioned to Nabi Zakariyyāh (A) the example of his own creation—he was nothing before his birth, but Allāh ﷻ made his birth possible. Childbirth is a wonderful miracle of Allāh ﷻ.

Nabi Zakariyyāh (A) still could not believe it. He asked for a sign from Allāh ﷻ. In response, Allāh ﷻ told him not to speak to anybody for three nights and three days.[3:41; 19:10] Zakariyyāh (A) was permitted only to give silent instructions to his people as to what work they should do. During this entire time, he glorified Allāh ﷻ through prayers and remembrance.

Birth of Yahyā (A)

Allāh ﷻ can do impossible things, but all such seemingly impossible things should be possible. Nabi Zakariyyāh (A) was an old man, but he could not become young again. The age of a person cannot move backwards, and Allāh ﷻ would

Time to Review

1. Why did Zakariyyāh (A) want to have a child?
2. What issues Zakariyyāh (A) have that would have prevented him from having a child?
3. Who named Zakariyyāh's (A) son?

not do that. Zakariyyāh's (A) wife was not able to give birth to a child, but she could be cured. Allāh﷿ cured her and made her fit to give birth to a child.[21:90] Allāh's﷿ wonderful miracles always work within the possibilities of nature.

$$ فَٱسْتَجَبْنَا لَهُۥ وَوَهَبْنَا لَهُۥ يَحْيَىٰ وَأَصْلَحْنَا لَهُۥ زَوْجَهُۥٓ $$

So We responded to him and gave him Yahyā and We cured his wife for him ... (21:90)

Interesting Facts

Sūrah Maryam contains details about the birth and life of Yahyā (A).

In the Bible, Yahyā (A) is known as John the Baptist. He is called this because he began baptism of newborn children in the River Jordan.

According to the Bible, Yahyā's (A) mother was Elizabeth, who was related to Maryam—'Isā's (A) mother.

According to the Bible, at the request of King Herod's stepdaughter, Yahyā (A) was beheaded.

In his childhood, Yahyā (A) learned many things and Allāh﷿ gave him wisdom. Allāh﷿ made him a nabi. He learned the Jewish scripture in detail. He was kind-hearted and dutiful to his parents. He was not arrogant nor disobedient to Allāh﷿ or his parents.[19:13–14] He achieved great dignity and honor among his people. Allāh﷿ blessed the day that he was born, the day he died, and the day he would be raised, the Day of Judgment. In this brief account of Zakariyyāh (A) and Yahyā (A), the Qur'ān reminds us that Allāh﷿ can make the most difficult things easier for us.

Points to Ponder

Instead of describing the teachings of Zakariyyāh (A), the Qur'an simply mentions his concerns and his wishes. What were some of his concerns and wishes? Ponder for a while how Allāh﷿ solved his concerns and wishes. What lessons can we learn from these accounts?

1. Who was the Roman king in Jerusalem during the time of Zakariyyāh (A), Yahyā (A), and ʿIsā (A)?

_____

2. Why did Zakariyyāh (A) pray for a son?

    A.   The son would inherit the teachings of Yaʿqūb (A).

    B.   The son would grow up and rule over the Romans.

    C.   The son would perform miracles.

    D.   The son would become Masih.

3. Zakariyyāh (A) asked for a sign from Allāh﷾ that he would have a son. In response, what did Allāh﷾ tell him to do?

_____

4. What were the two reasons that Zakariyyāh (A) believed he could not have a child?

    1. _____

    2. _____

5. Read āyah 19:4 of the Qurʾān. In this āyah, Zakariyyāh (A) mentions two things about his physical condition. What were the two conditions?

    1. _____

    2. _____

6. After seeing which child did Zakariyyāh (A) pray to Allāh﷾ to have his own child?

    A.   Child ʿIsa (A).

    B.   Infant Musa (A).

    C.   Child Maryam.

    D.   Child Yahyā (A).

7. Read āyāt 19:13 and 14 of the Qur'ān. In these āyāt, several of Yahyā's (A) qualities are mentioned. Mention five qualities from these āyāt.

1. _____

2. _____

3. _____

4. _____

5. _____

8. What was special about the name "Yahyā"?

   A. It was the name of an ancient king.

   B. It was the name of a spring in heaven.

   C. Nobody in Zakariyyāh's (A) family had this name before.

   D. It was the name of an Egyptian god.

9. After receiving the good news about the birth of a son, how many days and nights did Zakariyyāh (A) not speak?

   A. Five days and nights.

   B. Three days and nights.

   C. Seven days and nights.

   D. 10 days and nights.

10. How many people in Zakariyyāh's (A) family had the name "Yahyā" before his son was born?

   A. Many people.

   B. Three people.

   C. Five people.

   D. None.

Unit 4: Islam in the World

Wherever Muslims settled around the world, they built a masjid to pray to Allāhﷻ. Muslims continue to build masājid today. People assemble in masajid to perform salāt, to interact with other members, and to show their commitment to worshipping God. Some of these masājid are small, accommodating only a few people, while others are quite large, accommodating hundreds of thousands of worshippers in a single congregation. This lesson discusses some of the largest and most unique masājid in the world.

Lesson 20: Major Masājid in the World

Islam in the World

Major Masājid in the World

Throughout the world, Muslims have built a large number of masājid to perform salāt. Some of these masājid became landmarks in Islamic history. The architectural designs and majesty of the buildings are simply fascinating. This lesson introduces students to some of the most noteworthy masājid in the world.

Major Masājid in the World

Objective of the Lesson:

Throughout the world, Muslims have built a large number of masājid to perform salāt. Some of these masājid became landmarks in Islamic history. The architectural designs and majesty of the buildings are simply fascinating. This lesson introduces students to some of the most noteworthy masājid in the world.

When we perform salāt, we prostrate on the ground. Prostration on the ground is called sujud. The place where everyone performs sujud is called a masjid. The plural of masjid is **masājid**. The masjid is the foundation of Muslim society. It is the place where Allāh﷾ is remembered continuously. It is a dedicated place to worship Allāh﷾.

For this reason, wherever Muslims go, they build a masjid and establish the practice of worshipping Allāh﷾. Today, in almost every country you go, you will find a masjid—large or small. Whether it is in China, Russia, Korea, Norway, New Zealand, Argentina, Indonesia, or Sri Lanka, you will find a masjid.

When Rasūlullāhﷺ migrated to Madīnah, he rested for a few days in a place called **Quba**. He

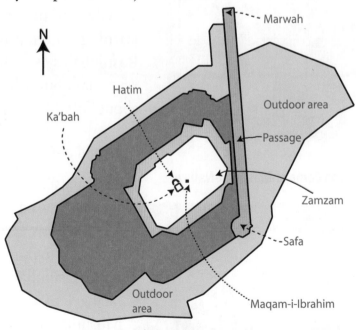

Outline view of Masjid al-Haram

built a masjid there. This masjid, known as **Masjid al-Quba**, was the first masjid Rasūlullāhﷺ built. He was moving away from Makkah, but he took the first opportunity he had to build a masjid. This shows the importance of having a masjid for every Muslim.

Over the past 1,000 years, Muslims have built fascinating masājid all over the world. Some of the masājid became centers of attraction as hallmarks of Muslim architecture. Let us take a brief look at some of the major masājid.

Masjid al-Harām

The foremost of all masājid in the world is Masjid al-Harām in Makkah, which surrounds the Ka'bah. It is called al-Harām because fighting, hunting, and many other activities are prohibited within its borders. Nabi Ibrāhīm (A) and his son, Ismā'īl (A), rebuilt the foundation of the Ka'bah. During the time of Hajj, millions of people perform salāt in this masjid. It is the largest masjid in the world. It has been expanded several times, and now can hold about one million people at one time.

Masjid al-Nabawi

After Rasūlullāhﷺ reached Madīnah, he built another masjid. This one is known as Masjid al-Nabawi. It became the center of all Muslim activities at that time. It also served as the center for education, learning, and training. The green dome on this masjid is located above Rasūlullāh'sﷺ tomb. The original masjid, during Rasūlullāh'sﷺ, time was small, but it has been expanded several times, and now can hold about 700,000 people.

The dome of Masjid al-Nabawi

Masjid al-Qiblatain

This masjid in Madīnah has historic significance. The name means "Masjid with two Qiblah." During the early years of Islam, the Muslims faced the direction of Jerusalem as their qiblah, or direction to pray. When the revelation about facing the Ka'bah was sent, Rasūlullāhﷺ was praying in this masjid.[2:144] He turned from facing Jerusalem to Ka'bah. The Jews were not happy to see the Muslims change the direction. This change of direction sparked a series of debates between the Muslim and the Jews.

Masjid al-Aqsa

This masjid is located in Jerusalem. It is mentioned in the Qur'ān as the Farthest Masjid.[17:1] During the famous Night Journey, Rasūlullāhﷺ traveled to this masjid. It was also used by Dāwūd (A), Sulaimān (A), and many other messengers. The nearby structure, known as the Dome of Rock, is not the Masjid al-Aqsa. Khalīfah 'Umar and many other Islamic rulers restored the masjid and dedicated it for salāt.

Muhammad Ali Masjid

This famous masjid is located in Cairo, Egypt. It is one of the famous landmarks of Cairo. Built by Muhammad Ali Pasha in the nineteenth century, it represents the architectural design of the Ottomans. Thousands of tourists visit this masjid every year.

Muhammad Ali Masjid

Masjid at Cordova

The Umayyad khalifahs built a famous masjid in the city of Cordova in the Andalusia region of Spain. After the Umayyad dynasty fell, the masjid was subsequently converted into a cathedral. Now it is mostly a tourist attraction.

Jama Masjid

There are many masājid in the world that are known as Jama Masjid. But the Jama Masjid in Delhi, India, is the most famous. This masjid is the largest and best-known masjid in India. It was built by the Mughal emperor, Shah Jahan, who also built the Tajmahal.

Jama Masjid in Delhi, India

King Faisal Masjid

This masjid is located in Islamabad in Pakistan. It is a relatively modern masjid famous for its architectural design. King Faisal bin Abdul Aziz of Saudi Arabia provided funds for the masjid. It was completed in 1986. It can accommodate about 300,000 people at one time for salāt.

Great Masjid of Xi'an

This is probably the oldest masjid in China. It was built in the eighth century C.E. The architecture of this masjid is totally Chinese. This masjid continues to draw both worshippers and tourists.

Another masjid in China, built around the same time, is Huaisheng Masjid in Guangzhou. The minaret of this masjid was also used as a lighthouse!

Some recent masājid

Sultan Qaboos Masjid in Muscat

Several new masājid show extraordinary beauty in architectural design. Some of these masājid (in alphabetical order of the country) are: Baitul Mukarram in Dhaka, Bangladesh; Sultan Saifuddin Masjid in Bandar, Brunei; Masjid Istiqlal in Jakarta, Indonesia; Hassan II Masjid in Casablanca, Morocco; National Mosque in Abuja, Nigeria; Sultan Qaboos Masjid in Muscat, Oman; and a new Grand Masjid in Abu Dhabi.

We have discussed only some masājid in today's lesson. There are many magnificent masājid around the world including North America. The next time you travel to a new city, try to visit the local masjid. We should all try to make a trip to Masjid al-Haram in Makkah, whether we go for a Hajj or, at a minimum, for an 'Umrah.

1. Look at the outline view of Masjid al-Haram in Makkah provided in the chapter. Then circle T if the sentence is true. Circle F if the sentence is false.

The passage between Safa and Marwah runs east to west. T (F)

The Ka'bah is east of the passage between Safa and Marwah. T (F)

Maqam-i-Ibrahim is east of the Ka'bah. (T) F

The passage between Safa and Marwah is located in the eastern part of the Masjid. (T) F

2. What is the name of the first masjid that Rasūlullāhﷺ built?

Quba

3. Allāhﷻ commanded Rasūlullāhﷺ to change the Qiblah while he was praying in a masjid. What was the name of the masjid?

Masjid al-Qiblatain

4. Mark with ☑, if the sentence is true. Mark with ☒, if the sentence is false.

Masjid al-Nabawi contains the tomb of the Messengerﷺ. ☑

Masjid al-Quba is located north of Masjid-al Nabawi. ☒

Masjid al-Aqsa is in Jerusalem. ☑

The minaret of the masjid at Xi'an was used as a lighthouse. ☑

5. Where did Nabi Muhammad ﷺ start building the very first masjid for the Muslims?

    A. Jerusalem.

    B. Quba.

    (C) Madinah.

    D. Makkah.

6. Which masjid contains the tomb of Nabi Muhammad ﷺ?

    A. Masjid Al-Haram.

    B. Juma Masjid.

    (C) Masjid Nabawi.

    D. Masjid Qiblatain.

7. Which masjid in the Qur'an is referred to as the Farthest Masjid?

    A. Masjid Nabawi.

    B. Masjid Quba.

    C. Masjid at Cordova.

    (D.) Masjid Al-Aqsa.

8. Unscramble the following letters to make meaningful words. Then rearrange the circled letters to make a secret word.

RCDOAVO   C O r d o v a

MARHA   H a r a m

HQABIL   Q b b l a h

ADWDU   D a v u d

Secret word   Q u b a

Unit 5: Islamic Values and Teachings

Islamic values and teachings are not intended to remain confined to the pages of theology books. They are intended to become a part of our heart, defining who we are and what we believe. Good moral values show that we are truly abiding the teachings of the Qur'ān and Sunnah of the Messenger. Maintaining good morals and demonstrating strong ethics are far more effective than society's laws or regulations. As Muslims, we face two fundamental questions: What moral values do we demonstrate that earn God's approval? What conduct do we guard against to avoid God's displeasure? The chapters in this unit discuss Islamic values and teachings to help students appreciate and emulate these values in their lives. Lessons on the significance of salāt, sawm, zakāt, and sadaqah will allow students to understand the underlying principles of these religious duties.

Islamic Values and Teachings

Upholding Truth: *A Duty of All Believers*
Muslims are always required to uphold the truth. Allāhﷻ says that when truth is revealed, falsehood vanishes. Islam always propagates truth. Allāhﷻ loves the truthful people. This lesson discusses why upholding truth is important and how we can do small things to establish and encourage truth.

Responsibility and Punctuality
Responsibility and punctuality are often forgotten values in our lives. According to the principles of the Qur'ān and Sunnah, Allāhﷻ and Rasūlullāhﷺ always encouraged punctuality. Punctuality derives from a sense of responsibility. This lesson shows students how and why they should be punctual and always encourage each other to maintain punctuality..

My Mind, My Body: *Body Is a Mirror of the Mind*
The mind and body are closely related. If the mind of a person is polluted, he or she will most likely pollute his or her body. Islam requires our minds to be clean just as our bodies should be clean. This lesson discusses various ways we can keep our minds and bodies clean.

Kindness and Forgiveness
Kindness and forgiveness are closely related. One cannot be kind without being forgiving. Islam requires us to be kind and forgiving in many ways. Forgiving someone does not mean undue encouragement of doing wrong. This lesson discusses various ways we can be kind and forgiving to others.

The Middle Path: *Ways to Avoid Two Extremes*
Islam always encourages us to adopt the middle path. What is the middle path and how can we adopt the middle path? Why is the middle path the blessed path of Allāhﷻ and favorite to the Messengerﷺ? This lesson discusses the importance of following the middle path in every matter in our lives.

Salāt: *Its Significance*
Performance of salāt is one of the most important duties of all Muslims. From a young age, children are required to perform salāt. It is not just a ritual to follow. Salāt purifies us and removes our sins. This lesson discusses the major significance of salāt.

Sawm: *Its Significance*
Sawm is not simply about being hungry all day and eating a full meal after breaking the fast in the evening. Sawm has more value in helping us become better Muslims. Its rewards are immense. This lesson discusses the significance of sawm.

Zakāt and Sadaqh: *Similarities and Differences*
One of the requirements of Islam is to pay zakāt. It is not a burden on the wealthy to part with a small portion of their surplus wealth. It is a useful system to share our wealth with the less fortunate. Zakāt also has spiritual benefit as it purifies our wealth. This lesson explains who can receive zakāt, how much to give, and when to give.

Upholding Truth: *A Duty of All Believers*

Objective of the Lesson:

Muslims are always required to uphold the truth. Allāh ﷻ says that when truth is revealed, falsehood vanishes. Islam always propagates truth. Allāh ﷻ loves the truthful people. This lesson discusses why upholding truth is important and how we can do small things to establish and encourage truth.

The teachings in the Qur'ān have several goals. Some of these goals are to establish justice, bring peace into the world, prohibit wrongdoing, stop evil, and so on. One of the most important goals of the Qur'ān is to establish the truth. Unless truth is established, falsehood cannot vanish. One of the beauties of truth is that it always defeats falsehood. It has the power to wipe out lies, untruths, and falsehood. As Muslims, it is our duty to uphold the truth.

A tough job

Throughout their lives, all of the messengers tried to uphold the truth. It was not easy. However, not a single messenger gave up the attempt to establish truth.

Allāh ﷻ always helps those who try to establish truth. He is always on the side of people who uphold the truth. One of Allāh's ﷻ finest names is **al-Haqq**, or "the Truth." This is because He loves Truth, He promotes Truth, and He is the Truth.

Challenge with friends and family

Our biggest challenge to stay truthful occurs when we are with our friends, family or people we know. In other words, people with whom we interact are the people with whom we sometimes lie. Some of these lies are very trivial in nature and they do not harm anybody. For example, a boy tells his friend that while going to school he saw a big spider on the sidewalk. If this is a lie, it is trivial and harmless. The school will not shut down because of the spider, nor will adults call for an emergency meeting, or will police show up where he saw the spider. His friend probably heard the comment and forgot it immediately. But it remains that the boy told a lie. A lie is a lie is a lie.

Everyday we interact with our parents and siblings. Everyday we interact with our friends and other people we know. Everyday situations arise when we can either be truthful or lie about trivial matters. With a little practice, we can always remain truthful. Our attempt to uphold truth might sometimes bring difficulties, but the rewards are endless. Abū Bakr (R) once said that if someone indulges in falsehood, the path to Paradise will be closed for him or her.

Realize your inner power

All animals have tongues, but human beings use their tongue to speak words and sentences. In an average day, men use about 7,000 words and women use about 20,000 words. Many of the words and sentences we use are idle talk and some are lies. Allāh says our tongues are likely to speak lies. However, Allāh gave human beings the inner power to stop telling lies. All of us have this inner power, but we might not realize it. With a little conscious effort, we can stop telling lies and be truthful.

$$\text{وَلَا تَقُولُوا لِمَا تَصِفُ أَلْسِنَتُكُمُ الْكَذِبَ هَٰذَا حَلَٰلٌ وَهَٰذَا حَرَامٌ لِّتَفْتَرُوا عَلَى اللَّهِ}$$
$$\text{الْكَذِبَ إِنَّ الَّذِينَ يَفْتَرُونَ عَلَى اللَّهِ الْكَذِبَ لَا يُفْلِحُونَ ﴿١١٦﴾}$$

And do not say—because your tongues are given to telling lies: "This is lawful and that is unlawful"—so that you forge a lie against Allāh. Surely those who forge a lie against Allāh do not prosper. (16:116)

Falsehood is afraid of truth

Upholding truth, no matter how difficult, should be our goal in life. As mentioned previously, our opportunity to uphold truth occurs when we are with our friends, family, and people we know. You should uphold truth when there is falsehood. Truth always exists as Allāhﷻ, al-Haqq, always exists. You do not have to create truth—it is there. On the other hand, falsehood has to be invented. Whenever falsehood is invented, it can never be proven right. Falsehood always fears examination because examination exposes falsehood. Once exposed, falsehood shatters. In contrast, truth always invites examination. It is not afraid of any amount of verification. The more you examine the truth, the more it is established.

Abū Bakr (R) was a truthful and honest person. For this reason, he understood the importance of upholding the truth. He once said that the greatest truth is honesty, and the greatest falsehood is dishonesty. Our Nabi Muhammadﷺ fondly gave him the title **As-Siddīq**, which means, "the Honest." In the Qur'ān, nabi Idrīs (A) is mentioned as As-Siddīq because he was also a man of truthfulness.[19:56] Our Messengerﷺ always spoke truth. For this reason, the Quraish fondly gave him the names **As-Siddīq** and **al-Amin**, which mean "the truthful." Honesty and truthfulness always go together.

The Qur'ān on truth

There are many verses in the Qur'ān that strongly emphasize truthfulness. Here are three of these verses:

$$\text{وَقُلْ جَاءَ الْحَقُّ وَزَهَقَ الْبَاطِلُ إِنَّ الْبَاطِلَ كَانَ زَهُوقًا ﴿٨١﴾}$$

And you say: "The Truth has come, and falsehood has vanished. Surely the falsehood does ever vanish away." (17:81)

بَلْ نَقْذِفُ بِالْحَقِّ عَلَى الْبَطِلِ فَيَدْمَغُهُ فَإِذَا هُوَ زَاهِقٌ وَلَكُمُ الْوَيْلُ مِمَّا تَصِفُونَ ۝

In fact, We cast the Truth against the falsehood, so that it knocks out its brains, and lo! it vanishes. And woe be to you on account of what you attribute. (21:18).

Say: "The Truth has come, and falsehood cannot originate, nor can it reproduce." (34:49).

Giving false evidence is prohibited

In our day-to-day life, we will be required to give evidence on certain matter. This evidence is not necessarily given in a court of law. This evidence could be in front of friends, family or people we know. The Qur'ān teaches us to give truthful evidence even if the issue is of little consequence.

Life cycle of truth

Truth often travels in a cycle. Great truths in the history of mankind always traveled through a specific cycle. Each of the stages in the cycle could last for months, years, and sometimes decades. In the beginning, when a major truth is first mentioned, people laugh at it and reject it as mere nonsense. Then seeing that truth still persists, they begin to oppose it. When truth still persists, people become scared of it and begin to resist it in the strongest terms. But, ultimately, a point comes when people fail to resist the power of truth—they give up resisting and the truth prevails.

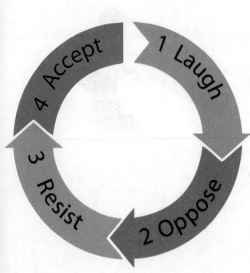

We can see examples of this in the life of Rasūlullāhﷺ. When he first preached Islam, everybody laughed and ridiculed the religion. They thought he was a madman, a crazy person. Next, seeing that truth continued to persist, people began to oppose it. The Quraish began to harass the Muslims in many ways. Then they became tough with Rasūlullāhﷺ and the Muslims. Some Muslims were physically tortured, while some others were forced into exile. Ridicule had turned into open hatred. Then they Quraish began fighting against truth. Several battles were fought against the Muslims. Ultimately, truth prevailed and falsehood vanished.

All the messengers were truthful

Truthfulness was the main quality of every messenger. The Qur'ān mentions Ibrāhīm (A) was a truthful person.[19:41] His son, Ismaʿīl (A), was a man of his word, which means he was truthful.[19:54] We already mentioned nabi Idrīs (A) was also truthful.[19:56] Nabi Yūsuf (A) was truthful.[12:46] Maryam, mother of 'Isā (A), was not a nabi, but she was a truthful woman.[5:75] The messengers were human beings. If these human beings could be truthful, then it is also possible for us to be truthful.

Practice being truthful

We should ask ourselves—are we truthful in our actions? If not, we have to practice truthfulness. We cannot become truthful all of a sudden one day. We can start by making sure we speak the truth. Sometimes truth may create trouble for us. But if we are truthful, Allāhﷻ will help us. Our trouble will go away.

Rasūlullāhﷺ was always truthful, which means he had to face difficulties in life. He never compromised on the truth—he never mixed truth with falsehood. Over a period of time, his difficulties ended and he received Allāh'sﷻ blessings and rewards.

Truthfulness means not only speaking the truth, but behaving in a truthful manner. If someone trusts us with a secret, we should keep that secret. If someone trusts us to keep an item safe, we should take care of it and return it when they ask for it. If we promise something, we must fulfill our promise.

Truthfulness leads to forgiveness

If we are truthful, we can expect forgiveness from Allāhﷻ. Our truthfulness will benefit us on the Day of Judgment. By practicing truthfulness, a person becomes better in the sight of Allāhﷻ. A truthful person is a righteous person. We must fear Allāhﷻ and always tell the truth.

Reward for upholding truthfulness

The greatest reward for being truthful in life is forgiveness from Allāhﷻ and entry to Paradise. In sūrah al-Ahzāb, Allāhﷻ says that He has forgiveness and a great reward for all truthful men and truthful women.[33:35]

From Hadīth

Abdullah bin Mas'ud (R) narrated that Rasūlullāhﷺ said, "Truth leads to piety and piety leads to Jannat."

1. Which of the following choices is correct about the meaning of truthfulness?

    A.   It is only about telling the truth.

    B.   It is about telling the truth and behaving in a truthful manner.

    C.   It is only about keeping the trust of other people.

    D.   It is only about doing good work.

2. In the first stage of the life cycle of truth, people react to truth in a certain manner. Based on the lesson, how do people first react when they hear the truth?

    A.   They accept it reluctantly.

    B.   They accept it wholeheartedly.

    C.   They ridicule it.

    D.   They violently oppose it.

3. Read āyah 21:18 of the Qur'ān. It says that truth destroys falsehood by attacking its main center. The center is compared to an organ of the body. What organ is mentioned as the center of truth?

Brain

4. When truth is revealed, something always happens. Read āyah 17:81. What happens after the truth arrives?

faleshood ~~ Vanishes and disapears

5. In āyah 2:42 of the Qur'ān, Allāh says not to do something regarding the truth. Read the āyah. What does Allāh tell us not to do regarding the truth?

dont not mix frath with faleshood and don not hide the ~~ truth

6. Based on the lesson, which three people had the title "As-Siddiq"?

1. Abu bakar (a)

2. Idris (a)

3. ~~mmh~~ Muhammad (swa)

7. Find the following words in the word search puzzle.

TRUTH   FALSEHOOD   HONEST   MESSENGER   SIDDIQ
IBRAHIM   LAUGH   PARADISE

```
F  S  T  V  Q  R  V  I  K  P  D  K  C
R  I  R  H  U  Y  P  X  S  W  O  Y  Q
O  D  B  T  O  L  A  W  Q  I  O  I  H
I  S  E  R  Q  Y  R  G  C  O  H  G  G
O  H  R  U  A  I  A  T  K  H  E  A  B
M  T  G  E  T  H  D  Z  J  V  S  Q  Q
N  U  Z  U  G  K  I  D  V  C  L  U  H
B  R  H  U  A  N  S  M  I  K  A  T  Z
X  T  O  R  O  L  E  X  I  S  F  J  I
M  A  N  D  M  J  I  S  Z  B  P  W  E
A  D  E  Q  O  Q  V  T  S  K  D  C  H
T  L  S  O  T  K  W  X  E  E  O  O  D
H  O  T  K  M  V  A  W  J  O  M  U  G
```

Responsibility and Punctuality

Objective of the Lesson:

Responsibility and punctuality are often forgotten values in our lives. According to the principles of the Qur'ān and Sunnah, Allāhﷻ and Rasūlullāhﷺ always encouraged punctuality. Punctuality derives from a sense of responsibility. This lesson shows students how and why they should be punctual and always encourage each other to maintain punctuality.

Responsibility means honoring, as well as performing or completing, a duty or obligation. Usually a responsibility is a duty given to you by someone else. Sometimes it is a duty created by one's own promise or circumstance. All these duties—whether given by someone else or self-created—need to be completed in a timely and orderly manner. Responsibility is a duty, therefore, not fulfilling one's duty should have a consequence or penalty. We are responsible for something that is under our control. When we complete our duties in a timely manner, we are punctual.

Responsibility increases with age and experience

For an individual, responsibility increases with age and experience. A baby has little responsibility, therefore, we should not expect much from a baby. A grown-up has more responsibilities than a child. Some grown-ups, because of their positions, have more responsibilities than other grown-ups. As a child, you are not responsible for driving a car, but you are responsible for riding your bike safely. If you have a pet, then you are responsible for feeding and taking care of the pet. As you grow older, your responsibilities will increase, and you should fulfill your duties.

Ability to make decisions

Responsibility also refers to our ability to make decisions on the matters for which we are responsible. For example, if we are responsible for packing our backpack or bag before going to school, we must do it before we leave for school in the morning. It is a decision-making process that your brother, sister or parents cannot do for you.

Being responsible requires you to think and act in a sensible way. If somebody asks you to do a bad thing, you should use your judgment. If you avoid doing the bad thing, you have acted responsibly. "I did that because my friend asked me to" is not a good excuse. Allāhﷻ tells us:

"And do not pursue that of which you have no knowledge. Surely the hearing and the sight and the heart—all these will be questioned about it." (17:36)

Allāhﷻ allows us to disobey our parents if they teach us anything against Islam.[29:8] Otherwise we are responsible for treating our parents with kindness and respect.[17:23-24]

Responsibility to society

We have responsibilities to our society. If you turn off a running water faucet, you prevented wasting water. You have acted responsibly. If we find someone who is injured, we are obligated to help him or her, and call an ambulance if needed.

We are responsible if we do what needs to be done. We live in a society, so we should take care of others in our society. We should tell others to do good deeds and follow the Truth.[103:3] We are responsible for helping the poor and needy, so they do not remain poor and needy all their lives.

Do not blame others

Sometimes we play the "blame game" regarding responsibility. Often people blame others, saying, "Whose responsibility is this?" But people fail to understand that the idea of "responsibility" involves taking ownership and making the best opportunity of the circumstance. Instead of trying to find out who is responsible, it is always better to take control of the situation by improving the situation.

For example, your masjid has a policy of placing a donation box at the entrance of the hallway. One particular day the donation box was not put in the right place, and as a result no donations were collected that day. Instead of trying to find out who was responsible for putting the box, and blaming others, you should take responsibility for putting the box in the right place on the right day.

Salāt teaches responsibility

Islam teaches responsibility in many ways. Salāt provides us such teachings. We can learn to be responsible by making salāt on time. Paying zakāh also teaches us to be responsible for our fellow human beings.

Sawm teaches responsibility

Self-control is an important part of responsibility. Every year, sawm, or fasting, gives us an opportunity to practice self-control. While in a masjid, we can practice self-control and responsibility. We learn to sit attentively during the khutbah. Salāt also teaches us to increase our attention span, as every salāh requires us to pay attention to Allāhﷻ.

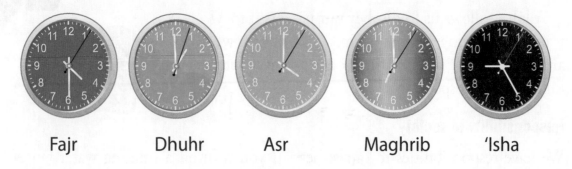

| Fajr | Dhuhr | Asr | Maghrib | 'Isha |

Sawm also teaches us punctuality. We cannot start fasting anytime we wish. We cannot stop a fast anytime we feel hungry. There is a need for discipline, and there is a need to be punctual. Allāhﷻ says that fasting should begin very early in the dawn hours. In the past, people did not have clocks, therefore, Allāhﷻ said that the time should be when a white thread appears distinct from a black thread in the early dawn.[2:187] We are also told to fast until nightfall.

Responsibility to keep promises

We are responsible for the promises that we make. We need to keep our word. Allāhﷻ says it is very important to keep our promises. When we make a promise, someone is depending on us. A failure to fulfill the promise creates trouble for that person. If we intentionally fail to keep our promise, then we should feed the poor, give clothing to the poor, or fast.[5:89]

Responsibility cannot be shifted

Each of us has our own individual responsibilities. No one can shift his or her responsibility to another. It is our duty to fulfill our own responsibilities. Your reward cannot be shared with another person, and another person's reward cannot be shared with you. It is acceptable to do a favor for someone, but it is not acceptable to take on his or her responsibilities.

Excuses will not help

Just as we should not blame others if they failed to do their responsibility, similarly we should not make excuses or blame others if we do not finish our job. Allāh عَزَّوَجَلَّ says that we are responsible for our own work. We should make good choices and do good deeds. Nobody is responsible for us if we do bad things.[16:111] Nūh (A) was a nabi, but his son and wife made bad choices. His son and wife were responsible for their own actions.[11:46, 66:10] They drowned in the big flood while the truthful people were saved.

Timeliness is responsibility

Everything must be done on time. Salāt should be performed on schedule. The prayer call for Fajr salāt says salāt is better than sleep. This means we must wake up and perform salāt. Allāh عَزَّوَجَلَّ said:

Surely salāt is made compulsory for the believers at its prescribed times. (4:103)

Similarly, fasting must also be done on time. Fasting teaches us the importance of managing time.

Time does not wait for us, and we do not know if we will get enough time in the future to do good deeds. Fir'awn lived his whole life rejecting Allāh. When he was about to die, he asked for forgiveness. He was not forgiven, but his body was preserved.[10:92] Maybe Allāh would have forgiven Fir'awn if he had used his time properly, and if he had asked forgiveness long before his death.

No one can achieve success in life without being responsible and punctual. If we study the biographies of people who achieved success, whether they are Muslim or non-Muslim, we will see that they were responsible and punctual. These are good qualities, and we should try our best to develop these qualities and maintain them in our lives.

From Hadith

It is reported In a hadīth that Rasūlullāh said: "The person who is punctual in the performance of [his or her] salāt will be a savior, a source of celestial light and proof for him or her on the Day of Judgment. The person who disregards salāt, will not be a savior or a source of celestial light or proof for him or her on the Day of Judgment."

1. On the Day of Judgment, who will be responsible for our actions? Who will be pleading for us? Find the answer in Sūrah An-Nahl, āyah 111.

Every soul will come pleading for itself

2. Read Sūrah As-Shūra (#42) āyah 48. Many people had turned away from Islam. What was Rasūlullāh'sﷺ responsibility toward them?

your only duty is romnuiation

3. Read āyah 73:20 of the Qur'ān. In the middle of this long āyah, our responsibility to the Qur'ān is mentioned. What is this responsibility?

Our responbility is to read the quron

4. Read Sūrah Al-'Ankabūt, āyah 8. What is our responsibility to our parents?

to respect and care for our parents

5. Read Sūrah Al-Baqarah, āyah 233. What is the responsibility of a father to his children?

to provide for them and clothe them in a proper prayer

6. We have certain obligations regarding money. Read āyah 67 from Sūrah Al-Furqān. What are some of these responsibilities?

dont be wastfull nur strngy with our ways

7. Unscramble the following letters to make meaningful words. Write the letters in the numbered boxes to discover the secret word. Your objective is to solve the secret message. If you can figure out the secret message, you can work backwards from the secret message to solve the jumbled words.

N D Y E

D	e	n	y
1	2	3	4

E V A G R S

G	r	a	v	e	s
10	5	6	7	8	9

C K W I E D

w	i	c	k	e	d
11	12				18

S O L U

s	o	u	l
	13	14	15

S A B T E N

a	b	s	e	n	t
16	17		e	n	19

P A S H D E

S	h	a	p	e	d
	20		21		

Secret message:

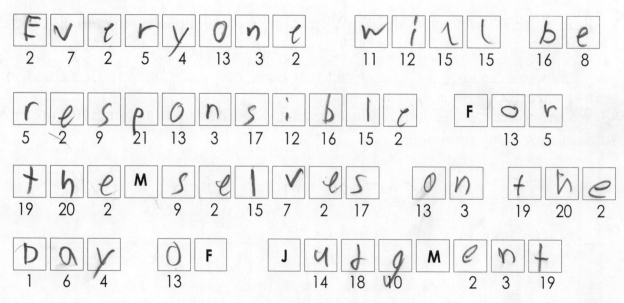

E	v	e	r	y	o	n	e		w	i	l	l		b	e
2	7	2	5	4	13	3	2		11	12	15	15		16	8

r	e	s	p	o	n	s	i	b	l	e		F	o	r
5	2	9	21	13	3	17	12	16	15	2		13	5

t	h	e	M	s	e	l	v	e	s		o	n		t	h	e
19	20	2		9	2	15	7	2	17		13	3		19	20	2

D	a	y		O	F		J	u	d	g	M	e	n	t
1	6	4		13			14	18	10		2	3	19

My Mind, My Body: *The Body Is a Mirror of the Mind*

Objective of the Lesson:

The mind and body are closely related. If the mind of a person is polluted, he or she will most likely pollute his or her body. Islam requires our minds to be clean just as our bodies should be clean. This lesson discusses various ways we can keep our minds and bodies clean.

Your mind is part of your body. The mind and body work together. If your mind is happy or sad, you might feel it in your body. Similarly, if your body is hurt or weak, you know it in your mind. If you constantly think about doing bad things, you might start doing some of those bad things that will hurt your body. To grow a healthy tree that will bear good fruit, we need to fertilize and prune it from time to time. If we do not fertilize it, the tree will die or it will not bear good fruit. Similarly, to help our minds and bodies develop properly, we need to take care of them by eating healthy food and avoiding food that is bad for us.

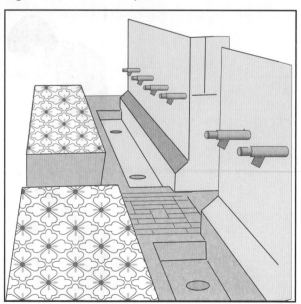

Islam teaches us to take care of our bodies just as it teaches us to take care of our minds. We can take care of our minds and bodies by keeping them pure. If we keep our bodies pure, our minds will automatically be healthy and stay pure. The question is: How do we keep our minds and bodies pure? Let us find out.

Purifying the body

We can purify, or cleanse, our bodies in three ways:

(1) **Wūdū**: this is called minor ablution
(2) **Ghusl**: this is called major ablution
(3) **Tayammum**: this is called dry ablution

Mind and body purified by wūdū

Wūdū is the most common form of purification. It is common because we are required to perform wūdū before every salāt. Sometimes we think that we can perform salāt two or three different times with one wūdū. Actually Allāh ﷻ teaches us that before every salāt we must perform wūdū.

يَـٰٓأَيُّهَا ٱلَّذِينَ ءَامَنُوٓاْ إِذَا قُمۡتُمۡ إِلَى ٱلصَّلَوٰةِ فَٱغۡسِلُواْ وُجُوهَكُمۡ وَأَيۡدِيَكُمۡ إِلَى ٱلۡمَرَافِقِ وَٱمۡسَحُواْ بِرُءُوسِكُمۡ وَأَرۡجُلَكُمۡ إِلَى ٱلۡكَعۡبَيۡنِ

O you who believe! when you stand up for Salāt then wash your faces, and your hands up to the elbows; and wipe your heads and your feet up to the ankles …(5:6)

By performing wūdū, we cleanse ourselves. We must also make sure our clothes are clean. Unless our bodies and clothes are clean, our salāt will not be valid. Wūdū can be completed with clean water. Colored water cannot be used for wūdū. Any natural water, such as rain, rivers, ponds, or lakes, can be used for wūdū. Tap water is also acceptable for performing wūdū.

Wūdū purifies our minds

When we perform wūdū, we prepare ourselves to serve Allāh. As a result, our minds become inclined to worship Allāh. The mind tells us to stay away from bad things. If you use the bathroom, pass gas, bleed, vomit, fall asleep, or pass out, you are required to perform wūdū again. You perform wūdū again because spiritual purification is important. For example, when you pass gas, you do not go to the bathroom to clean your body, but your wūdū is cancelled. This means your spiritual cleanliness is spoiled. Therefore, you are required to perform wūdū again. Similarly, when you use the toilet, you clean yourself as usual, but you are still required to perform wūdū to prepare your spiritual cleanliness.

Mind and body purified by ghusl

The meaning of *ghusl* is "bath." Wūdū only cleans minor impurities from your body. If your body has major impurities, then you are required to perform ghusl or take a bath or shower. In many ways our bodies can become impure, requiring a full bathing. For example, when you have played outside and you are dirty and sweaty, you need a shower. In the Qur'ān, Allāh says that with some forms of physical impurity, we cannot perform salāt until we make ghusl.[4:43]

Mind and body purified by tayammum

Tayammum means "dry purification." Islam allows tayammum as a symbolic way of purifying our minds. It can only be done under certain special circumstances, such as if water is not available, if water is dirty, or if the person is sick and he or she is not allowed to touch water. If you are not sick and water is available, tayammum is not an option. By performing this symbolic purification, we actually purify our minds.

Taking care of our minds

Wūdū, ghusl, and tayammum are three ways to care for our bodies and minds. There are many other ways to care for our minds. Such care is called spiritual purification. One of the main forms of spiritual purification is paying *sadaqah*, or giving to charity. When we give to charity, it purifies us.[92:18] Allāh told Rasūlullāh to take *sadaqah* from Muslims to purify them.

خُذْ مِنْ أَمْوَالِهِمْ صَدَقَةً تُطَهِّرُهُمْ وَتُزَكِّيهِم بِهَا وَصَلِّ عَلَيْهِمْ إِنَّ صَلَوٰتَكَ سَكَنٌ لَّهُمْ وَاللَّهُ سَمِيعٌ عَلِيمٌ ۝

You take for charity out of their wealth, that you may purify them and sanctify them with it, and you bless them. Your blessing is indeed happiness to them. And Allāh is all-Hearing, all-Knowing. (9:103)

Long ago, nabi Ibrāhīm (A) rebuilt the Ka'bah. Then he prayed to Allāh to choose a messenger from among the Arabs. The messenger might recite the divine revelation to the people, give them knowledge, and purify them.[2:129] In fulfillment of his prayer, Allāh sent Nabi Muhammad. One of the purposes of his mission was to purify the people from their spiritual diseases.[2:151]

How our minds and bodies are spoiled

Our minds and bodies are spoiled by things that we do, see, eat, or hear. To keep our minds pure, we should stay away from listening to bad things, including gossip, rumors, or disrespectful or negative music. We can keep our minds pure by not watching bad TV programs and not playing violent video games. There are many websites on the Internet that are harmful for our bodies and minds. We should stay away from them, too.

Good friendships for good bodies and minds

The types of friendships we have with people can influence our bodies and minds. Bad friends will influence our minds to do bad things that will ultimately damage

our bodies. Good friends can influence our minds to make us better people and better Muslims.

Good food for good body and mind

Allāh﷿ wants us to eat good and lawful food, and avoid bad and harmful food.[2:168; 16:114]

$$ يَـٰٓأَيُّهَا ٱلنَّاسُ كُلُوا۟ مِمَّا فِى ٱلْأَرْضِ حَلَـٰلًا طَيِّبًا وَلَا تَتَّبِعُوا۟ خُطُوَٰتِ ٱلشَّيْطَـٰنِ إِنَّهُۥ لَكُمْ عَدُوٌّ مُّبِينٌ ﴿١٦٨﴾ $$

O you mankind! Eat of what is on the earth, lawful, pure; and do not follow the footsteps of Shaitān. Surely he is to you an open enemy. (2:168)

Some lawful foods are bad for us if animals are slaughtered or prepared in the wrong manner. Such foods are not good for our spiritual health.

We should give importance to the care of our bodies and minds. We should purify ourselves both physically and spiritually. Spiritual purification cannot be achieved unless we physically purify ourselves.

From Hadith

Salih bin Abi Hassan narrated that, "I heard Sa'eed bin Musayyab saying: 'Indeed Allāh is Tayyib [good] and he loves Tayyib [what is good], and He is Nazif [clean] and He loves cleanliness, He is Karim [kind] and He loves kindness, He is Jawad [generous] and He loves generosity. So clean."

'Aishah (ra) narrated that the Messengerﷺ liked to start on the right whenever possible: when purifying himself, when putting on his shoes, and when combing his hair.

It is narrated in Sahih Muslim that Abu Huraira heard the Messengerﷺ say, "Allāh has forgiven my followers the evil thoughts that occur in their minds, as long as such thoughts are not put into action or uttered."

1. What are the three major forms of purification in Islam?

　1. _____

　2. _____

　3. _____

2. Which form of physical purification is most common and performed several times a day?

_____

3. You have running water at home, but you feel too lazy to perform wūdū. Can you perform tayammum? Explain your answer.

_____

_____

4. Which of the following forms of purification have a spiritual purpose?

　A.　Only wūdū.
　B.　Only tayammum.
　C.　Only *sadaqah*.
　D.　All of the above.

5. Name three things that you should avoid in order to keep your body and mind pure.

　1. _____

　2. _____

　3. _____

6. Read āyah 103 from sūrah at-Taubah. What can be done to purify one's wealth?

....

7. Make as many words having three or more letters from this word-wheel. Each word must use the letter in the center of the wheel plus two or more selections from the outer wheel. No letter may be used more than once in a word.

....

....

....

....

....

....

....

....

Kindness and Forgiveness

Objective of the Lesson:

Kindness and forgiveness are closely related. One cannot be kind without being forgiving. Islam requires us to be kind and forgiving in many ways. Forgiving someone does not mean undue encouragement of doing wrong. This lesson discusses various ways we can be kind and forgiving to others.

We are always dependent on Allāh﷿ for everything. We always look for one quality of Allāh﷿—His kindness. As human beings, we always make mistakes. Sometimes we commit sins knowingly, and sometimes we commit them unknowingly. If we ask for forgiveness, make **tawbah**, and return to Allāh ﷿, most of our sins will be forgiven. Our sins are forgiven because Allāh﷿ is most-Forgiving, most-Kind. In the Qur'ān, Allāh﷿ refers to Himself 84 times as *Ghafūr ar-Rahīm*.

وَكَانَ ٱللَّهُ غَفُورًا رَّحِيمًا

For Allāh is most Forgiving, most Rewarding.

Such emphasis on His kindness and forgiveness points to His extreme benevolence. The word *Ghafūr* not only means Allāh﷿ forgives, but also means He protects and shields us from the consequences of our evil actions. The word *Rahīm* means He is rewarding to the deserving people.

Kindness to all

We should always be kind to our friends and family. At the same time, we should also be kind to others, including our enemies.[17:53] This does not mean that we should allow our enemies to continue violence or verbal attacks against us. We should stand firm against those who are bad, but if they give up their evil ways, we should be kind to them.[2:190]

Control your anger—forgive others

We all have different types of emotions. Some emotions are positive and some are negative. Positive emotions bring happiness to us and those who are around us. Negative emotions not only make us unhappy, but they spread unhappiness to people around us.

Anger is one of the worst types of emotions. When angry, a person changes completely and behaves in a manner that he or she might regret later. When someone is angry, his or her eyes become red, blood pressure rises, the hart beats faster, and other physical changes occur. These are all harmful effects on the body. Anger could trigger a person to cause irreparable damage to oneself or to others. Allāh says He loves those who control their anger.[3:134] He says the best way to control anger is to forgive.[42:37]

وَٱلَّذِينَ يَجْتَنِبُونَ كَبَٰٓئِرَ ٱلْإِثْمِ وَٱلْفَوَٰحِشَ وَإِذَا مَا غَضِبُوا۟ هُمْ يَغْفِرُونَ ﴿٣٧﴾

and those who avoid the major sins and indecencies, and who when they feel anger—they forgive; (42:37)

Speak politely

We should always practice gentle speech. We should not hurt people with our words. Unless we have been harmed, Muslims should not speak badly about someone in public.[4:148] Allāh instructed nabi Mūsā (A) to speak politely to Fir'awn, even though Fir'awn was a cruel ruler.[20:44] Allāh also wants us to speak kindly and politely to others.[17:53]

Points to Ponder

Anger can cause irreparable damage to oneself and to others. What are some of the harmful changes anger causes in a person's behavior, his or her environment, and the people around him or her?

Forgiveness improves our society

The ability to forgive others can improve the quality of our lives. Allāh ﷻ commands us to practice forgiveness. In sūrah Al-Aʿrāf, Allāh ﷻ tells us:

$$ خُذِ ٱلۡعَفۡوَ وَأۡمُرۡ بِٱلۡعُرۡفِ وَأَعۡرِضۡ عَنِ ٱلۡجَٰهِلِينَ ۝ $$

Adopt forgiveness, and enjoin with goodness, and turn away from the ignorant. (7:199)

If we want to build a good society, we should learn to forgive others. However, forgiveness alone will not build a good society. We should ask and encourage others to do good deeds, and remind them not to make mistakes. The reason we forgive others is to allow them to understand their mistake. If they realize their mistake, they will most likely not make the same one again. But if they continue making the same mistake, then it is better to avoid them. Maybe later on they will realize their behavior is wrong and change it.

Rasūlullāh's ﷺ kindness

Rasūlullāh ﷺ was kind to his opponents.[5:13] He was so kind that he also told other Muslims to forgive the nonbelievers.[45:14] Because our Nabi Muhammad ﷺ was kind and gentle in his speech, this helped many nonbelievers want to become Muslims.[3:159]

There are many examples of kindness shown by our Nabi Muhammad ﷺ. Here are two situations where he demonstrated his extraordinary kindness.

Rasūlullāh ﷺ was still in Makkah, preaching the message of Allāh ﷻ. When the Makkan people did not listen, he went to Ta'if to tell the people to become Muslims. The people of Ta'if were cruel and attacked Rasūlullāh ﷺ. They started to throw rocks at him. Rasūlullāh ﷺ ran and escaped the city to save himself. Later, when he was safe, he sat down in a grape orchard to rest. He took off his shoes, and they were already filled with blood from running. He could have asked Allāh ﷻ to destroy the Ta'if community. Instead he asked Allāh ﷻ to guide them.

Another incident happened years later after Rasūlullāh ﷺ liberated Makkah. At that time he had vast military strength. Yet after liberating Makkah, he did not punish the idol worshippers or his enemies. He forgave them. He mentioned an āyah from sūrah Yūsuf about Nabi Yūsuf ﷺ forgiving his brothers.

$$\text{قَالَ لَا تَثْرِيبَ عَلَيْكُمُ الْيَوْمَ يَغْفِرُ اللَّهُ لَكُمْ وَهُوَ أَرْحَمُ الرَّاحِمِينَ (٩٢)}$$

He said: "No blame be on you this day. May Allāh forgive you; for He is the most Rewarding of the granter of rewards." (12:92)

Rasūlullāh☼ was never vengeful. During the incident at Ta'if, Rasūlullāh☼ had very few followers. Later, when he liberated Makkah, he had many followers. On both of these occasions, he did not abandon the quality of forgiveness.

Kindness of other messengers

All the messengers were gentle, kind, and forgiving. Nabi Ibrāhīm (A) was very caring. He prayed to Allāh☼ to forgive the nonbelievers.[14:36] Even though many people opposed Nabi Ibrāhīm (A), he was always gentle and forgiving.[11:75] The same was true of Nabi Shu'aib (A). Even his opponents considered him to be very kind and gentle.[11:87–88]

Kindness of the Sahābah

Kindness is a quality not limited to just messengers. Nabi Muhammad's☼ companions, or Sahābah were also kind to each other.[48:29] We can all practice kindness and compassion toward each other, to those who oppose us, and even to plants and animals. When Abū Bakr (R) was the Khalīfah of the Muslims, he advised his army not to destroy the crops or plants of the enemies and not to hurt children and the elderly. This shows he was a kind and compassionate person.

We want Allāh☼ to forgive our mistakes. Similarly, we should forgive others if they make mistakes. Forgiveness is such a noble quality that Allāh☼ asks us to adopt this quality.[7:199] Retaliation and hostility are not good qualities for building a good society. Allāh☼ will deal strongly with those people who are hostile and those who hurt others.[42:42]

When someone harms a person, that person has a right to act against the person who harmed him or her. Sometimes we go to court or to a mediator to

Time to Review

1. Who is the kind nabi mentioned in āyah 19:32 of the Qur'ān?
2. Who is the gentle, compassionate nabi mentioned in āyah 11:75 of the Qur'ān?
3. Provide two specific examples of kindness of any two nabi mentioned in the Qur'ān.

solve our issue. However, if the harmed person decides to forgive the aggressor, he or she will be rewarded by Allāh. [42:40]

Allāh reminds us that forgiveness is a great quality. [42:43] This quality can even be improved if we forgive someone and then forget the issue. [24:22] If we keep remembering that someone has harmed us, then we have not truly forgiven the person.

Some of Allāh beautiful names teach us about His kind and forgiving nature. The names **al-Ghaffar** and **al-Ghafur** indicate that He is the Forgiving and the Forgiver. His name **al-Wadud** indicates He is **the Loving**.

We should do our best to forgive other people. We should also always ask Allāh to forgive us. We are not always aware that we made a mistake. Therefore, we should follow the path of Rasūlullāh, and always seek Allāh's protection and His forgiveness. [4:106, 40:55, 47:19]

From Hadith

It is reported on the authority of 'Abdullah that the Messenger said, "the best of the deeds or deed is the [observance of] prayer at its proper time and kindness to the parents."

Jabir reported that the Messenger said, "Every act of kindness is sadaqah. Part of kindness is that you offer your brother a cheerful face and you pour some of your bucket into his water vessel."

1. Many people have good qualities. Read sūrah Al-Ahzāb, āyah 21. Who is an excellent example for us?

Prophet Muhemmad

2. Read sūrah Fussilat, āyah 41:34. How should we treat a friend even if we develop bad feelings about him or her?

see the good on the person

3. We learned in a previous lesson that Yūsuf's (A) brothers abandoned him. When Yūsuf (A) saw them again, how did he treat them? Find the answer in Sūrah 12, āyah 92.

Yusuf (A) forgave them

4. What are Rasūlullāh's two qualities in sūrah At-Taubah, āyah 128?

1. *kind*

2. *murecful*

5. In sūrah Maryam, āyah 47, a certain nabi prayed to Allāh to forgive a sinner. Who was the nabi? (Hint: find the answer in āyah 46.)

→ surah Al-maun

6. The title of a certain sūrah translates to "Acts of Kindness." Look for this sūrah in the Qur'an, and write the Arabic title. (Hint: it is one of the last ten sūrahs.)

Nebi Ibrahim

7. When the people of Ta'if humiliated Rasūlullāh ﷺ and made his feet bleed, how did he want to deal with the people of Ta'if?

    A.   He asked Allāh ﷻ to punish the culprits.

    B.   He prayed to destroy them.

    C.   He prayed to guide them.

    D.   He prayed to starve them.

8. After Rasūlullāh ﷺ liberated Makkah from idol worshippers, how did he deal with the Quraish who had opposed him and fought battles against him?

    A.   He forgave them.

    B.   He gave them very light punishment.

    C.   He simply asked them to give ransom money.

    D.   He asked them to surrender all arms.

9. Unscramble the following letters to make meaningful words. Then rearrange the circled letters to find a secret name.

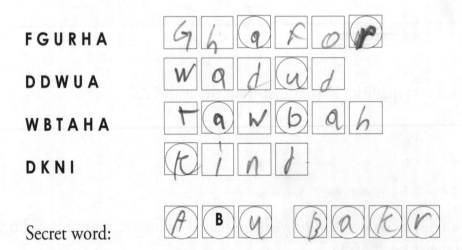

FGURHA   Ghafor

DDWUA   Wadud

WBTAHA   Tawbah

DKNI   Kind

Secret word: Abu Bakr

The Middle Path: *Ways to Avoid the Two Extremes*

Objective of the Lesson:

Islam always encourages us to adopt the middle path. What is the middle path and how can we adopt the middle path? Why is the middle path the blessed path of Allāhﷻ and favorite to the Messengerﷺ? This lesson discusses the importance of following the middle path in every matter in our lives.

If we read the teachings of the Qur'ān and the Sunnah in their entirety, we will find that Islam promotes the middle path. The middle path means a path that avoids the two extremes and maintains a balance. The middle path brings harmony to our every action and to our faith. Let us study the principle of the middle path in Islam.

What the middle path is not

First let us try to understand what the middle path is not. We should remember that the middle path is not a path of compromise. The middle path is not a path where we can get by with doing a little bit of good and a little bit of sin. The middle path is not a path where we can believe in some parts of Islam and ignore the rest. The middle path is not a path where we can partially worship Allāhﷻ and partially worship others.

The middle path is not a path for wrongdoers. It is not a path that can be taken at random. It is not a new path

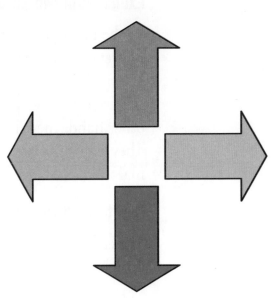

that has not been tested before. The middle path does not finish at a dead-end. It is not full of difficult and meaningless duties. It does not promise only suffering and bad luck. It is not a path that deprives us of rewards. It is not an aimless, pointless path.

Sūrah Fātihah and the middle path

We recite sūrah Fātihah every day in our salāt. Toward the end of the short sūrah, we pray to Allāh﷿ to guide us on the straight path. That straight path is the middle path. After asking Allāh﷿ to guide us on the straight path, we pray to Allāh﷿ to save us from the two extremes. In other words, we ask Allāh﷿ to guide us on the middle path. One extreme is the path of those who have earned Allāh's﷿ anger, and the other extreme is the path of those who have gone astray. Those who have earned Allāh's﷿ anger might still be doing some good deeds, but they made some big mistakes. Those who have gone astray have abandoned guidance from Allāh﷿ altogether. Both are extreme conditions. The following āyah is part of sūrah Fātihah:

Guide us on the Straight Path, the path of those on whom you have bestowed favors, not of those upon whom wrath is brought down, nor of those gone astray. (1:6–7)

Examples of two extremes

In the mission of nabi 'Isā (A), we can find two extreme examples. Isā (A) was a messenger for the Children of Israel—the Jews. But they rejected him altogether. They rejected his teachings and called him and his mother bad names. They criticized him for talking about their religion and attempted to kill him. On the other hand, the Christians accepted him and elevated him to the status of god. They call him the Son of God. Both extremes are serious sins. The Muslims maintain a balanced view of him—we believe he was a messenger of Allāh﷿

How to apply the middle path

The concept of the middle path teaches us to approach everything in life with an upright, unbiased attitude. Whenever we have a problem or challenge in life, we should approach it in a neutral, unbiased, and righteous manner. This will ensure that we establish balance in life. In Islam there is no provision for excessive worship that disrupts life, and there is no allowance for extreme ease and laxity. For this reason, Islam does not endorse severe self-discipline and avoidance of all forms of indulgence, typically practiced for religious reasons. The concept of **Asceticism** is not an Islamic teaching. Islam does not approve of self-denial and does not favor extreme pleasure. For this reason, we find all the rules and regulations in Islam do not intend to make our life difficult. Allāh﷿ says He wants ease for us, not difficulty.[2:185]

> **Definition**
>
> **Asceticism:** The doctrine that a person can attain a higher spiritual and moral state by denying themselves all good things in life, practicing self-mortification, and abstaining from all forms of indulgence.

Maintain balance

The Qur'ān repeatedly asks us to maintain balance. Let us read the translations of verses 7–9 from sūrah Ar-Rahmān.

وَٱلسَّمَآءَ رَفَعَهَا وَوَضَعَ ٱلْمِيزَانَ (٧)	*And the sky—He has raised it high, and He has set up the Balance,*
أَلَّا تَطْغَوْا۟ فِى ٱلْمِيزَانِ (٨)	*so that you may not transgress the Balance!*
وَأَقِيمُوا۟ ٱلْوَزْنَ بِٱلْقِسْطِ وَلَا تُخْسِرُوا۟ ٱلْمِيزَانَ (٩)	*And keep up the weighing with justice, and do not diminish the Balance.*

The significance of balance does not only mean that we weigh items correctly in a business or that we deliver fair justice. It means much more than that. It means that no matter what we do, we must do it in a balanced manner. The learned thinkers of Islam have selected four areas where we are required to follow the middle path. These four areas include everything we do, or need to do, in our daily lives. These four areas are:

> **Points to Ponder**
>
> Islam teaches us to adopt the middle path in all aspects of our daily lives. The middle path is not a path of compromise. When considering religion, how do we apply the concept of the middle path? As we adopt the middle-path approach, how do we take precautions so as not to stray from our religion?

- Beliefs ('Aqidah)
- Acts of worship ('Ibadah)
- Morals and manners (Akhlaq)
- Laws (Shari'ah)

The middle ummah

The Muslim community is one ummah. It is a requirement of the ummah to maintain balance and follow the middle path. In sūrah al-Baqarah, Allāh ﷻ says:

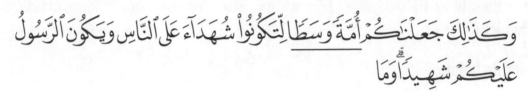

"Thus have We made of you a Middle Ummah, that you might be witnesses over the people, and the Messenger a witness over yourselves." (2:143)

The Arabic phrase used here is *ummatan wasatan*. It means a "community well balanced."

In another āyah, Allāh ﷻ asks the People of the Book to follow the middle path. The People of the Book are those who were given divine books earlier—such as the Jews and the Christians. Allāh ﷻ says:

"O People of the Book! do not exaggerate in your religion beyond the truth, and do not follow the low desires of people who went astray in the past, and who led a great many astray, and who went astray from the right path." (5:77).

To be successful in this life and in the Hereafter, we must follow the middle path and avoid the two extremes.

From Hadīth

It is narrated in Bukhārī that Rasūlullāh ﷺ said: "The religion is easy and whosoever will deal with religion harshly, it will defeat him. So be straight, follow the middle course, give good news, and seek help by moving [performing salāt] in the morning or the evening or part of the night."

1. Based on your understanding of the middle path, which of the following choices is correct?

   A.   The middle path is a path of compromise.

   B.   The middle path is a path of partial goodness.

   C.   The middle path is the straight path.

   D.   The middle path brings suffering and bad luck.

2. All of the following choices show people who followed the middle path except one choice. Which choice shows people who **did not** follow the middle path?

   A.   All the messengers, including 'Isā (A) and Muhammadﷺ.

   B.   All the companions of Rasūlullāhﷺ.

   C.   All the wives of Rasūlullāhﷺ.

   D.   Some of the People of the Book.

3. Which area or areas of our daily lives require us to follow the middle path?

   A.   Our beliefs.

   B.   How we worship.

   C.   How we deal with people.

   D.   Our beliefs, worship, manners, and laws.

4. Which of the following statements is correct about the middle path?

   A.   The middle path is a new religion to replace Islam.

   B.   The middle path was discovered by Rasūlullāhﷺ.

   C.   The middle path is a principle of Islam.

   D.   The middle path was tested and accepted by the Jews.

5. The Christians did not follow the middle path. What did they do? Write the answer in your own words.

_____

_____

6. Write two sentences to show what the middle path is not.

1. _____

2. _____

7. Find the following words in the word search puzzle.

PATH   MIDDLE   BALANCE   EXTREME   FATIHAH   PRINCIPLE
ABSTAIN   ASCETICISM   WORSHIP   MORALS   MANNERS   LAWS

E C N A L A B E T E D V
Z I M O R A L S Y W P D
P U Q M I D D L E R I L
A S C E T I C I S M H T
T A I B C O N H D E S S
H Q F A T I H A H M R L
P H X C A I Q G W E O A
N L N T B D H M N R W W
Y Z S R H R V N K T U S
Z B K A M P A B X X T L
A E L R A M L X B E E W
P R I N C I P L E P J T

Salāt: *Its Significance*

Objective of the Lesson:

Performance of salāt is one of the most important duties of all Muslims. From a young age, children are required to perform salāt. It is not just a ritual to follow. Salāt purifies us and removes our sins. This lesson discusses the major significance of salāt.

The first pillar of Islam is shahādah. It is a verbal declaration of faith. After a person declares his or her faith, the next important step is to demonstrate his or her faith in action. One way to do this is through the performance of salāt. Salāt is a pillar of Islam. Of all the pillars, salāt is most frequently mentioned in the Qur'ān.

As Muslims, we are required to perform salāt five times a day. We cannot miss salāt without a valid reason permitted by the Qur'ān. Think about the other pillars of Islam—fasting, paying zakāt, and performing Hajj. If you are sick and you cannot fast, there is no penalty. There are ways that you can feed the poor and still get the same reward for fasting. Zakāt is a required duty, but if you are poor and have no money, then it is not compulsory for you to pay. Zakāt is required only for people who have surplus income. Similarly, if you cannot afford to go to Hajj, there is no penalty. Hajj is obligatory only when a person can afford it and is in good health. You can shorten the salāt when it is necessary, but we should not miss it.[4:101] If a sick person cannot pray while standing, he or she may sit down and pray. If he or she cannot pray while sitting, then he or she may pray while lying down. Salāt has to be performed, even if we have great difficulty. We cannot engage someone else to perform salāt on our behalf. Salāt is a personal duty and personal form of worship.

Significance of salāt

Some of the significant aspects of salāt are listed below. The first and foremost significance is that salāt maintains a continuous and direct link with Allāh. As a result of establishing this link, people receive many other benefits as well. All of these benefits are important aspects of salāt:

1. Salāt maintains a continuous and direct link with Allāh.

2. Salāt protects believers from evil and bad actions.

3. Salāt promotes discipline in life.

4. Salāt creates awareness of Allāh.

5. Salāt strengthens belief.

6. Salāt is a great investment for the Hereafter.

7. Salāt, if performed in a group, helps establish a strong sense of equality and fellowship.

8. Salāt is the best form of personal jihād.

Definition

Jihad: Struggle or strive—particularly to achieve something better. It means internal as well as external efforts to be a good Muslims or believer. Any military action to make something better is a distant meaning of the word. The term is inaccurately overused to mean "holy war." Jihad is not a violent action, it is not declaration of war.

There are many more significant aspects of salāt. If you understand why salāt is significant, your salāt will become more sincere and you will receive a greater reward.

Salāt is not a new practice

Salāt is not a new religious duty given to Muslims. In the past, salāt was prescribed to the early communities, too. The previous communities also needed a continuous and direct link with Allāh. They also needed discipline in life. They also needed to strengthen their belief and invest in the Hereafter. The Qur'ān says the Children of Israel were instructed to perform salāt.[2:83; 5:12]

A continuous and direct link with Allāh

Salāt is a form of worship. It is not a du'ā or a personal communication with Allāh. In a du'ā we can say whatever we like. In salāt we say only sūrah and those statements that Rasūlullāhﷺ taught us to say. Salāt cannot be replaced by duʿā. Through salāt we establish a direct link with Allāhﷻ. Therefore, we are not allowed to talk, look sideways, or break away from the group and rejoin it later. Salāt helps us attain righteousness and nearness to our Creator. Allāhﷻ says:

$$قُلْ إِنَّ صَلَاتِي وَنُسُكِي وَمَحْيَايَ وَمَمَاتِي لِلَّهِ رَبِّ ٱلْعَالَمِينَ ١٦٢$$

Say: "Surely my Salāt and my sacrifice and my living and my dying are for the sake of Allāh—Rabb of all the worlds. (6:162)

Protection from evil and bad actions

Regular and timely performance of salāt protects us from evil and indecency. The word "indecency" (فحشا) means anything that is bad, inappropriate or not proper. In the Qur'ān, Allāhﷻ says:

$$وَأَقِمِ ٱلصَّلَوٰةَ إِنَّ ٱلصَّلَوٰةَ تَنْهَىٰ عَنِ ٱلْفَحْشَاءِ وَٱلْمُنكَرِ$$

...and establish the Salāt. Surely the Salāt restrains from indecency and evil... (29:45)

$$وَأَقِمِ ٱلصَّلَوٰةَ طَرَفَيِ ٱلنَّهَارِ وَزُلَفًا مِّنَ ٱلَّيْلِ إِنَّ ٱلْحَسَنَٰتِ يُذْهِبْنَ ٱلسَّيِّئَاتِ ذَٰلِكَ ذِكْرَىٰ لِلذَّاكِرِينَ ١١٤$$

And keep up the Salāt at two parts of the day, and at the early parts of the night. Surely good things carry away the evils. This is a reminder for the mindful. (11:114)

Think about it: How can we do something evil, knowing that within a few hours we are going to establish a direct link with Allāhﷻ? This thought itself can prevent us from doing something bad. Even if we are not aware of it, the performance of regular and timely salāt will help us avoid evil and bad actions.

Time to Review

1. What are the two main reasons for performing salāt?
2. How do we know that salāt is not a new practice given to the Muslims?
3. Why can a sick person engage someone else to perform salāt on his or her behalf?

Promotes discipline in life

Making salat on time helps us understand and appreciate the importance of discipline. If we do not have discipline, our lives will have innumerable problems. A disciplined person is also a successful person. This sense of discipline comes from performing salat in a timely manner. It also teaches us the importance of being punctual in life. Salat blends together our earthly activities with our spiritual activities. Salat helps reduce our negative emotions, such as anger or hatred. Curbing these negative emotions are also a form of disciplining ourselves.

Creates awareness of Allāh

The performance of salat helps us become fully aware of Allāh. If we are not aware of Allāh, we will start going in the wrong direction in life. Simply knowing about Allāh is not enough because even people of other faiths know about Allāh. We show awareness of Allāh by doing what Allāh wants us to do and by staying away from what is prohibited. Through such awareness of Allāh, we learn how to appreciate the blessings of Allāh, and show our utmost submission to the One who created us.

Strengthens belief

Salat helps us strengthen our belief. We say we believe, but unless we demonstrate our faith through righteous activities, our verbal declaration of faith is not enough. We are required to perform salat as proof of our faith. Therefore, salat helps us strengthen our faith.

Great investment for the Hereafter

Salat has benefits in this world and more in the Hereafter. Salat is a great investment for the Hereafter. If we perform salat regularly, its ultimate reward will be forgiveness from Allāh and admittance into Heaven. A hadīth mentions that on Judgment Day, the first deeds for which the people will be brought to account will be salat. If the obligatory salat are found to be sound, then the person will have an easy judgment. On the contrary, if the obligatory salat are lacking, then everything else will have less merit.

Establishes equality and fellowship

Human beings are social beings. We live in a society and interact with others in the society. We gather with our friends and other groups from time to time. Do we gather with them five times a day, every day? No. Group salat provides us the opportunity to meet with people who are in our group and with whom we are friendly. It also provides us the opportunity to meet with others who are

When we make du'ā, we make direct contact with Allāhﷻ—as we seek His help, mercy, and guidance. In du'ā, we also praise Allāhﷻ. In dhikr we remember Allāh. So why can du'ā or dhikr not become a substitute for salāt?

not in our group. Congregational or group salāt helps us establish equality and fellowship with people in our society.

Best form of personal Jihād

The Qur'ān wants us to do a personal jihād. We should understand that jihād is not necessarily an armed struggle. The main purpose of jihād is to improve ourselves. Salāt is the best form of personal jihād. It helps us to continuously improve ourselves by developing an awareness of Allāhﷻ, by strengthening our belief, and by avoiding the bad and evil things.

We should make it a point not to miss any salāt. We should try our best to perform salāt regularly and in a timely manner with the utmost dedication. We should remember that salāt is a form of worship of our Creator. We must never forget or ignore worshipping Him.

From Hadīth

Abu Huraira reported that Rasūlullāhﷺ said: "When Shaitān hears the call to prayer, he turns back and runs away so as not to hear the call being made, but when the call is finished he turns around and distracts [the minds of those who pray], and when he hears the Iqama, he again runs away so as not to hear its voice, and when it ends, he comes back and distracts [the minds of those who stand for prayer]."

1. Read āyah 2:153 of the Qur'ān. What are the two things for which we should seek help from Allāhﷻ?

1. _Patience_   2. _salah_

2. You are required to perform salāt. You are also required to ask others to perform salāt. Read āyah 20:132 of the Qur'ān. Who should you encourage to perform salāt?

Family

3. Why should you strictly guard your salāt? Write your answer in a short sentence.

Salah strengthens belief

4. Read āyah 2:239 of the Qur'ān. Salāt cannot be missed, even when we are busy doing something. What is the situation mentioned in this āyah, when we cannot miss salāt?

while riding, on foot

5. In the Qur'ān, Allāhﷻ says one particular salāt is the most excellent salāt. But the name of the salāt is not mentioned. Read āyah 2:238 and its commentary if available. Which salāt is mentioned in this āyah?

Asr

6. Read āyah 62:9 of the Qur'ān. Then answer the following questions:

Which salāt is mentioned in the āyah? _Juma_

What two things are you required to do when the call for this salāt is made?

1. _come to remembrance of Allah_

2. _first piaty_

7. Read āyah 11:114 of the Qur'ān. What does good things carry away, as mentioned in this āyah?

A. Evil.

B. Greed.

C. Self-destruction.

D. Pride.

8. In āyah 4:101 of the Qur'ān, Allāh﷾ provides a special concession about salāt. What is the special concession?

A. A person can skip salāt if he or she is sick.

B. A person can combine two salāt as needed.

C. A person can perform dry wūdū during travel.

D. A person can shorten salāt during travel.

9. Of all the pillars of Islam, which pillar is most frequently mentioned in the Qur'ān?

A. Salāt.

B. Zakāt.

C. Hajj.

D. Fasting.

10. All of the following choices about salāt are correct except one. Which one is incorrect?

A. Salāt is a direct link with Allāh﷾

B. Salāt restrains from indecency.

C. A sick person can do salāt lying down.

D. During travel all five salāt can be combined.

11. Read āyah 29:45 of the Qur'ān. According to this āyah, from what two things does salāt protects us?

A. Indecency and greed.

B. Inability and lack of discipline.

C. Indecency and evil.

D. Lethargy and unmindful conduct.

Sawm: *Its Significance*

Objective of the Lesson:

Sawm is not simply about being hungry all day and eating a full meal after breaking the fast in the evening. Sawm has more value in helping us become better Muslims. Its rewards are immense. This lesson discusses the significance of sawm.

The Arabic word for fasting is **sawm** (صيام plural: **siyām**). It means "to abstain" or "to stay away." In everyday usage, we understand sawm as fasting, particularly during the month of Ramadan. When we say sawm means fasting, we restrict the meaning of the word to not eating or drinking. However, the word sawm has a much deeper meaning. Let us try to understand the significance of sawm, and see why it is one of the pillars of Islam.

The goal of fasting

During sawm we do not eat or drink from early morning until the sun sets. The goal is not just to remain hungry. The goal is not to torture the body. The goal is not just the ritual of observing the fast. The main goal of fasting is to improve ourselves as human beings by attaining a "greater awareness" of Allāh﷾. The Qur'ān mentions this greater awareness as taqwā—on one hand it increases awareness of Allāh﷾, and on the other it helps to ward off evil and sins. In other words, it means guarding oneself against sins and harmful things, and using God as a shield or shelter.

> **Definition**
>
> **Taqwā:** Arabic word meaning protection, warding off evil, guarding against sins and harmful actions, honoring and observing the divine command in every aspect of life.

$$\text{يَـٰٓأَيُّهَا ٱلَّذِينَ ءَامَنُوا۟ كُتِبَ عَلَيْكُمُ ٱلصِّيَامُ كَمَا كُتِبَ عَلَى ٱلَّذِينَ مِن قَبْلِكُمْ}$$

$$\text{لَعَلَّكُمْ تَتَّقُونَ ﴿١٨٣﴾}$$

O you who believe! Sawm is prescribed for you, as it was prescribed to those who preceded you, so that you may practice reverence. (2:183)

Allāh could have simply ordered us to fast in the month of Ramadan, and as Muslims we would have been obligated to follow the command. But in the āyah above, Allāh orders us to fast and then gives us the reason behind the order—*so that you may practice reverence.*

In the previous lesson, we noted several aspects about the significance of salāt. With slight modifications, most of those significant aspects can be applied to sawm, too.

1. Sawm is a form of worshipping Allāh.
2. Sawm strengthens believers and helps them avoid evil and bad actions.
3. Sawm promotes discipline in life.
4. Sawm creates awareness of Allāh.
5. Sawm strengthens our belief.
6. Sawm is a great investment for the Hereafter.
7. Sawm earns blessings.

Why in Ramadan?

Why has Allāh prescribed fasting in the month of Ramadan but not during other months? The main reason is that the Qur'ān was revealed during the month of Ramadan.

$$\text{شَهْرُ رَمَضَانَ ٱلَّذِىٓ أُنزِلَ فِيهِ ٱلْقُرْءَانُ هُدًى لِّلنَّاسِ وَبَيِّنَـٰتٍ مِّنَ ٱلْهُدَىٰ وَٱلْفُرْقَانِ}$$

$$\text{فَمَن شَهِدَ مِنكُمُ ٱلشَّهْرَ فَلْيَصُمْهُ}$$

The month of Ramadan is the one in which the Qur'ān was revealed, as a guidance for mankind, and clear proofs of guidance, and the Discrimination. So whoever among you witnesses the month, he will then observe Sawm therein … (2:185)

The word Ramadan carries a special meaning. This word comes from the Arabic root word **ramida** or **ramada** (رمض), which means "to burn" or "to make burning-hot." In the month of Ramadan when we fast, it means much more than just being hungry. The core reason is we are required to symbolically burn all the bad feelings, bad instincts, and bad emotions in our minds and bodies, and thereby, become better individuals. Thus fasting is an annual practice to better ourselves as the best of Allāh's creations.

Abstain from all permissible things

In this blessed month, what other blessed thing can we do besides fasting that helps us become better individuals? During the period of sawm, we abstain from acts that are normally permissible and necessary for our survival. Now imagine, if we can give up eating and drinking for a certain period of time, we should be able to give up other things that are not necessary for our survival. For example, jealousy, hatred, anger, back-biting, lying, and many other emotional actions and reactions are not necessary for our daily living. Thus, fasting is a form of spiritual training. We receive this training once a year, every year.

Fasting increases taqwā

As mentioned previously, Allāh says the main purpose of fasting is to increase our **taqwā**.[2:183] In the previous chapter, we learned that salāt is not a new practice prescribed for the Muslims—past communities were also ordered to perform salāt. Similarly, fasting is not a specific command given to Muslims. Past communities were also ordered to fast. They, too, were required to have taqwā. They were also told to fast for a fixed number of days, and they were allowed to skip fasting if they were sick, on a journey, or would become extremely strained by it. They were advised to fast the missed days on other days or feed a needy person to compensate for their inability to fast.

On the list of four sacred months in Islam, Ramadan is not one of them. But Ramadan is a blessed month. Why was Ramadan made a blessed month but still not considered a sacred month?

أَيَّامًا مَّعْدُودَاتٍ ۚ فَمَن كَانَ مِنكُم مَّرِيضًا أَوْ عَلَىٰ سَفَرٍ فَعِدَّةٌ مِّنْ أَيَّامٍ أُخَرَ وَعَلَى ٱلَّذِينَ يُطِيقُونَهُ فِدْيَةٌ طَعَامُ مِسْكِينٍ

[Fast] for a fixed number of days. Then whoever of you is sick, or on a journey, there is then the counting out of the other days. And those who become strained by it, there is redemption by feeding the poor... (2:184)

Fasting promotes discipline

Fasting requires eating a pre-dawn meal, abstaining from food and water all day long, and eating at a specific time after sunset. It is a systematic process of disciplining ourselves. We train our bodies and minds. No matter how hot the day is, no matter how hungry or thirsty we are, no matter how tired we are, we cannot give up fasting. When we fast, we consciously stay away from bad habits. We not only increase stamina in our bodies by fasting, but we also develop our commitment to our faith.

Fasting strengthens belief

Fasting requires your time, commitment, and ability to withstand the difficulties of not eating or drinking all day. You cannot abstain from food and water for 30 long days unless your faith is strong. Therefore, fasting increases our faith.

Best investment for Hereafter

The benefits of fasting is mentioned in several ahādīth. In one hadīth collected by Imam Bukhārī, Ibn Majah, and Ahmad, it is mentioned that Rasūlullāhﷺ said, "Every work of a child of Adam is counted for him except fasting. It is for Allāh ﷻ and He rewards for it." Therefore, fasting is one of the finest investments we can make for our Hereafter. Imam Bukhārī and Muslim also reported that Rasūlullāhﷺ said those who fast during Ramadan by devoting themselves to Allāhﷻ will have their sins forgiven, and they will be as pure as a newborn baby.

Time to Review

1. In āyah 2:184, for how many days is fasting prescribed?
2. How do we know that fasting is not a new practice given to Muslims?
3. What could a permanently sick or disabled person do if he or she cannot fast during Ramadan or on other days?

Sawm earns blessings

The month of Ramadan is full of blessings. The revelation of the Qur'ān began on a blessed night called **lailatul qadr** in Ramadan. The blessings of *lailatul qadr* are endless. How can we expect to receive the blessings unless we fast? Therefore, fasting with a sincere mind is the key to earning blessings. These blessings are multiplied throughout the month, particularly during the last ten days of the month. Additionally, the blessings are multiplied many times on the night of *lailatul qadr*.

The importance of siyām cannot be described in a few words. The more you think about and study the blessings of siyām and Ramadan, the more you will understand why it is one of the finest forms of worshipping. We should always fast during the month of Ramadan in its true spirit.

From Hadīth

Abu Huraira reported that Rasūlullāhﷺ said: "Whoever fasts in the month of Ramadan with faith and seeks Allāh's pleasure and reward, they will have all their previous sins forgiven."

In another hadīth, Abu Huraira stated that Rasūlullāhﷺ said: "Allāh said: 'Every deed of man will receive 10 to 700 times reward, except sawm, for it is for Me and I shall reward it (as I like). There are two occasions of joy for one who fasts—one when he breaks the fast and the other when he will meet his Rabb.'" (Muslim)

1. What is the main purpose of fasting as mentioned in the Qur'ān?

    A.   To feel how the poor feel.
    B.   To increase our taqwā.
    C.   To lower our cholesterol.
    D.   To feel good.

2. The word siyām essentially means:

    A.   Fasting.
    B.   Abstaining.
    C.   Tarawih.
    D.   Only (a) and (c).
    E.   Only (a) and (b).

3. The root word of Ramadan is ramida or ramada. Which of the following is the correct meaning of the root word?

    A.   To burn.
    B.   To fast.
    C.   To abstain.
    D.   To attain taqwā.
    E.   To attain.

4. Read āyah 2:185 of the Qur'ān. Which two types of people are allowed to fast at other times of the year?

    A.   Those who are performing jihad and those who are working.
    B.   Those who are sick and those who are on a journey.
    C.   Those who cannot fast due to disability and those who are retired.
    D.   Students who have to study a lot and outdoor workers.
    E.   Those who work the night shift and those who are on a journey.

5. Read āyah 2:183 of the Qur'ān. What is the objective of siyām as mentioned in the āyah?

    A.   To attain goodness.

    B.   To become an Ansar of Allāh.

    C.   To attain success.

    D.   To attain taqwā.

    E.   To abstain from everything.

6. Read āyah 2:185 of the Qur'ān. What should one do when he or she witnesses Ramadan as stated in the āyah?

    A.   Announce the arrival of Ramadan.

    B.   Begin performing Tarawih.

    C.   Begin recitation of the entire Qur'ān.

    D.   Observe fasting.

    E.   Stop discrimination.

7. Unscramble the following to make meaningful words. Then rearrange the circled letters to make a secret word.

LMAE   Ⓜ a l e

QTWAA   r a q Ⓦ a

TSFNAGI   f Ⓐ Ⓢ t i n g

Secret word: Ⓢ Ⓐ Ⓦ Ⓝ

Zakāt and Sadaqah: *Similarities and Differences*

Objective of the Lesson:

One of the requirements of Islam is to pay zakāt. It is not a burden on the wealthy to part with a small portion of their surplus wealth. It is a useful system to share our wealth with the less fortunate. Zakāt also has spiritual benefit as it purifies our wealth. This lesson explains who can receive zakāt, how much to give, and when to give.

Zakāt is one of the five pillars of Islam. The root word of zakāt means "to purify."[9:103] The word also means "to make something grow and develop." In simple and ordinary usage, zakāt means giving alms, or giving to charity. There is another word that means alms-giving. It is **sadaqah** (صدقة). Literally, sadaqa means "to be sincere," "to be truthful." The word "siddiq," meaning a trustworthy person, is derived from the same root word. In the Qur'ānic usage, sadaqah means charity or alms. Giving to charity demonstrates sincerity for Allāhﷻ. A "musaddiq" is one who gives to charity.

Main difference

Both zakāt and sadaqah are repeatedly and sometimes interchangeably mentioned in the Qur'ān. In this lesson, let us explore the similarities and differences between zakāt and sadaqah. The main difference between zakāt and sadaqah is how it is given. Zakāt refers to obligatory charity. This charity is to be given from surplus wealth after all the expenses of the person or his or her family are met. Zakāt has to be given to the poor. It is obligatory upon those who have an **surplus**

> **Definition**
>
> **Surplus income:** A term used in economics to describe the amount of money left over after meeting a family's livelihood or expenses. Sometimes it is used to describe excess assets including other income, profits, capital, and goods.

income. Surplus income is any money left over after a family's expenses are met. Usually it is calculated for one calendar year. Therefore, people who do not have surplus money, or those who are poor, are not required to pay zakāt.

In contrast, sadaqah is voluntary charity. It can be given by anybody—whether one is rich or poor. Since it is voluntary, any amount can be given for any righteous cause. Our Rasūl Muhammadﷺ encouraged everyone to give sadaqah. If money cannot be given, then a smile, a word of sympathy, or time devoted to a good cause can be sadaqah.

Here is a short summary of the differences between zakāt and sadaqah:

Zakāt	Sadaqah
Literally means "to purify."	Means "sincerity for Allāhﷻ."
Obligatory charity.	Voluntary charity.
Time-bound, usually annual giving.	Has no time limits, can be given anytime.
Has a surplus income criteria.	No income cutoff or limits.
Once the required percent of charity is paid, the duty is fulfilled.	There is no required percent of charity. Any amount can be given.
An act of worship.	An act of worship.
Payments have conditions on them.	Payments do not have conditions on them.
Can be distributed only to the recipients clearly mentioned in the Qur'ān.	Can be distributed to any needy person or good cause.
If not paid, the person will be punished in the Hereafter.	If not paid or never paid, there is no punishment.

What zakāt is not

We should remember that zakāt is not a tax system. Under a tax system, everyone pays an expense based on income. In return they receive public services offered by the government. Zakāt is not a tax system because it is not based on one's yearly income. It is based on one's surplus economic assets that have been held for one year. It is also not *Social Security*, where taxpayers pay money to support the poor, disabled or older people who can no longer work.

Zakāt is not meant to promote a class of beggars. It is supposed to help people who have financial difficulties. Many people fall into financial hardship through no fault of their own. Sometimes a flood or an earthquake destroys a family's home. Sometimes a drought ruins a farmer's produce. A traveler might need help to complete his or her travels. A factory might close, leaving many people without jobs. Zakāt money might help the unfortunate overcome their difficulties. The day might come when these same people will have enough money to pay zakāt and help others. We should remember that poor people have a right to our wealth.[51:19, 70:24–25]

وَفِىٓ أَمْوَٰلِهِمْ حَقٌّ لِّلسَّآئِلِ وَٱلْمَحْرُومِ ﴿١٩﴾

And in their wealth is a share for the beggar and the abstainer. (51:19)

Zakāt is a better system of giving

The purpose of zakāt is to distribute one's surplus money or goods to those who are needy. It cannot be given to any needy people; eight categories of people qualify to receive zakāt. If a person does not have surplus money, he or she is not required to pay zakāt. The purpose of zakāt is to help the needy, not to cause difficulties for those who cannot pay zakāt. This is a much better system than the one practiced by Catholics or Jews. Both Catholics and Jews are required to pay 10% of their income to their church or synagogue. This is called the **tithe**, or "the tenth." The church or synagogue uses the money to support various humanitarian programs and help the needy. Let us look at two examples.

> **Definition**
>
> **Tithe:** A term used to denote one-tenth of one's annual produce or earnings, paid as a tax for the support of the church and clergy.

Consider a Catholic family of four that has an annual income of $20,000. Their entire annual income is spent on food, rent, gas, medicine, and so forth.

> **Points to Ponder**
>
> Zakāt must be paid on annual surplus income. A person calculates that his surplus income will be $12,000. In order to minimize his zakāt payment, he takes a $3,000 vacation, installs granite counter tops in his kitchen for $5,000, and buys a TV for $500. For the remainder amount he pays $87.50 in zakāt. Did he do right or wrong? What is your opinion?

There is nothing left at the end of the year. The family is still required to pay 10% of their income, that is, $2,000 to the church.

Now consider a Muslim family of four who has an annual income of $20,000. Their entire annual income is spent on food, rent, utilities, gas, medicine and so forth. There is nothing left at the end of the year. This family is not required to pay zakāt because there is no surplus money left. They can, however, pay any amount of sadaqah on their own.

Let us consider another example: a Catholic family of four who has an annual income of $100,000. Their annual expenses are $60,000 with a surplus of $40,000. This family is required to pay 10% of their income, that is, $10,000 to the church. Now consider a Muslim family of four that has an annual income of $100,000. They have annual expenses of $60,000 with a surplus of $40,000. This family will pay 2.5% of the surplus to a needy person or organization. This is equal to $40,000 X 2.5% = $1,000.

Christian Family	Muslim Family
Income $100,000	Income $100,000
less: 60,000	less: 60,000
Net $ 40,000	Net $ 40,000
10% of $100,000 = $ 10,000	2.5% of $40,000 = $ 1,000

The money paid as a *tithe* is used by the church to help the needy and also to support their projects, such as paying salaries to the clergy and maintaining the churches. The people who pay the tithe usually do not have much control over how the money is spent. When Muslims pay zakāt, they can decide whom they want to pay. Zakāt money is not spent on extravagant items, but is used to directly help the poor and the needy.

Time to Review

1. Which community is required to pay a tithe?
2. How is a tithe different from mandatory zakāt for Muslims?
3. Calculate how much zakāt a person should pay when his annual income is $65,000, and his surplus income is $5,000.

Many ways to give to charity

We can give charity in many ways. When we give to charity, we might want to announce it to others. This may encourage others to give to charity. You might also want to give to charity without anyone knowing about it. This protects us from becoming proud or seeking recognition. Giving to charity without telling others teaches us to be humble. Allāh ﷻ tells us that charity wipes evil away from us.[2:271]

When we give to charity, we should never feel proud about it. It is better to speak politely than to give to charity with pride.

﴿٢٦٣﴾ قَوْلٌ مَّعْرُوفٌ وَمَغْفِرَةٌ خَيْرٌ مِّن صَدَقَةٍ يَتْبَعُهَآ أَذًى ۗ وَاللَّهُ غَنِيٌّ حَلِيمٌ

A kind word and forgiveness is better than charity followed by hurtful words. And Allāh is self-Sufficient, Forbearing. (2:263)

Not a new practice

Zakāt is not something new introduced by our Nabi Muhammad ﷺ. Messengers before Muhammad ﷺ told the people in their communities to pay zakāt.[5:12] Nabi 'Isā (A) was asked by Allāh ﷻ to perform salāt and pay zakāt.[19:31]

Who can receive zakāt

As mentioned previously, the Qur'ān sometimes uses the terms zakāt and sadaqah interchangeably. In āyah 9:60, eight categories of people are mentioned who are qualified to receive zakāt. The term used here is sadaqah. These categories are: 1) the poor, 2) the needy, 3) the workers who collect and distribute zakāt, 4) those who are interested in becoming Muslim, 5) prisoners, 6) those in debt, 7) those who are in the way of Allāh ﷻ, and 8) the traveler.

بِسْمِ اللَّهِ الصَّدَقَـٰتُ لِلْفُقَرَآءِ وَالْمَسَـٰكِينِ وَالْعَـٰمِلِينَ عَلَيْهَا وَالْمُؤَلَّفَةِ قُلُوبُهُمْ وَفِى الرِّقَابِ وَالْغَـٰرِمِينَ وَفِى سَبِيلِ اللَّهِ وَابْنِ السَّبِيلِ فَرِيضَةً مِّنَ اللَّهِ وَاللَّهُ عَلِيمٌ حَكِيمٌ ﴿٦٠﴾

Charities are only for—the poor, and the needy, and the workers upon it, and those whose hearts are made to incline, and for the captives, and those in debt, and in the way of Allāh, and the wayfarer: an ordinance from Allāh. And Allāh is all-Knowing, most Wise. (9:60)

Giving money to charity does not make us poor. Our wealth comes from Allāh﷿. If we give to charity for the sake of Allāh﷿, He rewards us. It is only Shaitān who tries to convince us that we will become poor if we give money to charity.[2:268]

From Hadith

It is narrated by 'Adi Ibn Hatim that Messengerﷺ said: "Save yourself from Hell-fire by giving even half a date-fruit in charity."

It is narrated by Abu Hurairah that the Messengerﷺ said, "The best charity is that which is practiced by a wealthy person. And start giving first to your dependents."

It is reported in several ahādīth that the Messengerﷺ said, "Do not withhold your money, [for if you did so] Allāh﷿ would withhold His blessings from you."

1. Read Sūrah Maryam, āyah 55. Who is the messenger who used to ask his family to pay zakāh?

Ismail

2. Read āyah 2:277 of the Qur'ān. What are the four tasks that can help us earn rewards from our Rabb?

Do righteous deeds establish prayer give zakat belive

3. In Sūrah Al-Anbiyā, āyah 73, Allāh mentions other messengers who would pay zakāh. Write the names of three messengers from the previous few verses.

ibrahim (a) isaac (a) Yacub (a)

4. A Catholic family has an annual income of $60,000. Their annual expenses are $40,000 and their total savings is $20,000. At a 10% rate, calculate how much money they should pay to the church.

Use a calculator to calculate the zakāt for a Muslim family that has the same income, annual expenses, and savings. Use the zakāt rate of 2.5% for the Muslim family.

Catholic family: 6000 $

Muslim family: 500 $

5. Allāh does not like those who collect money and count it without spending it on a good cause. This is mentioned in Sūrah Al-Humazah. Please copy the translation of the first two verses of this sūrah.

who pile up wealth and think his wealth would last him forever

6. If we spend our wealth on charity and on good causes, what does Allāhﷻ promise to give us? Find the answer in sūrah Al-Baqarah, āyah 268.

forgiveness and Blessings

7. What is the meaning of the word "tithe"?

   A. Fifth.
   B. Tenth.
   C. Seventh.
   D. One-twentieths.

8. What is the meaning of "economic surplus"?

   A. Anything left over after guests leave.
   B. Anything left over after growing crops.
   C. Anything left over after meeting a family's expenses.
   D. Anything left over in the bank after a year.

9. Read āyah 2:43 of the Qur'ān. Who were commanded to pay zakāt? (Hint: go back a few verses to identify them.)

Bani- Israel

10. What eight categories of people are qualified to receive zakāt? List them.

1. the poor

2. the needy

3. the workers who collet and distribute zakat

4. those who are intrested for become muslim

5. prisoners

6. those in debt

7. those who are in the way of Allah

8. the traveller

Appendix
Steps of Salāt

Physical preparation for salāh:

Physical cleanliness: Before performing salāh, make sure your body is clean. You must complete *wudu*, and be in the state of *wudu*. During the salāh, do not look sideways, do not look at others, and do not talk to others. Do not make unnecessary movements. Do not scratch, yawn, laugh, or smile. If you must sneeze or cough, that is fine, but try to minimize the noise.

Clean clothes: Your clothes should be clean and should cover your body. For boys, clothes should cover the body at least from the navel to the knees. For girls, clothes should cover the body from the neck to the ankles, and to the wrists. The head should be covered, but the face can remain uncovered. Clothes should not be transparent. Avoid any clothing that has pictures of people, animals, or offensive writing.

Clean place: You should find a clean place to make your salāh. A prayer rug is not necessary. A prayer rug should always be clean, so it ensures a clean place while you are praying.

Direction to face: You should face *Qiblah*, which is the direction of the Ka'bah in Makkah.

Time: *Fard* (compulsory) prayers are performed at the proper time. It is preferable to perform the prayer as soon as the *Adhān* (call to prayer) is announced.

Mental preparation: We begin the prayer with full mental and physical attention. During salāh, we are worshipping and talking directly to Allāh, therefore, we must provide our total attention. Avoid any place or object that diverts your full attention.

What is a raka'ah? Each salāh can be divided into cycles of physical postures, or raka'at. Each raka'ah involves the positions of *qiyam* (standing), *ruku* (bowing), *sujud* (prostration), *jalsa* (sitting), another *sujud* (prostration), and associated recitations. The chart shows the specified number of raka'at for the five daily salāh. Some variation in the number of Sunnah prayers exists among the madhhab.

	Sunnah raka'at before Fard raka'at	Fard raka'at	Sunnah raka'at after Fard raka'at
Fajr	2	2	
Dhuhr	4	4	2
'Asr	4	4	
Maghrib		3	2
'Isha	4	4	2, then 3 (wajib)

Description for a salāh of two raka'at:

The following description of steps is for a salāh with two raka'at (for example, the Fard prayer of Fajr). At the end of this description, there are brief notes about how to perform three or four raka'at of salāh.

Step 1

(Figures above)

When you stand up for salāh, make an intention to perform the salāh for the sake of Allāh. Say to yourself (in any language) that you intend to offer this *Salāh* (*Fajr, Dhuhr, Asr, Maghrib,* or *Isha*), *Fard, Sunnat,* or *Witr,* and the number of raka'ahs (example—"I intend to offer two *raka'ah* of *Fard, Fajr* prayer for Allāh").

Position: *Qiyam.* Stand upright. Raise both hands up to the ears (palms and body facing the direction of the Ka'bah).

What to say: *"Allāhu Akbar."* (Allāh is the Greatest).

Step 2

(Figures on the right)

Position: Place your left hand over your belly, place your right hand on top of the left hand, and grip the wrist of the left hand.

What to say:

1. *"Subhanaka Allāhumma wa bihamdika, wa tabārakasmuka, wa ta'āla jadduka, wa lā ilāha ghairuka."* (This part is known as *thana.* It means "Glory be to you, O Allāh, and praise to You. Blessed be Your Name, exalted be Your Majesty and Glory. There is no god but You.")

2. *"A'ūdu billāhi mina ash-Shaytānir rajim."* (I seek the protection of Allāh against Shaitān, the condemned.)

3. *"Bismillāhir rahmānir rahīm."* (In the Name of Allāh, Most Gracious, Most Merciful.)

4. Now recite Sūrah Al-Fātihah. We must recite Sūrah Al-Fātihah during each raka'ah. A salāh is not valid if Sūrah Al-Fātihah is not recited.

"Al humdu li-llahi rabbi-l 'alamīn. Ar-rahmāni-r rahīm. Māliki yawmi-d dīn. Iyyāka na'budu wa iyyāka Nāsta'īn. Ihdina-s sirāta-l mustaqīm. Sirātal ladhīna an'amta 'alaihim, ghairil maghdūbi 'alaihim, wa la-d dāllīn. (Āmīn.)"

(The Praise belongs to Allāh, The Rabb of all the worlds; the Rahman; the Rahim. Malik of the Day of Judgment. You alone do we serve, and to You alone we seek help. Guide us on the Right Path—the path of those upon whom You have bestowed favors; not of those upon whom wrath is brought down, nor those gone astray.)

5. After reciting sūrah Fātihah, we now recite any short sūrah or a few verses from the Qur'ān. This additional recitation of part of the Qur'ān is done during the first two raka'ah only. It is always good to memorize as many sūrah as you can, so you can recite them during your salāh.

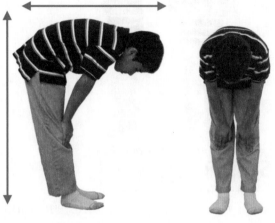

Step 3 (Figures above)

What to say: *"Allāhu Akbar."*

Position: This position is called *ruku*. Bow with your back perpendicular to your legs. Place your hands on your knees. Do not bend the knees.

What to say: *"Subhana rabbiyal 'Adhīm."* Say this three times. (Glorified is my Rabb, the Great.)

Step 4 (Figures below)

While going back to the *qiyam* (upright) position,

What to say: *"Samia Allāhu liman hamidah."* (Allāh listens to him who praises Him.)

Position: In *qiyam* position.

What to say: *"Rabbanā wa laka al hamd."* (Our Rabb, praise be for You only.)

Step 5 (Figure above)

What to say: While moving to the next position of *sujud*, say *"Allāhu Akbar."*

Position: This position is *sujud*. Place both of your knees on the floor. Try not to move the position of your feet, that is, do not move your feet away from the *qiyam* position. After placing the knees, place your two hands on the floor with palms touching the floor. Do not glide your hands on the floor. Your elbow is not on the floor. Your hands should be sufficiently apart to leave room for your head. Now place your forehead on the floor. Both your nose and forehead should touch the floor. Your hands are on the side of your head. Your stomach will not touch the floor. You should be the most humble in this position.

The most powerful part of our body is our brain, the site of our intelligence. We submit our full selves, with full understanding, to Almighty Allāh. We realize that our strength, power, wealth, and everything that we have is from Allāh. To emphasize this physical and spiritual humility, we will repeat the *sujud* position again in Step 7.

What to say: *"Subhana rabbiyal A'ala."* (Say this three times. Glory be to Allāh, the Exalted.)

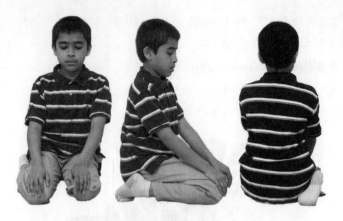

Step 6
(Figures above)

The next position is *jalsa*.

What to say: While moving to the *jalsa* position, say *"Allāhu Akbar."*

Position: To move to *jalsa* position, rise from *sujud*. First you will raise your head off the floor, then you will raise your hands. Now you are sitting on the floor— this posture is called *jalsa*.

What to say: *"Rabbi-ghfir lī wa rhamnī."* (O my Rabb, forgive me and have mercy on me.)

Step 8
(Figures above)

Rise to the *qiyam* (standing) position. The movement should be in a systematic, graceful manner. First you will raise your forehead from the floor, next you will raise your hands and then you will raise your knees. Try not to move your feet—that is, the position of your feet should be the same as it was during the first raka'ah.

What to say: While moving to the *qiyam* position, say *"Allāhu Akbar."*

Position: Stand upright. Hold the left hand with the right hand on top.

What to say: Sūrah Al-Fātihah, then any short sūrah or a few verses from the Qur'ān.

Step 7
(Figure above)

We will repeat *sujud* again. Every *raka'ah* has two *sujud*.

What to say: While moving to the sujud position, say *"Allāhu Akbar."*

Position: *Sujud.* Place your palms on the floor and then your forehead. Both the nose and the forehead should be touching the floor.

What to say: *"Subhāna rabbiyal A'ala."* Say this three times. (Glory to Allāh, the Exalted.)

This completes one raka'ah.

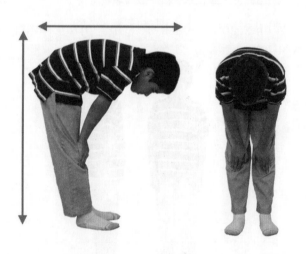

Step 9

(Figures on the previous page)

What to say: *"Allāhu Akbar."*

Position: *Ruku.* Bow with your back perpendicular to your legs. Place your hands on your knees.

What to say: *"Subhāna rabbiyal 'Adhīm."* Say this three times.

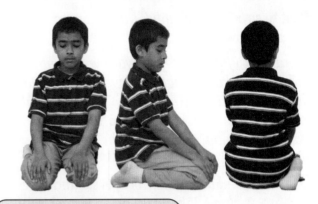

Step 10

(Figures above)

Position: While moving back to the *qiyam* (standing) position,

What to say: *"Sami'a Allāhu liman hamidah."*

Position: In *qiyam* position. You are upright.

What to say: "Rabbanā wa lakal hamd."

Step 11

(Figure below)

What to say: While moving to the sujud position, say *"Allāhu Akbar."*

Position: *Sujud.* Follow the same sequence as in Step 5.

What to say: *"Subhāna Rabbiyal A'ala."* Say this three times.

Step 12

(Figures above)

What to say: While moving to the jalsa position, say *"Allāhu Akbar."*

Position: Rise from the *sujud* position. Now you are sitting in the *jalsa* position.

What to say: *"Rabbi-ghfir lī wa rhamnī"* (O my Rabb, forgive me and have Mercy on me.)

Step 13

(Figure above)

What to say: While moving to the sujud position, say *"Allāhu Akbar."*

Position: *Sujud.* First place your hands and then your forehead on the floor.

What to say: *"Subhāna Rabbiyal A'ala."* Say this three times.

Step 14

(Figures in the next page)

What to say: While going to the jalsa position, say *"Allāhu Akbar."*

Position: Rise from the *sujud* position. Now you are sitting in the *jalsa* position.

What to say: Say *Tashahud, Durūd,* and a short prayer as follows:

"At-tahiyātu lillahi was-salawātu wattaiyibātu. Assalāmu 'alayka ayyuhan-nabiyu wa rahmatullāhi wa barakātuhu. Assalāmu 'ainā wa 'ala 'ibadi-llāhis-sālihīn. Ashhadu an lā ilāha illallāhu wa ashhadu anna Muhammadan 'abduhu wa rasūluhu."

(All these salutations, prayers, and nice comments are for Allāh. Peace be on you, O Nabi, and the blessings of Allāh, and His grace. Peace on us and on all the righteous servants of Allāh. I bear witness that none but Allāh is worthy of worship, and I bear witness that Muhammad is the servant and messenger of Allāh.) This is known as *Tashahud.*

Position: Raise your right index finger, so it is pointing upward, while reciting the last part of this prayer.

Next you will recite the *Durūd.*

"Allāhumma salli 'ala Muhammadin wa 'ala āli Muhummadin, kamā sallayta 'ala Ibrāhima, wa ala āli Ibrāhima, innaka hamidun majid. Allāhumma barik 'ala Muhammadin wa 'ala āli Muhummadin, kama barakta ala Ibrāhima, wa 'ala āli Ibrahīm, innaka hamīdun majīd."

(O Allāh, send your Mercy on Muhammad and his posterity as you sent Your mercy on Ibrāhīm and his posterity. You are the Most Praised, The Most Glorious. O Allāh, send your Blessings on Muhammad and his posterity as you have blessed Ibrāhīm and his posterity. You are the Most praised, The Most Glorious.)

Now you may add a short prayer, such as:

"Rabbanā ātinā fi-d dunyā hasanatan wa fi-l ākhirati hasanatan, wa qinā 'adhāban nār."

(Our Rabb, give us the good of this world, and good in the Hereafter, and save us from the chastisement of Fire.)

Step 15 (Figure above left)

Position: Slowly turn your head and face right. This is called *salam.*

What to say: *"As-salāmu 'alaikum wa rahmatullāh."* (Peace and mercy of Allāh be on you.)

Step 16 (Figure above right)

Position: Slowly turn your head and face left. This is called *salam.*

What to say: *"As-salāmu 'alaikum wa rahmatullāh."*

This completes the two raka'at of salāh.

How to pray three raka'at (Maghrib)

In order to perform a three-raka'at salāh, use all the postures and prayers up to step 13.

In step 14, recite up to *"At-tahiyātu lillahi was-salawātu wattaiyibātu. Assalāmu 'alayka ayyuhan-nabiyu wa rahmatullāhi wa barakātuhu. Assalāmu 'ainā wa 'ala 'ibadi-llāhis-sālihīn. Ashhadu an lā ilāha illallāhu wa ashhadu anna Muhammadan 'abduhu wa rasūluhu."* This is known as *Tashahud.*

After saying *"Allāhu akbar,"* return to the *qiyam* position, step 8. This time recite only *Al-Fātihah* (in step 8), but do not recite any sūrah or part of the Qur'ān. All prayers and postures are the same as shown in steps 9–16.

How to pray four raka'at (Dhuhr, 'Asr, and 'Isha)

In order to perform a four-raka'at salāh, use all the postures and prayers up to step 13.

In Step 14, only the *Tashahud* prayer will be recited, and the *qiyam* position, in step 8, will be resumed.

In step 8, only *Al-Fātihah* will be recited without adding any sūrah. Steps 8–13 complete the third raka'ah. The *qiyam* position in step 8 will be resumed.

In step 8, only *Al-Fātihah* will be recited without adding any sūrah. Steps 8–16, complete the fourth raka'ah.

From the Qur'an

...keep up the salāt, as salāt controls indecent and unacceptable behaviors... *(Sūrah Al-'Ankabūt, 29:45)*

Take care to do your salāt, praying in the best way, and stand before Allāh with full devotion. *(Sūrah Al-Baqarah, 2:238)*

Summary of Prayer Postures

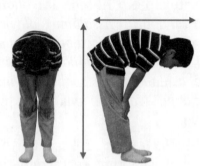

Standing for salāt facing the direction of the Ka'bah.

Front and lateral view

Raising hands for takbir. Folding them back to recite sūrah.

Bending position for ruku.

Front and lateral view

Rising from ruku.

Performing *sujud*.

Sitting down from the *sujud*, this is *jalsa* position.

Front, lateral and back view

Second *sujud* from the *jalsa* position.

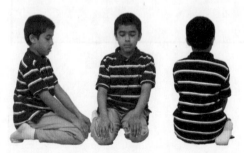

At the end of the second raka'at, sitting down after the second *sujud* to recite *tashahud*.

Completing salāt—turning face first to the right and then to the left.

Test Your Knowledge - 1
(All questions are based on the lessons taught in this book.)

1. Who is Allāh's partner in the management of the universe?

2. Before the Battle of Badr, who traveled with a caravan from Syria to Makkah?

3. Which sūrah discusses the history of to the Battle of Uhud?

4. In which year was the Treaty of Hudaibiyah signed?

5. In which year was the famous Farewell Khutba delivered?

6. During which battle did the archers leave their positions on the hill?

7. Who advised the Muslims to dig a trench around Madīnah before a battle?

8. Which famous Makkan warrior accepted Islam soon after the Treaty of Hudaibiyah?

9. In which city was Ibrāhīm (A) born and where did he spend his early years?

10. Who was Yūsuf's (A) youngest brother?

11. When Iblīs tempted Adam (A) to eat the fruit, he said the fruit would make Adam (A) immortal or become something else. What was the "something else" he promised?

12. In the temple, Ibrāhīm (A) broke all the idols except one. Which idol was left unharmed?

13. In which year was the final revelation sent to Nabi Muhammad?

14. Who was the leader of the Makkan army when they came to fight at Badr?

15. In which year was the Battle of Uhud fought?

16. Who was Yahyā's (A) father?

17. During which battle did the Jewish tribe Banu Qurayzah want to attack the Muslims?

18. On what type of path, as mentioned in sūrah Fātihah, do we ask Allāh to guide us?

Answers:

1. Nobody; Allāh does not have any partners   2. Abu Sufyān   3. Sūrah Al-i-'Imrān
4. 628 C.E. / 6 A.H.   5. 632 C.E. / 10 A.H.   6. Battle of Uhud
7. Salmān al-Fārisī   8. Khālid Ibn Walīd   9. Ur
10. Binyamin   11. Adam would become an angel.   12. The largest idol
13. 632 C.E. / 10 A.H.   14. Abu Jahl   15. 624 C.E. / 2 A.H.
16. Zakariyyāh (A)   17. Battle of Khandaq   18. The Straight Path

Test Your Knowledge - 2

(All questions are based on the lessons taught in this book.)

1. What is the meaning of the word "al-Qur'ān"?

2. In what language did all the nabi and rasūls speak?

3. How many Muslim armies participated in the Battle of Badr?

4. During the Battle of Uhud, how large was the Makkan Quraish army?

5. How many years of peace were agreed upon in the Treaty of Hudaibiyah?

6. With which king did Ibrāhīm (A) argue about the power of Allāh﷿?

7. In which sūrah is the story of Luqmān (A) narrated?

8. What is the name of the night on which the Qur'ān was first revealed?

9. Of one's surplus money, what percent should be given in zakāt?

10. How many brothers conspired to kill Yūsuf (A) by dropping him in a well?

11. In the Battle of Uhud, the Muslims started with a 1,000-man army. How many men were left when the battle actually began?

12. Which famous nabi's father was an idol worshipper?

13. During which battle did Abdullah Ibn Ubayy abandon the Muslim army with 300 of his men?

14. In which country can you find the famous mosque known as the King Faisal Mosque?

15. Which famous masjid has two Qiblah?

16. Where was Yūsuf (A) sent for nine years after some women accused him of wrongdoing?

17. During Maryam's childhood, who was her guardian?

18. Iblīs refused to bow down to Adam (A) because Iblīs was made of something. What was Iblīs made of?

Answers:

1. The Reading	2. Their local language	3. One 313-man army
4. 3,000 men	5. 10 years of peace	6. Nimrod
7. Sūrah Luqmān	8. Lailatul Qadr	9. 2.5% of one's surplus money
10. 10 brothers	11. 700 men	12. Ibrāhīm's (A) father
13. Battle of Uhud	14. Pakistan	15. Masjid al-Qiblatain
16. To prison	17. Zakariyyāh (A)	18. Fire

Outline of Curriculum – Levels 1, 2 and 3

Each year the curriculum begins with a few topics on Allāh✿, the Qur'ān, the Nabi✿, the Hadīth, or Sunnah. In the early years, emphasis is placed on the five-pillars, and each year, this emphasis increases. Every year, a history of some of the messengers is introduced in an age-appropriate manner. Several lessons are devoted to Islamic manners, values, and morals so that children grow up with a good understanding of Islamic culture. Each lesson includes a short homework assignment.

Level 1	Level 2	Level 3
Unit 1: Aqaid: Our Belief	**Unit 1: The Creator–His Message**	**Unit 1: Knowing About Allah**
Allah✿: Our Creator	Allāh✿: Our Creator	What Does Allāh✿ Do?
Islam	How Does Allah✿ Create?	What Allāh✿ Is and Is Not
Our Faith	Allāh✿: What Does He Do?	Allāh✿: The Most-Merciful
Nabi Muhammad✿	What Does Allah✿ Not Do	Allāh✿: The Best Judge
The Qur'an	The Qur'an	**Unit 2: What Islam Says**
Unit 2: Knowing Allah✿	Hadith and Sunnah	We Are Muslims: We Have 'Imān
Allāh✿ Loves Us	**Unit 2: Our Ibadat**	What Does Allāh✿ Want Us to Do?
Remembering Allāh✿	Shahadah: The First Pillar	Hadīth
Allāh✿ Rewards Us	Salah: The Second Pillar	Jinn
Unit 3: Our Ibadat	Zakah: The Third Pillar	Muslims in North America
Five Pillars of Islam	Sawm: The Fourth Pillar	The Right Path: The Straight Path
Shahadah: The First Pillar	Hajj: The Fifth Pillar	**Unit 3: Why Do We Worship**
Salah: The Second Pillar	Wudu: Keeping Our Bodies Clean	Shahādah: Allāh✿ is One
Zakat: The Third Pillar	**Unit 3: Messengers of Allah**	Types of Salāt
Fasting: The Fourth Pillar	Ibrahim (A): A Friend of Allah	Why We Make Salāt
Hajj: The Fifth Pillar	Yaqub (A) and Yusuf (A)	Why Do We pay Zakat?
Unit 4: Messengers of Allah	Musa (A) and Harun (A)	Why Do We Fast?
Adam (A): The First Nabi	Yunus (A)	Why Do We Go for Hajj?
Nuh (A): Saved From Flood	Nabi Muhammad✿	**Unit 4: Life of Nabi Muhammad✿**
Ibrahim (A): Never Listen to Shaitan	**Unit 4: Learning About Islam**	The Nabi✿ in Makkah
Musa (A): Challenging A Bad Ruler	Obey Allāh✿ Obey Rasul✿	The Nabi✿ in Madīnah
Isa (A): A Great Nabi of Allah✿	Day of Judgment	How Rasulullah✿ Treated Others
Unit 5: Other Basics of Islam	Our Masjid	**Unit 5: Messengers of Allah**
Angels: They Always Work for Allah✿	Islamic Phrases	Ismā'īl (A) and Ishāq (A)
Shaitan: Our Enemy	Food that We May Eat	Dāwūd (A): A Nabi of Allāh✿
Makkah and Madinah	**Unit 5: Akhlaq and Adab in Islam**	'Isā (A): A Nabi of Allāh ✿
Eid: Two Festivals	Truthfulness	**Unit 6: Akhlaq and Adab in Islam**
Unit 6: Akhlaq and Adab in Islam	Kindness	Being Kind: A Virtue of the Believers
Good Manners	Respect	Forgiveness: A Good Quality
Kindness and Sharing	Responsibility	Good Deeds: A Duty of the Believers
Respect	Obedience	Cleanliness: A Quality of Believers
Forgiveness	Cleanliness	A Muslim Family
Thanking Allah✿	Honesty	Perseverance: Never Give Up
		Punctuality: Doing Things on Time

Outline of Curriculum – Levels 4, 5 and 6

By Level 5, students have learned the biography of the Nabi Muhammad☆, including a summary of the events that shaped his life and early Islam. By Level 6, students will have read the biographies of most of the prominent messengers. At this stage, students will have learned all the fundamental principles and key concepts of Islam. Even if students do not attend weekend schools after Level 6, they have already gained significant knowledge about Islam.

Level 4	Level 5	Level 6
Unit 1: Knowing the Creator	**Unit 1: The Creator, His Message**	**Unit 1: The Creator–His Message**
Rewards of Allāh☆: Everybody Receives Them	Tawhīd, Kāfir, Kufr, Shirk, Nifāq	Attributes of Allāh☆
Discipline of Allāh☆	Why Should We Worship Allāh☆?	The Promise of Allāh☆
Names of Allāh☆	Revelation of the Qur'ān	**Unit 2: The Qur'ān and Hadith**
Books of Allāh☆	Characteristics of the Messengers	Objectives of the Qur'ān?
Unit 2: How Islam Changed Arabia	**Unit 2: The Battles, Developments**	Compilation of the Qur'ān
Pre-Islamic Arabia	Pledges of 'Aqabah	Previous Scriptures and the Qur'ān
The Year of the Elephant	The Battle of Badr	Compilation of Hadīth
Early Life of Muhammad☆	The Battle of Uhud	**Unit 3: Fundamentals of Deen**
Life Before Becoming a Nabi	The Battle of the Trench	Importance of Shahādah
First Revelation	The Treaty of Hudaibiyah	Khushū in Salāt
Makkah Period	Liberation of Makkah	Taqwā: A Quality of Believers
Hijrat to Madīnah	**Unit 3: The Messengers of Allāh**	**Unit 4: Messengers of Allāh**
Madīnah Period	Adam (A): The Creation of Mankind	Nūh (A)
Unit 3: The Rightly Guided Khalīfah	Ibrāhīm (A) Debate with Polytheists	Tālūt, Jālūt, and Dāwūd (A)
Abū Bakr: The First Khalifah	Ibrāhīm (A): Plan Against Idols	Dāwūd (A) and Sulaimān (A)
'Umar ibn al-Khattāb	Luqmān (A): A Wise Man's Lifelong Teachings	Mūsā (A) and Fir'awn
'Uthmān ibn 'Affān	Yūsuf (A): His Childhood	Mūsā (A) and Khidir
'Ali ibn Abū Tālib	Yūsuf (A): His Righteousness	'Isā (A) and Maryam (ra)
Unit 4: The Messengers of Allāh	Yūsuf (A): Dream Comes True	**Unit 5: Some Prominent Muslimah**
Hūd (A): Struggle to Guide People	Ayyūb (A): Patience, Perseverance	Khadījah (ra)
Sālih (A): To Guide the Misguided	Zakariyyāh (A), Yahyā (A)	'A'ishah (ra)
Mūsā (A): His Life and Actions	**Unit 4: Islam in the World**	Fātimah (ra)
Sulaimān (A): A Humble King	Major Masājid in the World	Some Prominent Muslimahs
Unit 5: Fiqh of Salāt	**Unit 5: Islamic Values, Teachings**	**Unit 6: Knowledge Enrichment**
Preparation for Salāt	Upholding Truth: A Duty for All Believers	Al-Qiyamah: The Awakening
Requirements of Salāt	Responsibility and Punctuality	Rūh and Nafs: An Overview
Mubtilāt us-Salāt	My Mind My Body	Angels and Jinn: An Overview
How to Pray Behind an Imām	Kindness and Forgiveness	Shaitān: The Invisible Enemy
Unit 6: General Islamic Topics	The Middle Path: Ways to Avoid Two Extremes	**Unit 7: The Current Society**
Compilers of Hadīth	Salāt: Its Significance	My Friend Is Muslim Now
Shaitān's Mode of Operation	Sawm: Its Significance	Friendship
Day of Judgment	Zakāt and Sadaqah: Similarities and Differences	Muslims Around the World
Eid: Its Significance		People of Other Faith
Truthfulness: A Quality of Muslim		**Unit 8: Developing Islamic Values**
Perseverance: Keep on Trying		Greed and Dishonesty
		Avoiding Extravagance

Outline of Curriculum – Levels 7, 8 and 9

In these levels, the application of knowledge is increasingly emphasized by offering carefully selected topics. Specific details about some of the messengers are introduced to highlight the abiding morals in their lives. In Level 8, early Muslim struggles are discussed in detail. Increased depth and informaiton in the lessons require focused attention from students. Age-appropriate moral lessons are also covered including gossip, friendship, peer pressure, dating, indecency, encouraging good and forbidding evil.

Level 7	Level 8	Level 9
Unit 1: The Creator	**Unit 1: Knowing the Creator**	**Unit 1: A Reflection on the Divine**
Why Islam? what is Islam?	Divine Names	Signs of Allāh in nature
Belief in Allāh	Sunan of Allāh	Pondering the Qur'ān
The Qur'ān: Its Qualitative Names	Objectives of the Qur'ān	Preservation and Compilation of the Qur'ān
Istighfar: Seeking Forgiveness of Allāh	Sūrah Hujurat: Its Teachings	Ibadat—Easy Ways to Do It
Allāh: Angry or Kind	True Piety: Analysis of Verse 2:177	**Unit 2: An Islamic Perspective**
Unit 2: Stories of the Messengers	Ayātul Qursi	Why Human Beings Are Superior
Ādam (A): Trial of the Messenger	**Unit 2: Knowing the Messenger**	Is Islam a Violent Religion?
Life of Ibrāhīm (A)	The Person Muhammad	Shariah
Sacrifice of Ibrāhīm (A)	Farewell Pilgrimage	Justice in Islam
Lūt (A): Message for Modern Societies	Finality of Prophethood	**Unit 3: Ethical Standard in Islam**
Yūsuf (A)—The Will to Overcome Temptation	Hadīth: Collection, Classification	Peer Pressure
Unit 3: Stories from the Qur'ān	**Unit 3: Challenges in Madīnah**	Choices We Make
The Companions of the Cave	Hypocrites	Islamic Perspective on Dating
Dhul Qurnain: Journey of a King	Banu Qaynuqa	Indecency
Effective Debate and Negotiation Styles in the Qur'ān	Banu Nadir	Alcohol and Gambling
Unit 4: Two Companions	Banu Qurayzah	Permitted and Prohibited Food
Abū Sufyān	Mission to Tabūk	Food of the People of the Book
Khālid Ibn Walīd (R)	**Unit 4: Islamic Ethical Framework**	Family Values
Unit 5: Knowledge Enrichment	Friends and Friendship	**Unit 4: Essays on Rasulullah**
The Character of the Messengers	Friendship With Non-Muslims	Khadījah (ra)
Rasūlullāh's Marriages	Dating in Islam	Rasūlullāh's Multiple Marriages
Lailatul Qadr	Hold Firmly the Rope of Allāh	Marriage to Zainab (ra)
Fasting During Ramadan	Elements of Bad Life	The Prophet: A Great Army General
My Family is Muslim Now	**Unit 5: Islamic Values, Teachings**	Prophecy of Muhammad in the Bible
Science in the Qur'ān	Duties Toward Parents	Allegations Against Rasūlullāh
Lessons from Past Civilizations	Hope, Hopefulness, Hopelessness	**Unit 5: A Reflection on Islam**
Unit 6: Teachings of the Qur'ān	Trials in Life	God's Chosen People
Amr Bil Ma'rūf	Permitted and Prohibited Food	Mūsā's Personality
Guard Your Tongue	Performance of Hajj	Essentials of Salah
Islamic Greetings	Parables in the Qur'ān	Life Cycle of Truth
How to Achieve Success	**Unit 6: Islam After the Rasūl (S)**	How Ramadan Makes Us Better
Permitted and Prohibited	Origin and History of Shī'ah	Muslims in North America
Types of Behavior Allāh Loves	Ummayad Dynasty	
	Abbasid Dynasty	

Outline of Curriculum – Levels 10, 11–12

In Level 10 and 11–12, Islamic topics increasingly prepare youths to fine-tune their spiritual and social lives. Significant issues that have real-life implications are introduced. The application of knowledge continues to be emphasized. The lessons in the Level 11–12 book strongly promote the application of Islamic knowledge. This is achieved through carefully selected topics. All lessons teach core Islamic beliefs and understandings based on the Qur'ān and authentic Hadith.

Level 10*	Level 11–12*
Unit 1: Knowing the Creator	**Unit 1: Understanding Our Belief**
Understanding the Word "Allāh"	Islam
Al-Fātihah: An Analysis of its Message	Muslim
Al-Fātihah vs The Lord's Prayer	Shahādah
Muhkam and Mutashābihat Āyāt	Belief in Allāh
Al-'Asr: The Formula of Success	Belief in the Angels
Qur'ānic Calligraphy	Belief in the Revealed Books
Unit 2: Interfaith Studies	Belief in the Messengers
The Bible and the Qur'ān	Belief in the Hereafter
The Ten Commandments and Islam	**Unit 2: The "Driver" Within Us**
Our Faiths: Key Differences	Life's Ultimate Purpose
Unit 3: Marriage and Family in Islam	Wealth Is The "Driver"
The Status of Women in Islam	The "Driver" Within Us
Marriage to Non-Muslims	**Unit 3: A Heart for Allāh**
Marrying Four Women	When Allāh Seems Distant
Difficult Questions on Marriage	Tawakkul: Trust in Allāh
A Muslim Family	Du'ā: How Does Allāh Respond?
Unit 4: General Islamic Topics	A Heart for Allāh
Who are the Khalīfah on Earth?	**Unit 4: Controlling Our Thoughts**
False Piety	Controlling Your Thoughts
Superstition	Maintaining a Relationship
Do Not Transgress Limits	The Power of Forgiveness
Secular and Religious Duties	Reading the Qur'ān
Islamic Views on Racism	Afraid to Think, Forbidden to Ask
Unit 5: Principles of Finance in Islam	**Unit 5: A Review of Key Concepts**
Public Finance in Early Islam	Lower Your Gaze
Wealth in The Qur'an	'Ā'ishah (ra): The Child Bride
Islamic Investment	"Strike" in Sūrah An-Nisā'
Language of Investment	The Myth About the Satanic Verse
Faith-Based Wealth Building	How Jesus Became Christ
Managing Earning and spending	Rūh and Nafs
Leading an Interest Free Life	**Unit 6: Faith-Based Wealth Building**
Unit 6: Islam and the World	Taking financial control early
Islamic Architecture	Fundamental of Finance
Islam in Spain and Portugal	Islamic Investment

*Proposed topics in the Revised Edition. Actual topics may change at the time of publication.